Understanding
Rabbinic Midrash

THE LIBRARY OF JUDAIC LEARNING
VOLUME V

EDITED BY

JACOB NEUSNER

University Professor
Professor of Religious Studies
The Ungerleider Distinguished Scholar of Judaic Studies

BROWN UNIVERSITY

Understanding
Rabbinic Midrash

Texts and Commentary

by

Gary G. Porton

KTAV PUBLISHING HOUSE, INC.
HOBOKEN, NEW JERSEY
1985

Library of Congress Cataloging in Publication Data
Main entry under title:

Understanding rabbinic midrash.

(The Library of Judaic learning. ISSN 0190-5635 ;
v. 5)
  Includes bibliographies and indexes.
  1. Halakhic Midrashim. 2. Midrash. I. Porton,
Gary G. II. Series.
BM514.U53 1985   296.1'405   84-26147
ISBN 0-88125-055-4
ISBN 0-88125-056-2 (pbk.)

MANUFACTURED IN THE UNITED STATES OF AMERICA

For Samson H. Levey

Table of Contents

Acknowledgments

My teacher and the editor of this series, Professor Jacob Neusner, University Professor and the Ungerleider Distinguished Scholar of Judaic Studies at Brown University, suggested that I undertake this anthology. I wish to thank him for his continued support of my work in general, and of this volume in particular. I owe him a special debt here, for the following pages have been greatly informed by his studies on Babylonian Jewry and his literary analyses of the rabbinic collections.

Professors William S. Green of the University of Rochester and Alan Avery-Peck of Tulane University read earlier drafts of this study. Professor Green, always the careful and artful editor and thoughtful critic, spent a great deal of time working on and improving the English text of this volume. In addition, he added to this study through his many conversations with me. I greatly appreciate his support and friendship. Professor Avery-Peck's working through of the translations prevented me from making several errors in my rendition of the Hebrew. I am deeply indebted to his careful reading of the original manuscript and for his thoughtful and penetrating suggestions for its improvement. The present volume is much better than the original manuscript because of the work of these two scholars.

My colleague Professor William R. Schoedel read the original manuscript and offered several suggestions which have been incorporated in the present version. In addition, Ms. Nancy Tepper and Ms. Linda C. Weingart read the original manuscript, and many of their suggestions and insights can be found on the following pages. I am grateful for the help of these friends, and the readers of this book have benefited greatly from their insights.

I was able to complete my work on this volume while I was an Associate of the Center for Advanced Study at the University of

Illinois and while I had a fellowship from the John Simon Guggen-
heim Memorial Foundation. I am greatly honored by both of these
awards.

As always my family, Fraeda, Avi, Zipporah, provided the environment in which I could complete my work. They gave up a good deal
so that I might complete this study. What they have given and the
love I feel for them is something to which I can refer but which I
cannot fully express in this space.

This volume is dedicated to my teacher Rabbi Samson H. Levey,
Professor of Rabbinics at the Hebrew Union College–Jewish Insti-
tute of Religion, Los Angeles. Rabbi Levey was the first to introduce
me to the careful reading of rabbinic texts and to the critical study of
these documents. He spent a good deal of time with me so that I
might learn what he had to offer. His work with me exhibited his
extensive knowledge of rabbinic Judaism, the environment in
which it developed, and the critical study of the text and culture
produced by the rabbis of late antiquity. His care, thoughtfulness,
and patience were always evident in our work together. In addition,
he has remained a constant friend and careful critic. The dedication
of this book is a scant recognition of what Rabbi Levey has given me
over the years.

Abbreviations of Names of Biblical Books

Gen.	Genesis
Ex.	Exodus
Lev.	Leviticus
Num.	Numbers
Deut.	Deuteronomy
Josh.	Joshua
Jdgs.	Judges
Hos.	Hosea
Obad.	Obadiah
Mic.	Micah
Nah.	Nahum
Hab.	Habakkuk
Zeph.	Zephaniah
Hag.	Haggai
Zech.	Zechariah
Mal.	Malachi
Ps.	Psalms
I Sam.	I Samuel
II Sam.	II Samuel
I Kgs.	I Kings
II Kgs.	II Kings
Isa.	Isaiah
Jer.	Jeremiah
Ezek.	Ezekiel
Prov.	Proverbs
Cant.	Canticles
Qoh.	Qohelet
Lam.	Lamentations

Esth.	Esther
Dan.	Daniel
Neh.	Nehemiah
I Chr.	I Chronicles
II Chr.	II Chronicles

Transliteration of Hebrew

א = ʾ
ב = b
ג = g
ד = d
ה = h
ו = w
ז = z
ח = ḥ
ט = ṭ
י = y
כ ך = k
ל = l
מ ם = m
נ ן = n
ס = s
ע = ʿ
פ ף = p
צ ץ = ṣ
ק = q
ר = r
שׁ = š
שׂ = ś
ת = t

Rabbinic Masters

The information which follows was culled from M. Margolioth, *Encyclopedia of Talmudic and Geonic Literature, Being a Biographical Dictionary of the Tanaim, Amoraim and Geonim* (Tel Aviv, 1962), and A. Hyman, *Toldoth Tannaim Ve'Amoraim* (Jerusalem, 1964). In addition, readers should consult the works cited below and the articles in the *Jewish Encyclopedia* and the *Encyclopaedia Judaica*.

The term *Tanna* applies to sages who lived from the turn of the era until about 220 C.E. The term *Amora* applies to sages who lived from about 220 until the end of the sixth or seventh century of the common era.

Abba the Son of Kahanah. Third-generation Palestinian Amora.
Abbahu. Third-generation Palestinian Amora. One of Yoḥanan's most important students. Head of the academy in Caesarea.
Abin. Third- and fourth-generation Amora who was born in Babylonia and studied in Palestine. Abin's son was also called Abin; therefore, it is difficult to determine to whom the name refers when it appears in our texts. The son was a leading Palestinian sage of the fifth generation of Amoraim.
Aḥa. Fourth-generation Palestinian Amora.
Aḥai the son of Yoshiah. Fifth-generation Babylonian Tanna. He appears frequently in the Mekhilta deRabbi Ishmael and Sifre Numbers.
Aibu. Third-generation Palestinian Amora. One of the most important aggadists of his generation. He appears most frequently in *Genesis Rabbah.*
Ami. Third-generation Palestinian Amora. Head of the academy in Tiberias. Student of Rabbi Hoshiyah.
Aqiba. Aqiba (the son of Joseph) was a leading figure in Palestinian

Judaism in the period from the destruction of the Temple until the Bar-Kokhba War. The authoritative line of Palestinian Tannaitic Judaism traces its origin from Aqiba back to Hillel. C. Primus, *Aqiva's Contribution to Law of Zera'im* (Leiden, 1977). Compare with L. Finkelstein, *Akiba: Scholar, Saint and Martyr* (New York, 1936).

Banayah. Palestinian rabbi who lived during the transition from the tannaitic to the amoraic period. His most famous student was Yoḥanan.

Bar Qapara. (Eleazar) bar Qapara was a Palestinian rabbi who lived during the transition from the tannaitic to the amoraic period. He was a student of Judah the Patriarch (Rabbi), and the teacher of Hoshiyah and Hoshiyah the son of Levi.

Berekhyah. Fourth-generation Palestinian Amora.

Berekhyah the Elder. Some scholars identify this sage with Berakhyah, while others claim he was a second-generation Palestinian Amora.

Dosa. Dosa (the son of Harkinos) traditionally is placed in the first generation of Palestinian Tannaim; however, tradition states that he lived to be a very old man. It is unclear to me whether the references to the Tanna Dosa refer to one or to several individuals.

Eleazar. Eleazar (the son of Shamoa') was a fourth-generation Palestinian Tanna who studied with Rabbi Aqiba. Tradition states that he was one of Aqiba's five students whom Judah the son of Baba ordained after Aqiba's death at the hands of the Romans.

Eleazar. Eleazar (the son of Pidat) was a second-generation Babylonian Amora who migrated to Israel. Succeeded Yoḥanan as the head of the academy in Tiberias.

Eleazar the son of Aḥwai. I could find no information on this Palestinian Tanna.

Eleazar the son of Azariah. Third-generation Palestinian Tanna. Patriarch who participated in the overthrow of Rabban Gamliel. R. Goldenberg, "The Deposition of Rabban Gamliel II," *Journal of Jewish Studies*, XXIII (1972), 167–190. T. Zahavy, *The Traditions of Eleazar ben Azariah* (Missoula, 1978).

Eleazar the son of Menaḥem. Third-generation Palestinian Amora.

Eleazar the son of Parta. Third-generation Palestinian Tanna.

Eleazar HaQappar. Fifth-generation Palestinian Tanna.

Eliezer. Eliezer (the son of Hyrcanus) was a second-generation Palestinian Tanna. He was one of Yoḥanan the son of Zakkai's most important students. He is often in dispute with Rabbi Joshua. J. Neusner, *Eliezer ben Hyrcanus: The Tradition and the Man* (Leiden, 1973).

Eliezer the son of Jacob. There were two Tannaim with this name. One was a second-generation Palestinian Tanna, and the other was a fourth-generation Palestinian Tanna. Tradition states that the former was important in the creation of Mishnah *Middot.*

Elisha the son of Abbuyah. Third-generation Palestinian Tanna. Known as 'Aḥer, "the other one," Elisha rejected his Judaism in favor of Greek philosophy. Rabbi Meir was his teacher. M. Steinberg, *As a Driven Leaf* (New York, 1939).

Gamliel. Patriarch in Yavneh for the first ten years following the end of the Bar-Kokhba War in 135 C.E. His grandfather was Gamliel the Elder, who was Patriarch in Yavneh for the ten years preceding the Bar-Kokhba War.

Ḥama the father of Hoshiya. Ḥama (the son of Bisa) lived during the last generation of the Palestinian Tannaim.

Ḥama the son of Hanina. Second-generation Palestinian Amora. Like his father, Ḥanina the son of Ḥama, lived in Sepphoris.

Ḥanana the son of Isaac. Also known as Ḥinah the son of Isaac, Ḥanana was a third-generation Palestinian Amora. He does not appear at all in the Babylonian Talmud.

Ḥanana the son of Pappa. Also known as Ḥaninah the son of Pappa and Ḥinnah the son of Papai. He was a third-generation Palestinian Amora. He may have studied with Rabbi Samuel the son of Naḥman.

Ḥananyah the son of Joshua's brother. Third-generation Palestinian Tanna.

Ḥanina. Ḥanina (the son of Ḥama) was a first-generation Palestinian Amora. He was born in Babylonia but migrated to Palestine. He was a student of Judah the Patriarch.

Hilkiah. Fourth-generation Palestinian Amora. A student of Rabbi Simeon.

Hillel. Although born in Babylonia, Hillel stu   ı as an adult in Palestine. He is traditionally counted as the founder of the Pharisaic movement in Palestine. Hillel lived before the destruction of the Second Temple in 70 C.E. J. Neusner, *The Rabbinic*

Traditions About the Pharisees Before 70 (Leiden, 1971), I, 212–340; III, passim, idem, *From Politics to Piety: The Emergence of Pharisaic Judaism* (Englewood Cliffs, N.J., 1973), 13–44.

Ḥiyya. Lived during the last generation of the Palestinian Tannaim. He was born in Babylonia but migrated to Palestine. J. Neusner, *A History of the Jews in Babylonia*, I, *The Parthian Period*, 2d printing, rev. (Leiden, 1969), 149–151.

Ḥiyya the son of Ada. Second-generation Palestinian Amora.

Hoshiya. Also known as Oshiya. Third-generation Amora who was born in Babylonia and was a student of Rav Judah and Rav Hunah. He migrated to Palestine. Sometimes he is confused with Hoshiya the Great, a first-generation Palestinian Amora.

House of Hillel. Name given to Hillel's anonymous students.

House of Shammai. Name given to Shammai's anonymous students. Shammai and Hillel, as well as the House of Hillel and the House of Shammai, often dispute with each other. Neusner, *Rabbinic Traditions*, II, III, passim.

Hunah. The name of a second-generation Babylonian Amora, a fourth-generation Palestinian Amora, and a third-generation Babylonian Amora. The first Hunah was the head of the school in Sura.

Hunah the Great of Sepphoris. Third-generation Palestinian Amora. He was a student of Rabbi Yoḥanan.

Isaac. Fourth-generation Palestinian Tanna. Traditionally counted among the students of Rabbi Ishmael.

Ishmael. Third-generation Palestinian Amora. His major antagonist was Rabbi Aqiba. Although Ishmael is said to be the originator of thirteen exegetical principles, recent work has cast doubt on this theory. G. Porton, *The Traditions of Rabbi Ishmael* (Leiden, 1976–82).

Ishmael the son of Ami. Mentioned only in the opening of *Leviticus Rabbah.*

Ishmael the son of Eleazar the son of Azariah. Palestinian Tanna who rarely appears in the rabbinic texts.

Issacar of the Village of Mandi. Palestinian Amora whose dates are uncertain.

Jacob of Kefar Ḥanan. Third-generation Palestinian Amora.

Jeremiah the son of (E)leazar. Palestinian Amora who may have lived during the third generation.

Joshua. Joshua (the son of Ḥananyah) was a second-generation Palestinian Tanna who was one of Yoḥanan the son of Zakkai's most important students. Joshua is often in dispute with Eliezer. W. S. Green, *The Traditions of Joshua ben Hananiah* (Leiden, 1981).

Joshua of Siknin. Fourth-generation Palestinian Amora. A student of Rabbi Levi.

Joshua the son of Levi. First-generation Palestinian Amora. A student of Bar Qapara. A major figure in Lod.

Joshua the son of Nehemiah. Fourth-generation Palestinian Amora.

Joshua the son of Qorḥa. Fourth-generation Palestinian Tanna. A student of Rabbi Yoḥanan the son of Nuri.

Judah (the son of Ezekiel). Second-generation Babylonian Amora who founded the school in Pumbadita.

Judah (the son of Ilai). Fourth-generation Palestinian Tanna. He was one of Rabbi Aqiba's most important students.

Judah the son of Bathyra. There may have been two sages with this name; one who lived before the Temple was destroyed in 70 C.E., and one who flourished in the third generation of the tannaitic period. Neusner, *A History of the Jews,* I, 130–134.

Judah the son of Simeon. Third- and fourth-generation Palestinian Amora. In the Palestinian Talmud he is known as Judah the son of Pazzai, while in the Babylonian Talmud he is known as Judah the son of Simeon the son of Pazzai.

La. Also known as Ilai, Ila, Hila, he was a third-generation Palestinian Amora. He was one of Yoḥanan's students.

Leazar. See Eleazar.

Levi. The name may refer to a Palestinian sage who lived during the transition from the tannaitic to the amoraic period or to Levi the son of Sisi, who was a third-generation Palestinian Amora. The latter studied with Rabbi Yoḥanan.

Levi the net-maker. He is mentioned only twice in the rabbinic texts.

Meir. Fourth-generation Palestinian Tanna. One of Aqiba's most important students, he is counted among the leaders of the mainstream of Tannaitic Judaism. R. Goldenberg, *The Sabbath-Law of Rabbi Meir* (Missoula, 1979).

Naḥman. Rav Naḥman (the son of Jacob) was a second- and third-generation Babylonian Amora.

Nathan. Fourth-generation Palestinian Tanna. He was the son of the Exilarch in Babylonia and eventually migrated to Palestine. Neusner, *A History of the Jews*, I, 141–144.

Nathan the son of Joseph. Also known as Yonatan the son of Joseph, or of Yosi, he was a fourth-generation Palestinian Tanna. He may have been one of Aqiba's students.

Nehemiah. This is the name of a fourth-generation Palestinian Tanna and a fourth-generation Palestinian Amora. The former was ordained by Judah the son of Baba after the Bar Kokhba War.

Phineḥas. Phineḥas (the priest, the son of Ḥama) was a fourth-generation Palestinian Amora.

Rabbah. Fourth-generation Babylonian Amora, the son of Joseph the son of Ḥama. Rav Naḥman was his most important teacher; he also studied with Rav Ḥisda.

Rabbi. Rabbi (Judah the Patriarch) was the leader of the Palestinian Jewish community at the end of the second century and the beginning of the third century. He was the most important Patriarch of the tannaitic period. Tradition states that he edited the Mishnah; however, recent scholarship has rejected this claim. J. Neusner, *The Modern Study of the Mishnah* (Leiden, 1973), idem, *Judaism: The Evidence of the Mishnah* (Chicago, 1982).

Rav. Rabbi Abba the son of Aibo founded the academy in Sura and was the founder of the Amoraic movement in Babylonia. J. Neusner, *A History of the Jews in Babylonia*, II, *The Early Sasanian Period* (Leiden, 1966), 126–134.

Samuel the son of Naḥman. Second- and third-generation Palestinian Amora. He was a student of Yonatan.

Samuel the son of Tanḥum. Fifth-generation Palestinian Amora.

Simeon (Simon). Second- and third-generation Palestinian Amora. He was known as Simeon the son of Pazzai in Babylonia. He was the father of Judah the son of Simeon.

Simeon the son of Azzai. Also known as the son of Azzai, he was a third-generation Palestinian Tanna. His teacher was Joshua the son of Ḥananyah.

Simeon the son of Laqish. Also known as Resh Laqish, he was a second-generation Palestinian Amora and one of Yoḥanan's students. Both Yoḥanan and Resh Laqish served as head of the academy in Tiberias.

Simeon the son of Menasya. Fifth-generation Palestinian Tanna.

Simeon the son of Yohai. Also known simply as Simeon, he was a fourth-generation Palestinian Tanna and one of Aqiba's most important students.

Simlai. Second-generation Amora who was born in Babylonia but migrated to Palestine and settled in Lod.

Tabyomi. Two sages are known by this name. One was a fourth-generation Palestinian Amora, and the other was a fifth-generation Babylonian Amora. Our texts probably refer to the first sage with this name.

Tanḥuma. Tanḥuma (the son of Abba) was a fifth-generation Palestinian Amora. He was a student of Hunah, Judah the son of Shalom, and Phineḥas.

Tanḥuma the son of Hanilai. Second-generation Palestinian Amora.

Tarfon. Second-generation Palestinian Tanna. J. Gereboff, *Rabbi Tarfon: The Tradition, the Man, and Early Rabbinic Judaism* (Missoula, 1979).

Tifdai. Seldom-mentioned sage; dates uncertain.

Yassai. I could find nothing on this sage who is mentioned in our selection from *Genesis Rabbah.*

Yoḥanan. Yoḥanan (the son of Napha [Napah]) was a second-generation Palestinian Amora. A pivotal figure in the transmission of Palestinian tannaitic traditions in the early amoraic period. He apparently studied with Judah the Patriarch.

Yoḥanan the son of Bag Bag. Also known as the son of Bag Bag, he was apparently one of Hillel's contemporaries.

Yoḥanan the son of Beroqa. Third-generation Palestinian Tanna. He was one of Joshua's students.

Yoḥanan the son of Godgada. Second-generation Palestinian Tanna.

Yoḥanan the son of Nuri. Third-generation Palestinian Tanna. He may have studied with Eliezer.

Yoḥanan the son of Zakkai. One of the founders of the Pharisaic movement in Palestine. The first major teacher, after Hillel, of whom we have knowledge. J. Neusner, *A Life of Yohanan ben Zakkai* (Leiden, 1970), idem, *Development of a Legend: Studies in the Traditions Concerning Yohanan ben Zakkai* (Leiden, 1970).

Yonatan. Fourth-generation Palestinian Tanna. He studied with Ishmael.

Yonatan the son of Joseph. See Nathan the son of Joseph.

Yoshiah. A fourth-generation Tanna who was born in Babylonia but migrated to Palestine, a third-generation Palestinian Amora, and a fifth-generation Babylonian Amora were known by this name. The Tanna was one of Ishmael's most important students. The Palestinian Amora was a student of Yoḥanan's. The Babylonian Amora was one of Rabba's students.

Yosi. Yosi (the son of Ḥalaftah) was a fourth-generation Palestinian Tanna. He was one of the students of Aqiba. A fourth-generation Palestinian Amora was also known merely as Yosi.

Yosi the Galilean. Third-generation Palestinian Tanna. J. Lightstone, *Yose the Galilean, I, Traditions in Mishnah-Tosefta* (Leiden, 1979).

Yosi the net-maker. I could find no information on this Tanna.

Yosi the son of Biba. Also known as Yosi the son of Bibi, he was a Palestinian Amora; however, his dates are uncertain.

Yosi the son of Judah. Fifth-generation Palestinian Tanna, he was the son of Judah the son of Ilai and a contemporary of Judah the Patriarch.

Yosi the son of Zimra. A Palestinian who lived during the transition from the tannaitic to the amoraic period. Some speculate that through the marriage of his son he was related to Judah the Patriarch.

Commentators and Commentaries

Bartinoro. Obadiah the son of Abraham Yare was an Italian rabbi who lived approximately 1450–1516. He was the author of one of the standard commentaries to Mishnah.

David Luria. Lithuanian rabbi and scholar who lived 1798–1855. Head of yeshivah in his hometown of Bykhow in the Mogilev region. He wrote a commentary to Mishnah; however, he appears in this volume as the author of a commentary to Midrash Rabbah known as the *Ḥiddushei HaReDaL.*

David Moses Abraham. This sage from Rohatyn wrote the *Merkevet HaMishnah,* a commentary to the Mekhilta deRabbi Ishmael.

Issachar Ber Ashkenazi. He lived in the sixteenth and seventeenth centuries and wrote a commentary to Midrash Rabbah known as *Matnat Kehunah.*

Maimonides. Moses the son of Maimon lived 1135–1204. He was born in Spain but lived in Fez and eventually Cairo. He wrote philosophical and legal compendia as well as a commentary to Mishnah.

MaLBiM. Rabbi Meir Loeb the son of Jehiel Michael, 1809–1879, was born in Volochisk (Volhynia)

Qorban Aaron. Commentary of Aaron the son of Ḥyyim, first published in Venice in 1609.

Rabbenu Hillel. Hillel the son of Eliakim lived in the twelfth century in Greece and wrote commentaries to Sifra and Sifre.

RaDaK. Rabbi David Kimḥi a grammarian and exegete of Narbonne, Provence, who lived 1160(?)–1235(?). He wrote a commentary to many of the biblical books.

RaLBaG. Rabbi Levi the son of Gershom, who lived 1288–1344, was a mathematician, astronomer, philosopher, and biblical commentator. He was probably born at Bagnols-sur-Cèze (Langue-doc), France.

Rashi. Rabbi Solomon the son of Isaac, 1040–1150, is one of the most famous talmudic and biblical commentators. He was born in Troyes, France, and eventually headed a yeshivah there.

Toledot Adam. The commentary of David Moses Abraham (see above) to Sifre.

Wilna Gaon. Elijah the son of Solomon Zalman, 1720–1797, was one of the leading spiritual and intellectual figures of his age. Among his many works were commentaries and glosses to Mekhilta, Sifra, Sifre, Tosefta, the Babylonian Talmud, and the Palestinian Talmud.

Ze'av (Zev) Wolf [Einhorn]. Author of a nineteenth-century commentary to Midrash Rabbah.

Zeh Yenaḥamu. Eighteenth-century commentary to Mekhilta by Moses of Frankfurt.

1 Introduction

A book entitled *Understanding Rabbinic Midrash* should begin with a definition of its subject matter. To what, exactly, does the term "rabbinic midrash" refer?

Let us focus first on the adjective, "rabbinic." Most people probably have an idea of what a rabbi is. Many certainly would describe a rabbi as a Jewish clergyman employed by a congregation or synagogue to perform several or all of the following functions: leading the congregation in its ritual activities, officiating at its life-cycle ceremonies (circumcision, Bar Mitzvah, Bat Mitzvah, confirmation, wedding, funeral), counseling its members, directing its growth, overseeing its educational programs, and the like.[1] Our conventional picture of a rabbi is one of an individual who delivers sermons and conducts services on the Sabbath and holidays in front of the congregation. However, this type of rabbi is quite modern. Rabbis did not assume many of these functions before the nineteenth century.[2] The rabbis with whom we are concerned, the sages who flourished in Palestine and Babylonia (modern-day Iraq) during the first seven centuries of the common era, were much different from present-day rabbis; therefore, in this volume the adjective "rabbinic" has a meaning different from the one that probably first comes to mind.

The defining characteristic of the rabbi in late antiquity was his knowledge; what he knew distinguished him from the rest of the Jews.[3] The rabbis taught that Moses had received a dual revelation from God on Mount Sinai. Part of this revelation, the Written Torah, was available to all and was contained in the biblical books of

1

Genesis, Exodus, Leviticus, Numbers, and Deuteronomy, which were written on the Torah scrolls housed in the synagogues. The second part of this revelation, the Oral Torah, was in the possession of the rabbis alone. Each rabbi had received the Oral Torah from his master, who had received it from his master, who, in turn, had received it from his master. The unbroken chain stretched all the way back to the first rabbi, *mosheh rabbenu*,[4] Moses our rabbi, who had learned Torah directly from God, face to face,[5] on Mount Sinai. Thus, to know the whole revelation it was necessary to consult a rabbi. The rabbis' possession of the Written and the Oral Torah gave them special knowledge and constituted the basis of their power and authority.

A rabbi's knowledge began with the Written Torah, with the five books of Moses'; the public record of the perfect revelation from the perfect God. This document had to be taken seriously; it had to be read and reread, studied and restudied.[6] Because God's revelation to Moses on Sinai was, by definition, complete and perfect, it contained all that one needed to know, or should know.[7] But those who read the holy scroll encountered problems, for the Written Torah is laden with unfamiliar technical terms, vague commandments, repeated phrases, sentences, and even pericopae, and multiple, different, and often contradictory versions of the same story or accounts of the same event. Because this scroll contained an accurate record of what the One and Only God had revealed to Moses, these difficulties had to be faced and explained. The Torah had to make sense, and it was the rabbi's task to make it comprehensible.

The Oral Torah was the record of the rabbinic attempts to solve the difficulties mentioned above. It filled in the details, explained unclear matters, and expanded upon enigmatic passages. It brought forth material relevant to the biblical accounts and detailed all that was explicit and implicit in the Written Torah. In addition, it offered rules and methods according to which the Torah should be interpreted and upon which an understanding of it should be based. The Oral Torah provided the guidelines that made possible the application of Scripture's lessons to everyday, contemporary life, and it offered countless examples of such applications. The Oral Torah was the key to unlocking the mysteries of the Written Torah, and the rabbis were the only ones who possessed this key.

Because the rabbis believed that they alone possessed both parts of revelation—the Written and the Oral Torah—they claimed that they were the only people who could follow the word of God completely and exactly: They alone knew all that God expected of human beings, they alone could follow the commandments correctly, they alone could practice the rituals in their minutest details, they alone knew the correct ways in which people should interact, and so on. As a result of the Jewish population's acceptance of the rabbis' claims that they fulfilled the duties and responsibilities of human beings more completely than anyone else, the rabbis were considered to be among those most favored by God. The rabbi possessed extraordinary powers because he could be counted among God's "closest friends." This enabled the rabbi to cure people, to curse people, to foresee the future, to construct amulets, to bring rain, to create food out of nothing, and the like.[8] He was believed to be, in the final analysis, a man of power.

The rabbi knew more than other people, and this led him to act differently from the majority of Jews. The rabbis were scrupulous about their dress, their food, their language, their prayers, and their daily actions. They knew the fine points of God's law, and they ardently strove to fulfill their potential as the type of human beings God had intended to create. The differences in dress, language, and dietary habits helped to make a rabbi recognizable and to keep the rabbinic class distinguishable from the rest of the Jews.[9] In addition, the rabbis' actions became part of the Oral Torah, for these traits illustrated what the rabbi knew; they were the concretization of the Oral Torah.

A man acquired the status of rabbi by studying with a rabbi. In fact, the classical rabbi's primary task was not to lead a congregation or to deliver sermons every Friday night; rather, the rabbi's highest goal was to create other rabbis.[10] True, membership in the rabbinic class was open to everyone, and in theory, the rabbis wanted all Jews to acquire the knowledge of the Oral Torah so that they would be able to follow God's word correctly. But not everyone could spend time studying with a rabbi, and not everyone had the intellectual ability to succeed in his rabbinical studies. Therefore, the rabbis had to go out into the community and become active in its life in order "to spread the word." Many of the rabbis were the civil servants of the Babylonian and Palestinian Jewish communities. They ran the courts, supervised the markets, prepared and witnessed official documents, and the like.[11] As a result of their being the civil servants of the Jewish community, the rabbis were involved in the everyday public affairs of that community, and they strove to ensure that at least the community's public life conformed to the Oral Torah. For example, a rabbi who was a market supervisor could see to it that all of the butchers sold meat that was ritually acceptable and properly slaughtered. However, the rabbi could not enter a Jew's private home in order to determine whether or not that particular Jew was eating only permitted meat. A rabbi who served as a judge in a Jewish court could adjudicate the cases that came before *his* court according to the Torah; however, he had no control of cases that did not appear before him or were tried in non-Jewish courts. In fact, he could not even force Jews to appear before rabbinic courts instead of gentile tribunals. In brief, the rabbis of late antiquity could not interfere in a Jew's private life unless the latter asked them to do so. The rabbis exercised control only over the public affairs of the Jewish community unless specifically requested to deal with a person's private affairs.

There was, however, one segment of the ancient Jewish community over which the rabbis had absolute and complete control, the rabbinic class. Because membership in the class was a privilege conferred by other members, an individual rabbi had to "toe the line" if he wished to remain part of the rabbinic circle. The rabbinic way of life, therefore, was probably a reality at least for the rabbis, since they probably did live their lives according to the Oral Torah, but it is unlikely that the average Jew followed the minutiae of the rabbinic traditions. Thus, only a small portion of the ancient Jewish community were rabbinic Jews and followed the details of the Oral Torah. [12]

The term "rabbinic" refers to the way of life, the beliefs, the ideas, the ideals, and the behaviors of the rabbis of late antiquity. Rabbinic midrash, therefore, is the type of midrash produced by this small segment of the Jewish population of Palestine and Babylonia during the first seven centuries of the common era.

The meaning of "midrash" is much less well-known than the meaning of "rabbinic." Even to those familiar with Hebrew terminology, the word "midrash" has a variety of connotations. It has been used to describe biblical interpretations or exegesis, sermons, and haggadic (nonlegal) discussions. [13]

For the purposes of this volume, "midrash" refers to statements, comments, or remarks that are juxtaposed to the accepted authoritative Jewish Scriptures. From this point of view, rabbinic midrash

refers to a literary phenomenon—the juxtaposition of rabbinic statements with the biblical text in a way that suggests that the latter is
intimately related to the former.

For the rabbis, the authoritative Jewish Scriptures were all contained in the *TaNaKh*—Torah, Nevi'im (Prophets), Ketuvim (Writings, Hagiographa)—the three sections of the Hebrew Bible, which
achieved final canonical status sometime during the first three
centuries of the common era.[14] This collection of material was
considered to be the sum total of God's public revelation to humans.
As stated above, this public revelation contained obscure passages
and posed difficulties for those who wished to understand it. However, the process of interpreting the material which eventually
achieved canonical status within the Jewish community did not
begin with the rabbis. On the contrary, examples of the interpretation of older, accepted material is found within each of the three
major sections of the Hebrew Bible.[15] There is virtual agreement
among scholars that the process of interpreting Scripture is as old
as the Hebrew Bible itself. Thus, we should view the rabbis' midrashic activity as a continuation of a process begun at the genesis
of the Hebrew Bible.

Just as we should not view the rabbinic interpretations of the
Bible as a process begun only after the Bible had been canonized, so
also we should not conclude that the small group of Jews we have
described as "rabbis" were the only Jews of the postbiblical period to
exegete the Hebrew Bible. That those Jews and non-Jews who
eventually became known as Christians elucidated the Hebrew Bible
is a well-known fact.[16] In addition, the small community of Jews who
lived on the bluff overlooking the north end of the Dead Sea at
Qumran also explained the Bible, and some of their interpretations,
known as *pesharim* after the word *pesher* ("interpretation") with
which many of the relevant passages open, have come down to us.[17]
Furthermore, we have several anonymous documents from the
period between 400 B.C.E. and 200 C.E. which rewrite, summarize,
paraphrase, or expand upon the accounts contained in Scripture.[18]
One could also argue that the translations of the Hebrew Bible into
Greek (the Septuagint)[19] and into Aramaic (the *targum*)[20] contain as
much interpretation as translation. In each of these examples the
relationship between the biblical text and the comment is clear and
unambiguous.

The central feature of a midrashic comment is its *explicit* relationship to the Bible. Let me explain this point with reference to the rabbinic texts. The primary document of first- and second-century Palestinian Judaism is the Mishnah, the first collection of rabbinic teachings. Much of the material found in Mishnah is based on the Hebrew Bible, and there is no doubt that the framers of Mishnah knew the Hebrew Bible and believed that they were producing a document that somehow was based on it.[21] However, Mishnah seldom explicitly refers to the biblical verse upon which its statements are based or to the scriptural text from which its laws are derived. For this reason alone, most of the comments found in Mishnah are not midrashic. In fact, most of them are the opposite of midrash, for they seem to consciously avoid drawing a *clear* relationship between themselves and the Bible.

The difference between a midrashic and a nonmidrashic statement may be determined by context. If a remark that does not refer to a biblical verse appears in Mishnah with others that also make no reference to Scripture, the remark is nonmidrashic. On the other hand, if the same remark in the same form appears in a midrashic collection as one of several comments juxtaposed to a specific biblical verse, the remark becomes midrashic. The defining characteristic of a midrashic statement is its explicit relationship (real or constructed) and formal juxtaposition to the biblical text, and neither its content nor its particular language.

Let me illustrate. We find the following passage in Mishnah *Nega'im* 1:2:

> The variegation that is in snow-white [leprosy] is like wine that is mixed with snow. "The variegation that is in lime-like [leprosy] is like blood mixed with milk"—the words of Rabbi Ishmael. Rabbi Aqiba says: "The reddish color that is in this and in that is like wine mixed with water."

This passage offers opinions about the different colors of skin that is infected by disease. Notice that nothing in this passage connects it to a biblical text; therefore, it is a nonmidrashic pericope. However, the same statements appear in Sifra, a collection of rabbinic interpretations of Leviticus. Because in their context in Sifra the statements are *presented* as an exegesis of a verse from Numbers, the pericope becomes a midrash:

And like what is the intermediate color [of skin disease? It appears] like snow, for it is said: *Miriam was leprous, as white as snow* (Num. 12:10). From here they said the signs [of leprosy] are two, which are four. "[Spot *(bhrt)* in Leviticus and Numbers refers to] a spot which is an intensely bright spot [white] as snow. The second is [a color] like the lime [on the outside] of the Temple. The swelled sore [is a color] like the membrane surrounding an egg. The second is like white wool"—the words of Rabbi Meir. But sages say: "The swelled sore is like wool and the second is like the membrane surrounding an egg." The variegation that is in snow-white [leprosy] is like wine that is mixed with snow. "The variegation that is in lime-like [leprosy] is like blood mixed with milk"— the words of Rabbi Ishmael. Rabbi Aqiba says: "The reddish color that is in this and in that is like wine mixed with water."

In the passage from Sifra, *Tazri'a* 2:4–5, the statements of Ishmael and Aqiba are joined with other comments *that are placed in the context of an explanation of Num. 12:10.* The editors of this section of Sifra had redacted the rabbis' remarks to make them appear as interpretations of Num. 12:10. For that reason, they may be classified as midrashic comments, for in this context they are clearly related to a biblical verse.

Mishnah *Ketubot* 1:1 states:

A virgin should be married on a Wednesday and a widow on a Thursday, for in towns the court sits twice a week, on Mondays and on Thursdays; so that if the husband would lodge a complaint about his bride's virginity, he may go in the morning immediately to the court.

The Mishnah states that a virgin should be married on a Wednesday and a widow on a Thursday, and it explains that this is the practice so that it will be easy for the new groom to bring any questions about his bride's virginity before the court. However, in Genesis Rabbah 8:28 we read:

And God blessed them (Gen. 1:28). There [in the Mishnah] we learn that a virgin is married on the fourth day (Wednesday), but a widow [is married] on the fifth day (Thursday). Why [were these

days designated as wedding days? They were so designated because the word] "blessing" is written with regard to them. But
"blessing" is written with regard to the fifth day (Thursday) [Gen.
1:22] and the sixth day (Friday) [Gen. 1:28]. Bar Qapara said: "The
fourth day is the eve of the fifth, and the fifth is the eve of the
sixth."

This is not the place to discuss the awkward nature of this passage;
we shall do that below when we review chapter 8 of Genesis Rabbah.
My point here is that the same law appears in Mishnah *Ketubot* and
in Genesis Rabbah. In the former it is in a nonmidrashic passage,
while in the latter it is clearly a midrashic statement, for the passage
attempts to find the reason for the law in specific and clearly
identifiable biblical passages.

To summarize: Midrash, the subject matter of this book, com-
prises a body of statements pertaining to Scripture and juxtaposed
to the scriptural text that were made by the small group of Jews of
late antiquity whom we have called rabbis.

II

Although, as we have seen, many types of Jews commented upon the
Bible in late antiquity, we can identify important *literary* features
that distinguish rabbinic midrash from other types of Jewish scriptural interpretation. First, the rabbinic texts are collections of independent units whose sequential or thematic arrangements are the
work of the editors. It is doubtful that the individual pericopae or
statements were originally parts of a consecutive commentary to the
Bible. Second, we often find more than one comment per biblical
unit in the rabbinic collections. Several synonymous, complemen-
tary, or contradictory remarks may appear in connection with a
single verse, word, or letter. No comparable phenomenon appears in
the nonrabbinic documents. Third, a large number of the rabbinic
statements are assigned to named sages. Unlike the other types of
midrashim, rabbinic midrashic statements are not all anonymous.
However, the editors and authors of the rabbinic collections are
unknown to us, just as the creators of the majority of the other
forms of Jewish exegesis from this period are also unknown to us.
Fourth, the rabbinic comment may be a direct and clearly recogniz-

able discussion of the biblical text or it may be part of a dialogue, a story, or an extended soliloquy which has been artificially juxtaposed to Scripture. The comment may answer a question that derives directly from the Bible or it may deal with an issue which was raised in another interpretation of the biblical passage. In some instances, the midrashic comment is so loosely connected to the biblical text that the former would be totally comprehensible in another context where it was not associated with any biblical verse. Fifth, the rabbinic commentator may mention the specific method which forms the basis of his remark. The methods are never explicit in the other forms of midrashic activity.

The selections included in this volume illustrate several presuppositions that underlie the rabbinic interpretation of the Bible. Because the rabbis believed that the Bible was the accurate and complete public record of a direct revelation from the One, Only, and Perfect God to His people, nothing in the Bible could be frivolous. Every element of the text—every letter, every verse, every phrase—was important and written as it was for specific reasons. The Bible contained no needless expressions, no "mere" repetitions, and no superfluous words or phrases. If something appeared to be superfluous, repetitious, or needless, it had to be explained and interpreted in order to demonstrate that this was not the case. The assumption that every element of the biblical text was written in a specific way in order to teach something underlies all of the comments found in rabbinic midrash.

A second major rabbinic presupposition is that everything in the whole Bible—the Torah, the Prophets, and the Writings—is interrelated. Over and over again we shall see that one cannot explain a particular verse without taking other verses into consideration. Frequently we shall be told that a given verse needed to appear in order to modify another sentence or phrase.

A third concept that underlies our texts is that there may be more than one possible interpretation for any given biblical verse. Again and again we shall encounter several interpretations of a given text, with no resolution among them.

A fourth idea that runs through our texts, especially through Sifra, Mekhilta, and Sifre, is that reason unaided by revelation is fallible. A common technique in our midrashim is to refute a reasonable or logical conclusion merely by citing a verse from Scripture. The midrashic activity was important, for without it, people might not act in proper ways and might misunderstand the realities of the world, man, and God.

A fifth assumption of the authors of our texts is that the midrashic activity was a religious, God-centered activity. It should be obvious that Jews were not the only people who interpreted an ancient text. In fact, at exactly the same time that the rabbis in Palestine and Babylonia were elucidating the Holy Writings, the Greek rhetoricians in Alexandria, Egypt, were commenting upon the classical Greek authors.[22] Indeed, many of the techniques employed by the rhetoricians were applied to the Bible by the rabbis. Scholars have pointed out that many of the technical terms of rabbinic exegesis are merely Hebrew translations of the names the Greek rhetoricians applied to their own methods of interpretation.[23] However, at its core rabbinic midrash was based on the word of the One and Only God. For the rabbis, the Bible contained all the secrets of the universe, and it was the source of all knowledge and wisdom. Midrash thus was a means of discovering these secrets, of attaining true knowledge and wisdom. The Bible was the ultimate guide for human action; it was the standard against which one measured one's deeds, the final arbiter of true and false, right and wrong. The rabbis dealt with only one book, and that book was not of human origin. With the passing of time, the study of the Torah became the most holy task possible to humans and, thus, the goal of a well-led life. Its rewards were found in this world; but, more importantly, they were bestowed fully in the world-to-come. The rabbis' interest in the Bible was not merely historical or antiquarian. The rabbis were not merely interested in explaining difficult words or passages, in identifying unknown places, in solving problems within the text. Their interpretation and study led to salvation, not only for the Jews, but for the whole world. Midrash was the product of rabbinic theology. It focused on the word of the One and Only God who had created the world, revealed His will on Mount Sinai, and who would eventually perfect His creation. In all of its forms, midrash was a religious exercise. Midrash reached its zenith only after the Temple in Jerusalem lay in ruins. Just as the Torah replaced the Temple as the locus for meeting God, so also the midrashist replaced the priest as the intermediary between God's word and humanity. Midrash replaced the sacrifices as the means of securing God's favor and of joining the upper and the lower worlds. While the rabbis might "play" with the biblical text, this was holy "play."[24] Midrash was, above all, a means of confronting God and of bringing Him into contact with His people.

III

Now that we have an initial picture of rabbinic midrash, we should ask why it is important. What do we learn if we "understand rabbinic midrash"? We saw above that rabbinic Judaism is Torah-centered and that rabbis were rabbis because they studied and lived Torah. Therefore, by examining how they dealt with the Torah, how they interpreted it, how they read it, how they studied it, we shall achieve a better understanding of the rabbis themselves, for we shall discover how they dealt with the central symbol of their system of thought.

All Jewish groups of late antiquity had to confront the Hebrew Bible and deal with it. In fact, the different ways in which the various types of Jews interpreted the Bible were major factors in their self-understanding.[25] By examining rabbinic midrash, we shall gain better insight into how the rabbis understood themselves and the type of Judaism they created. By studying rabbinic midrash we shall begin to understand what it means to say that rabbinic Judaism was "Torah-centered," and what the rabbis meant when they suggested that the study of Torah was the most important activity in which a human could be engaged.

Understanding the rabbinic Judaism of late antiquity is important because contemporary Judaism is its direct descendant. The realities of contemporary Judaism were first encountered by the rabbis of the first seven centuries of the common era. It was then that the Temple in Jerusalem was destroyed and replaced by the synagogues. With the end of the Temple came the cessation of the sacrificial cult and the creation of the prayer services designed to take its place. It was then that the priests were replaced by the rabbis. It was then that the center of Judaism moved from Palestine to the Diaspora, so that instead of living under an independent government of their own, the Jews were obliged to subsist in foreign countries under non-Jewish rulers. The responses which the rabbis made to these changes still play a role in contemporary Judaism. The rabbinic texts still form the basis of our Judaism. We study their writings and we pray their prayers. Their use of the Bible, the ways they read it and interpreted it, was central to Judaism's surviving the trauma of the Temple's destruction in 70 C.E.

Rabbinic Judaism, like many religions, was based on a revealed text that had been given to humans in the distant past. By looking at the ways in which one group of people, the rabbis, dealt with a specific revealed document, the Torah, we shall gain insight into the broader problem of the relationship between a "revealed text" and those who lived a long time after the revelation but still considered the revealed document to be valid and important. Thus, our study of rabbinic midrash will help us to understand both rabbinic Judaism in particular and other text-oriented religions in general.[26]

In addition, midrash constitutes one of the primary corpora of rabbinic literature. It stands apart from other rabbinic literary creations because all of its statements are juxtaposed clearly and directly to the Bible. For this reason, it can be studied independently of the other types of rabbinic texts, such as Mishnah or Talmud. As we shall discover below, despite the variety of midrashim, this category of literature is sufficiently coherent to provide an independent subject of study. Rabbinic midrash as a general literary category and the individual midrashic collections as discrete documents deserve the same attention that has been paid to Mishnah, Tosefta, the Talmuds, the liturgical statements, and the mystical texts of Judaism of late antiquity.

IV

We have explained above what the reader is going to encounter in this volume and why the subject of this book is worthy of concern. It is now time to turn to the method for studying rabbinic midrash which will be employed below. How are we going to undertake the process of "understanding rabbinic midrash"? Our discussion of rabbinic midrash will focus on three aspects: the processes by which statements were juxtaposed to the Bible, the statements themselves, and the rabbinic collections of these statements. Let us now look at each of these issues in turn.

The processes by which statements were juxtaposed to the Bible are complex. Some rabbinic comments are merely restatements of the "literal" meaning of the biblical text, and the process that brought them into being was the simple rewriting of the biblical verse in different words. Others derive from a real or perceived problem in the biblical text. The process that produced them was the master's identifying the problem and then solving it. In these cases the midrashic statements may explain an obscure word, an enigmatic reference, or an unusual spelling in the biblical verse. In other cases, however, the problem "discovered" in the biblical text may be artificial and merely an "excuse" for the master to make his exegetical comment. Furthermore, some rabbinic comments appear to be attempts to ground a particular theological, political, social, or economic point or ritual in the Bible. In these instances the midrashist began with the nonbiblical reality and then discovered a biblical proof-text which justified that reality. Finally, some passages in the rabbinic midrashic collections seem to have little relationship to the verses to which they have been joined. In these instances, the process by which the remark became "midrashic" was the work of the editors of the texts. These different processes created different types of midrashic statements, each of which relates to the biblical verses in different ways.

The second issue we shall discuss is the formal structure of the midrashic statements. Here our interest will be in the way in which they are formulated, to whom they are attributed, to whom they are addressed, and how they substantially and formally are related to the biblical text. We shall find some statements that are closely and carefully juxtaposed to biblical verses, and others that are related to a particular biblical text only by the context in which they occur. In addition, we shall discover midrashic statements, disputes, and debates. Furthermore, we shall see that some midrashic statements are set in a narrative framework, while others are short pithy remarks. In brief, we shall discover that midrashic statements and pericopae are not formally different from any other rabbinic comments, with the exception of their juxtaposition to the biblical text.

The last broad subject with which we shall deal concerns the nature of the collections of the rabbinic interpretations. Below, the reader will encounter examples taken from the six major rabbinic midrashic collections. We shall discover that each document asks its questions in a unique manner, has its own presuppositions, and constructs its exegetical comments in its own ways. Although, all of the texts share some common features and presuppositions, and even deal with the same issues, they are each distinctive. Upon finishing this volume, the reader should have a good idea of the variety of rabbinic midrashic collections.

The selections that appear in this anthology have been chosen because they allow the reader to understand the three aspects of midrash mentioned: the process of creating interpretations, the interpretations themselves, and the collections of these interpretations. Each example presents a variety of rabbinic interpretive techniques and exhibits a wide range of rabbinic presuppositions about revelation and reason. Some examples merely repeat the literal meaning of the biblical text, while others seem to ignore the actual words of Scripture.

In order to address the issues raised above, I have provided passages lengthy enough to allow the reader to acquire a sense of the different collections. The differences in approach, language, and presuppositions among the various rabbinic midrashic collections are clearly evident on the following pages. Throughout, I have tried to maintain terminological consistency. The translations are uninterrupted by comments or notes so that the reader can confront each text on its own terms. All translations are original for this volume. Although I have been sensitive to the need to render the passages into idiomatic English, I have attempted to reflect distinctive language, technical terminology, and syntax in the translations. I have transcribed the Tetragrammaton as YHWH. This noun is a proper name, and the usual translation of "Lord" does not convey this to the modern reader. Because the rabbinic tradition prohibited the pronunciation of God's name, I have omitted the vowels when transcribing the Hebrew consonants. It is well to observe that the midrash often reads a biblical verse in a specific way, sometimes by altering either the vocalization of words or the syntax of a verse. If the flow of the midrash demands that a verse be rendered in a way different from its conventional English translation, I have offered the translation required by the text. However, if the midrash only reads a particular verse in a unique manner, I have placed the midrash's understanding of the verse in the notes. Words enclosed by brackets [] are not found in the Hebrew text but are required in English to make sense out of the passage.

Each selection is introduced by a brief discussion of the collection in general. These remarks make it clear that there is much we do not know about the rabbinic collections. We do not know the names of their editors, nor do we know the exact dates of their compilation. In addition, the introductions present a short summary of the midrash so that the reader will have an idea of what he or she will encounter in the rabbinic text.

My comments follow the translations. In these comments, I explain the rabbinic exegeses, the issues that are explicit or implicit in the interpretations, the methods the rabbis employed, the stories and the issues that are assumed by the masters, and the ways the various comments fit together and relate to one another and to the biblical text to which they are juxtaposed. Some of the comments draw on the traditional commentaries to these collections, but many present my own interpretations. Unlike most traditional commentaries, my commentary seeks to interpret each portion of a midrashic text in its own terms. It does not presuppose that rabbinic midrash is monolithic, and that scriptural interpretations can be understood apart from their immediate literary contexts. It therefore makes only occasional use of parallels or passages outside of the document under discussion. Although I sometimes rely on medieval and modern commentators, I consistently note the century in which the commentator flourished. Therefore, a twelfth-century explanation of a third-century text is identified as such, and the reader is left to decide on the value of the explanation. The comments are meant only as an aid to the reader; they are not designed to offer a complete and definitive analysis of the midrashim which appear in this volume. Their purpose is to raise issues as well as to answer questions.

My conclusions appear following the comments. In these paragraphs I summarize the midrashic text, pointing out how I believe each section relates to each other section. I explain how I view the collection: how it is structured, what questions it asks, to whom it is addressed, and I draw attention to the sociological, historical, and political realities I believe were in the minds of the authors of our texts. The "conclusions" aim to be suggestive rather than definitive or comprehensive and indicate possibilities for further study and research.

Each chapter concludes with a section of notes. The notes refer to other versions of the passages quoted in the midrash, documents and passages mentioned or assumed by the midrash, the commentators and scholars from whom I have drawn my remarks, and some secondary sources that more fully discuss the issues raised either in the midrashim themselves or in my comments to these selections. In addition, the notes contain references to parallel versions of the accounts found in the midrashic texts.

I have provided only the first step of the intellectual journey through rabbinic midrash. I have presented the texts in a complete and, I hope, comprehensible manner. I expect interested readers to take this first step with me and to proceed on the remainder of the journey on their own, preferably with the guidance I have provided on the following pages. Rabbinic midrash is interesting because it offers us a wide variety of the intellectual creations of the rabbis. It shows how they dealt with the holiest of texts, the Bible, and it allows us to see how this text functioned in their minds and worldview. Rabbinic midrash is important because Judaism is a text-oriented system; it is based on the supposed accurate record of God's revelation to Moses on Mount Sinai. Rabbinic midrash shows us how the rabbis, the founders of contemporary Judaism, dealt with the revelation on Sinai so that that revelation could indeed have everlasting value, meaning, and importance.

NOTES

1. M. Sklare, *Conservative Judaism: An American Religious Movement,* new, augmented ed. (New York, 1972), 159–198. J. Neusner, *Understanding American Judaism: Toward the Description of a Modern Religion* (New York, 1975), I, 115–216.

2. D. Philipson, *The Reform Movement in Judaism* (London, 1907), especially 36–37, 72–102. W. G. Plaut, *The Rise of Reform Judaism: A Sourcebook of its European Origins* (New York: 1963), 228–233.

3. My description of a rabbi in late antiquity is derived from the picture drawn by Jacob Neusner. J. Neusner, *A History of the Jews in Babylonia* (Leiden, 1965–70), especially vols. II–III. J. Neusner, *There We Sat Down* (Nashville and New York, 1972).

4. See, Mishnah, *Pirqe Avot* 1:1 ff.: "Moses received the Torah from Sinai and transmitted it to Joshua, and Joshua to the elders, the elders to the prophets, the prophets transmitted it to the men of the Great Assembly. . . . Simon the Just was of the remnant of the Great Assembly. . . . Antigonus of Soko received [the Torah] from Simeon the Just. . . . Yosi the son of Yoezer of Zeredah and Yosi the son of Yoḥanan of Jerusalem received [the Torah] from them," etc. J. Neusner, *The Rabbinic Traditions About the Pharisees before 70* (Leiden, 1971), I, 11–23. For a discussion of "Moses our rabbi," see Neusner, *There We Sat Down,* 73–74.

5. Deut. 34:10: *And there has not arisen a prophet since in Israel like Moses, whom YHWH knew face to face.*

6. Mishnah, *Pirqe Avot* 5:22: "Ben Bag Bag said: 'Turn it [the Torah] and turn it again, for everything is in it; and contemplate it and grow gray and old over it and stir not from it, for you can have no better rule than it.' "

7. Neusner, *History,* III, 94–194.

8. Neusner, *There We Sat Down,* 72–97.

9. Ibid., 90–92.

10. On the training of rabbis, see D. Goodblatt, *Rabbinic Instruction in Sasanian Babylonia* (Leiden, 1974).

11. Neusner, *History,* III, 272–338.

12. Ibid., III, 95–194.

13. G. Porton, "Midrash: Palestinian Jews and the Hebrew Bible in the Greco-Roman Period," in *Aufstieg und Niedergang der römischen Welt,* ed. H. Temporini and W. Haase (Berlin and New York, 1979), II.19.2, 103–138. G. Porton, "Defining Midrash," in *The Study of Ancient Judaism,* ed. J. Neusner (New York, 1981), 55–92. Neusner has suggested that so many

17

meanings have been applied to the term "midrash" as to render the word virtually useless as a descriptive term. J. Neusner, *Midrash in Context: Exegesis in Formative Judaism* (Philadelphia, 1983)

14. On the canonization of the Hebrew Bible and the significance of this process, see S. Leiman, *The Canonization of Hebrew Scriptures: The Talmudic and Midrashic Evidence* (Hamden, 1976). J. Sanders, *Torah and Canon* (Philadelphia, 1972).

15. S. Sandmel suggested that certain portions of Genesis are "haggadic expansions" of earlier sections, G. Vermes suggested that Deuteronomy was a kind of midrash on Exodus and Numbers, J. Halperin considers Ezekiel 10:9–17 to be a type of midrash, Bevard Childs argued that the titles given to some of the Psalms should be viewed as a type of midrash on Psalms, and L. Zunz in the last century was one of the first to claim that the books of Chronicles are a midrash on the books of Kings. For a discussion of this issue and references to the works cited, see Porton, "Defining Midrash," 67–69; "Midrash," 118–119.

16. R. Ruether has argued that the difference between the nascent Christian community and rabbinic Judaism was a matter of midrash, the way in which each group expounded the Hebrew Bible. R. Ruether, *Faith and Fraticide* (New York, 1974), 23–116.

17. For a dicussion of the *pesher,* see Porton, "Defining Midrash," 75–77; "Midrash," 125–127.

18. Porton, "Defining Midrash," 72–75; "Midrash," 122–125.

19. C. Rabin, "The Translation Process and the Character of the Septuagint," *Textus,* VI (1968), 1–26. E. Bickerman, "The LXX as a Translation," *Proceedings of the American Academy for Jewish Research,* XXVIII (1959), 9 ff.

20. Porton, "Defining Midrash," 70–72; "Midrash," 119–122.

21. J. Neusner, *Judaism: The Evidence of the Mishnah* (Chicago, 1981), 167–229.

22. R. Pfeiffer, *History of Classical Scholarship* (Oxford, 1971).

23. D. Daube, "Rabbinic Methods of Interpretation and Hellenistic Rhetoric," *Hebrew Union College Annual,* XXII (1949), 239–264. S. Lieberman, *Hellenism in Jewish Palestine* (New York, 1950), 20–46.

24. I. Heinemann, *The Paths of the Aggadah* [Hebrew] (Jerusalem, 1954), 2.

25. J. Blenkinsopp, "Interpretation and the Tendency to Sectarianism: An Aspect of Second Temple History," in *Jewish and Christian Self-Definition,* II, *Aspects of Judaism in the Greco-Roman Period,* ed. E. P. Sanders, A. I. Baumgarten, and A. Mendelson (Philadelphia, 1981), 1–26.

26. G. F. Moore described Judaism as a "Revealed Religion," and his comments are important in the present context. G. F. Moore, *Judaism in the First Centuries of the Christian Era: The Age of the Tannaim* (Cambridge, 1966), I, 219–356.

2 Sifra

Sifra, organized as a running commentary to the Book of Leviticus, is one of our oldest midrashic collections.[1] However, the exact date of its compilation and its final editor are unknown to us.[2] Sifra means "the Book," and the name has been applied to the Book of Leviticus itself as well as to our midrashic collection.[3] Similarly, the Palestinian Talmud (edited approximately 500 C.E.) calls the Book of Leviticus and the midrashic material on it *torat kohanim* ("the priestly torah," or "the priestly law"). Although today Sifra is a running commentary to virtually the whole Book of Leviticus, some portions of the text appear to be older than others; therefore, the text seems to be constructed from various layers of exegetical comments.[4]

The selection which follows comments upon Leviticus 1:1–2: *And YHWH called to Moses and spoke to him from the Tent of Meeting saying: "Speak to the Children of Israel and say to them, 'When a man among you . . .'"*

The comments with which Sifra opens reflect an extremely detailed reading of the biblical text. The midrash asks why the verbs "call" and "spoke" both appear in Lev. 1:1, amplifies the phrase *to him* in the same verse, and plays with the preposition *from* in the phrase *from the Tent of Meeting*. The conclusions reached in these discussions were nonlegal. Although at one point the midrash suggests that a teacher learns from the way God spoke to Moses on Mount Sinai to give his students time to contemplate what they have learned, for the most part this section of the midrash does not attempt to reach any conclusions concerning normative action. The first sections of this exegetical text show us how much the rabbis read "from" or "into" a simple biblical text.

When Sifra moves to Lev. 1:2 it takes up legal matters; however, these issues are again based on a concern for the details of the biblical text. From an analysis of the phrase *Children of Israel* we learn that men and women

19

did not practice the same rites with regard to the sacrifices. By juxtaposing this phrase with Lev. 24:14, we also learn that gentiles and Jews did not perform the same rituals with the offerings they brought to the Temple in Jerusalem. Our selection ends with a detailed discussion of the phrase *a man among you*, Lev. 1:2. Here we learn that proselytes are considered to be like Jews, while apostates are to be rejected.

One of the most important features of the following selection is that much of it follows the same pattern: The anonymous midrash offers an interpretation of the verse, that interpretation is challenged by the text's offering a number of "logical" arguments, and these arguments are rejected with a citation of Scripture. Jacob Neusner has explained the significance of this pattern:

> One polemic fundamental to Sifra's purpose is to demonstrate the inadequacy of reason unaided by revelation. Time and again Sifra asks, Does this proposition, offered with a proof-text, really require the stated proof of revelation? Will it not stand firmly upon the basis of autonomous reason unaided by Scripture? Sometimes Scripture will show that the opposite of the conclusion of reason is the result of exegesis. Therefore, the truth is to be discovered solely through exegesis. At other times, Sifra will show that reason by itself is flawed and fallible, not definitive. At important points it will seek to prove not only a given proposition, but also that the proposition is to be demonstrated solely through revelation, through exegesis of Scripture.[5]

Thus, for Sifra, the Bible is necessary because it teaches us by means of revelation what we could not necessarily learn through our reason. In addition, the Bible often corrects or prevents mistakes which might result from our use of reason alone.

In addition, we shall see that Sifra is much more than a commentary to Leviticus. While portions of our text offer a detailed analysis of the words which appear in Leviticus, other sections do not even refer to Leviticus. Whole units of the text have little or nothing to do with the text of Leviticus; they have been included because they are thematically or linguistically related to the material which surrounds them. In addition, in many places several interpretations of a verse are presented and no choice is made among the several possible interpretations.

And[6] [YHWH] called [to Moses] and spoke [to him] (Lev. 1:1). [This teaches us] that "calling" precedes "speaking." But cannot [this be established by means of] an argument by analogy, [so that we do not need to learn it from this verse? Here is the argument: The holy] speech is mentioned here, and [the holy] speech is mentioned in connection with the [burning] bush, [for Ex. 3:4 states: *When YHWH saw that he turned aside to see, God called to him out of the bush. . . . Then He said: . . .].* Just as with regard to the [holy] speech which was mentioned at the [burning] bush, "calling" preceded "speaking," so also with regard to the [holy] speech which was mentioned here, "calling" preceded "speaking."

No, [these two instances are not analogous]. If you say concerning the [holy] speech at the [burning] bush, which was the first time [that God] spoke [to Moses and that God's calling preceded His speaking], need you reason that, with regard to the speech at the Tent of Meeting, which was not the first time [that God] spoke [to Moses], that He likewise began by calling [to Moses? Rather], the [holy] speech at Mount Sinai supports [your claim that you can use an argument by analogy], for [Mount Sinai] was not the first occasion on which God spoke to Moses, yet, even so, [God] began there by "calling" and followed by "speaking."

No, [these two instances are not analogous]. If you say concerning the [holy] speech at Mount Sinai, which [was addressed] to all of Israel [and that "calling" preceded "speaking"], need you reason [that "calling" preceded "speaking] in the case of the [holy] speech at the Tent of Meeting, which was [addressed to Moses alone and] not to all of Israel? [You need not.] Behold, you can argue [that "calling" always should precede "speaking"] by means of a prototype. [You can] not [claim that] the [holy] speech at the [burning] bush where He first spoke [to Moses] is like the [holy] speech at Mount Sinai, which was not the first occasion on which God spoke [to Moses], and [you can] not [claim that] the [holy] speech at Mount Sinai, where He spoke to all of Israel, is like the [holy] speech at the [burning] bush, where He did not speak to all of Israel.

The common element between [the speech at Mount Sinai and the speech at the burning bush] is that they are [both holy] speech[es] and [that they] were from the mouth of the Holy One to Moses and that "calling" preceded "speaking" [in both places]; therefore, in every [place] where there is a [holy] speech which is from the mouth of the Holy One to Moses [one might reason that] "calling" preceded "speaking."

Not [necessarily. You could argue] that just as the common element between [the speech at Mount Sinai and the speech at the burning bush] is that they are [holy] speech[es spoken] through fire from the mouth of the Holy One to Moses and [in both places] "calling" preceded "speaking," so also only [in] a [place where] there is a [holy] speech [spoken] through fire from the mouth of the Holy One to Moses will "calling" precede "speaking." [And this would] exclude the [holy] speech at the Tent of Meeting, for it was not [spoken] through fire. [Therefore], Scripture [must] say: [*And YHWH] called [to Moses] and spoke [to him]* (Lev. 1:1) [to teach us that also here, where the holy speech was not spoken through fire,] "calling" preceded "speaking."

You might think that "calling" [occurred] only with reference to this [act] of speaking alone. And on what basis [do we learn that "calling" preceded] all [acts of] "speaking" which are in the Torah? Scripture says: [*YHWH called to Moses and spoke to him] from the Tent of Meeting* (Lev. 1:1). On the basis of this passage let us hold that "calling" preceded "speaking" in the case of all [the words of God] which [came] from the Tent of Meeting.

You might think that "calling" preceded only "speaking"; on what basis [do we learn that "calling" preceded] "saying" and "commanding"? Said Rabbi Simeon: "Scripture says, [*And YHWH called to Moses] and spoke [to him from the Tent of Meeting saying:] 'Speak . . .'* (Lev. 1:1) to include [the fact that] 'saying' and 'commanding' [were] also [preceded by 'calling']."

You might think that [the term "calling" is used only to indicate] a [preceding] interruption [in the text; however,] Scripture says, *And spoke* (Lev. 1:1) [to indicate] that the "calling" was [done] as a function of the "speaking" and that the "calling" was not [done to indicate] an interruption.

But, what [then] was the function of the interruptions [that is, the spaces between the words and the sentences in the written Torah? They served] to give Moses [time to] rest, so that he [could] reflect [on God's words] between the sections and between the [individual] topics. And behold, [Moses' actions can be used as the basis of] an *a fortiori* argument: Now, if someone [such as Moses] who hears [God's words directly] from the mouth of the Holy One, blessed be He, and who speaks [directly] with the Holy Spirit needs [time] to reflect between the sections and between the topics, how much the more does a common person [who hears something] from [another] common person [need time to reflect between hearing individual verses and subjects].

And on what basis [do we learn] that all the callings [from God] were [begun by God's calling] "Moses, Moses"? Scripture says: *God*

called to him from the midst of the bush and said: "Moses, Moses"
(Ex. 3:4–5). For Scripture does not [normally say] "and said." And
why did Scripture [here] say *and said?* [This was said to] teach [us]
that all the callings [from God to Moses were begun by God's calling]
"Moses, Moses."

And on what basis [do we learn] that [in response to] every
"calling" [Moses] would say, "Here I am *(hnny)*"? Scripture says: *And
God called to him from the midst of the bush and said: "Moses,
Moses." And he [Moses] said, "Here I am"* (Ex. 3:4–5). Scripture
does not [normally] say "and he said, here I am." And why does
Scripture say [here], *And he said, "Here I am"*? [This was said to]
teach [us] that [in response] to every "calling" [Moses] would say:
"Here I am."

[The repetition of the name, as in] Moses, Moses; Abraham,
Abraham; Jacob, Jacob; Samuel, Samuel, is an expression of en-
dearment and encouragement.

Another matter: *Moses, Moses* [indicates that] he [was called]
Moses before he spoke with Him and [that] he [was called] Moses
after he spoke with Him [to teach that his character did not change].

[*And YHWH called to Moses and spoke] to him* (Lev. 1:1). [This
was said] to exclude Aaron.

Said Rabbi Judah the son of Bathyra: "Thirteen 'speakings' were
said in the Torah to Moses and to Aaron. Corresponding to them,
thirteen ['speakings'] were said [which were] limited [to Moses alone]
to teach you that they were not said [directly] to Aaron but [were
said] to Moses, who [then] said [them] to Aaron."

And these are they: *And when Moses came to the Tent of Meeting
to speak with Him* (Num. 7:89), *And he heard the voice speaking to
him* (Num. 7:89), *And It spoke to him* (Num. 7:89), *[There] I will
meet with you and I will speak with you* (Ex. 25:22), *Where I will
meet with you, to speak to you there* (Ex. 29:42), *On the day that
He commanded him* (Lev. 7:38), *That which YHWH commanded
Moses* (Lev. 7:38), *And all that I command you for the Children of
Israel* (Ex. 25:22), *And on the day that YHWH spoke to Moses in the
Land of Egypt* (Ex. 6:28), *And these are the generations of Aaron
and Moses on the day that YHWH spoke to Moses on Mount Sinai*
(Num. 3:1), *And YHWH called to Moses and spoke to him* (Lev. 1:1).
[These] exclude Aaron from [directly receiving] the speeches at
Mount Sinai. With regard to [the speeches at] the Tent of Meeting
what does it say? [It says:] *And YHWH called to Moses* (Lev. 1:1),

[which] excludes Aaron from [directly receiving] the speeches at the Tent of Meeting.

Rabbi Yosi the Galilean says: "With reference to three places in the Torah 'He spoke to Moses' is said: In the Land of Egypt, on Mount Sinai, and at the Tent of Meeting. [This is all] in the whole Torah. [Concerning] the Land of Egypt what does it say? [It says:] *On the day that YHWH spoke to Moses in the Land of Egypt* (Ex. 6:28), [which] excludes Aaron from [directly receiving] the speeches in the Land of Egypt. [Concerning] Mount Sinai what does it say? [It says:] *And these are the generations of Aaron and Moses on the day that YHWH spoke to Moses on Mount Sinai* (Num. 3:1), [which] excludes Aaron from [directly receiving] the speeches on Mount Sinai. [Concerning] the Tent of Meeting what does it say? [It says:] *And YHWH called to Moses* (Lev. 1:1), [which] excludes Aaron from [directly receiving] the speeches in the Tent of Meeting; therefore, [we must conclude that God] spoke to Moses and not to Aaron."

Rabbi Eleazar says: "*There I will meet with the Children of Israel and it will be sanctified by My glory* (Ex. 29:43). [This means] in the future I will be witnessed to by them and I will be made sanctified by them. When was this? [This was] the eighth day of [Aaron's] inauguration [as a priest], for it is said, *And all the people saw and shouted and fell on their faces* (Lev. 9:24)."

Or [perhaps I should reason that this means that] only [the honor of] witnessing the speeches was given to them; [however,] Scripture says: *Where I will meet with you (lk)* (Ex. 25:22). [Contrary to reason, it is therefore clear that] to you *(lk)* [Moses] was [given the honor of] witnessing [the speeches, and the honor of] witnessing [the speeches was] not [given] to all of Israel.

[Or perhaps it is logical that] I should [assume that God] excluded [only] Israel [from witnessing the speeches, because] they were ritually unfit to ascent Mount [Sinai], but I should not exclude the elders, for they were ritually fit to ascent Mount [Sinai. Or, perhaps it is logical that] I should exclude the elders, for they were not seen during the speeches with Moses, but I should not exclude the sons of Aaron, for they were seen during the speeches with Moses. [Or, perhaps it is logical that] I should exclude the sons of Aaron, for they did not witness the speeches with Moses, but [I should not exclude] Aaron himself, for he did witness the speeches with Moses; [however, contrary to all logical reasoning,] Scripture says, *Where I will meet with you (lk) there* (Ex. 30:6) [which indicates that the honor of] witnessing [the speeches was given] to you [Moses alone, and the honor of] witnessing [the speeches] was not given to all of them.

Or [perhaps it is logical] that I shall exclude them from witnessing, but I should not exclude them from [hearing] the speeches [directly; to the contrary, however,] Scripture says, *I will speak with you ('tk)* (Ex. 25:22). [Perhaps it means] I should exclude Israel but I should not exclude the elders. [Or, perhaps it means that] I should exclude the elders, but I should not exclude the sons of Aaron. [Or, perhaps it means that] I should exclude the sons of Aaron but I should not exclude Aaron himself; [however,] Scripture says, *To speak with you ('lyk)* (Ex. 29:42) [which proves, contrary to all logic, that] the speech was with you [Moses], and the speech was not with all of them.

You might think that [even though] they did not hear the speech, they did hear the sound of [His] voice; [however,] Scripture says, *The voice was sent to him* (Num. 7:89). [Perhaps it means that] I should exclude all of Israel [from having heard the sound] but I should not exclude the elders. [Perhaps it means that] I should exclude the elders but I should not exclude the sons of Aaron. [Perhaps it means that] I should exclude the sons of Aaron but I should not exclude Aaron himself; [however, to show that this reasoning is incorrect,] Scripture says, *The voice was [sent] to him* (Num. 7:89).

[Perhaps this means that] I should exclude all of them but I should not exclude the ministering angels, for Moses was not able to enter into their midst until he was called; [however,] Scripture says, *The voice was [sent] to him* [which means that the voice was directed] to him. Moses heard the voice but all of these others did not hear the voice.

From the Tent of Meeting (Lev. 1:1). [This] teaches that the voice would stop and would not leave the Tent of Meeting. You might think that [it did not leave the Tent of Meeting] because it was [too] soft; [however,] Scripture says, *And he heard the voice* (Num. 7:89). But Scripture does not [normally] say, "the voice." Why did Scripture say *the voice* [here? It said this to indicate that it was] the [same] voice which was specified in the Writings. And to what [does] "which was specified in the Writings" [refer? It refers to the statement that] *the voice of YHWH is powerful, the voice of YHWH is full of majesty. The voice of YHWH breaks the cedars, the cedars of Lebanon, the voice of YHWH flashes forth flames of fire* (Ps. 29:5–7). If [this] is so [that the voice was not soft], why was *from the Tent of Meeting* said?

[This was said to] teach that the voice would stop, and it would not leave the Tent.

Similarly, you say, *The voice from above the wings of the cherubim was heard as far as the outer court* (Ezek. 10:5). You might say that [it was not heard any farther than this] because the voice was [too] soft; [however,] Scripture says, *Like the voice of God Almighty when He spoke* (Ezek. 10:5)—at Sinai. And if [this] is so, why was *as far as the outer court* said? [This was said] only [to teach us] that when [the voice] reached the outer court, it would cease.

From the Tent of Meeting (Lev. 1:1). "You might think [that the voice came] from every [place within the] structure; [however,] Scripture says: *[There I will meet with you], and from above the mercy seat, [from between the two cherubim] that are upon the ark of the testimony, I will speak with you* (Ex. 25:22). If [it had said only] *from above the mercy seat*, you might think [that He spoke with Moses] from above the whole mercy seat; [however,] Scripture says, *From between the two cherubim*"—the words of Rabbi Aqiba. Said Rabbi Simeon the son of Azzai: "I do not [speak] in order to refute the words of my teacher, but as one who adds to his words, for regarding the glory [of God] it is said, *Do I not fill the heaven and the earth?* (Jer. 23:24). See how precious Israel is [to God]. How was this honor demonstrated? It is as if He compressed [Himself] to be [able] to speak from above the mercy seat, from between the two cherubim."

Rabbi Dosa says: "Behold it says, *For a man shall not see Me and live* (Ex. 33:20) [which means] they do not see Me during their lifetime but they [will] see Me at their death. And thus it says, *Before Him shall bow all who go down to the dust and whose soul is not alive* (Ps. 22:30)."

Rabbi Aqiba says: "[Behold it says,] *For a man shall not see Me and live* [which tells us] that even the holy beings who carry the throne of glory do not see the glory [of God]."

Said Rabbi Simeon: "I do not [speak] in order to refute the words of my teacher, but as one who adds to his words. [Behold it says,] *For a man shall not see Me and live.* Even the angels, who live an everlasting life, do not see the glory [of God]."

Saying (Lev. 1:1) [which means He said to Moses,] "Speak humble words. 'Because of you [Israelites] He speaks with me.'" "For thus we find that for all thirty-eight years that Israel were like those who had been excommunicated, He did not speak with Moses, for it is said,

*When all the men of war had perished and were dead . . . YHWH
said to me* (Deut. 2:16–17).

Another matter: *Saying* [means He said to Moses]: "Go and speak
to them and bring [their] answer to Me." On what basis [do we learn
that] Moses used to go out and speak with them? [We learn this from
Ex. 34:34,] for it is said: *[But whenever Moses went in before YHWH
to speak with Him, he took off the veil, until he came out; and then
he came out,] and told the Children of Israel what he was commanded.* And on what basis [do we learn that] Moses used to bring
back the[ir] words before the Mighty One? Scripture says, *And
Moses reported the words of the people to YHWH* (Ex. 19:8).

Eleazar the son of Aḥwai says: "You might think that [God] spoke
with him because of His own needs; [however], Scripture says
saying, [which means] 'saying to Israel.' For the sake of Israel He
used to speak with him, and not because of His own needs."

Another matter: *Saying* [means He said to Moses:] "Go and say to
them and bring [their] answer to Me." And on what basis [do we
learn that] Moses went and spoke with them? [We learn it from Ex.
34:34:] *And then he came out and told the Children of Israel.* And
on what basis [do we learn that] Moses used to bring back the[ir]
words before the Mighty One? [We learn it from Ex. 19:8], for it is
said, *And Moses reported the words of the people to YHWH.*

Speak to the Children of Israel (Lev. 1:2) *and they shall place
their hands on the sacrifices* (Lev. 24:14). The Children of Israel lay
their hands [on sacrifices], but gentiles may not lay their hands [on
sacrifices]. Is this really so? Which act is more frequent, the act of
waving or the act of the laying on of the hands? The act of waving is
more frequent than the act of the laying on the hands, for waving is
practiced for a thing which contains the spirit of life and for a thing
which does not contain the spirit of life; but the laying on of the
hands is practiced only for a thing which contains the spirit of life. If
[the gentiles] are excluded from the act of waving [a sacrifice before
God], which is the more frequent [act with regard to the sacrifices],
should I not exclude them also from the laying on of the hands,
which is the less frequent act? You might say, on the one hand, let
the waving be increased and the laying on of the hands be decreased. Or, [perhaps you say] on the other hand, let the laying on of
the hands be increased and the waving be decreased, for the laying
on of the hands is practiced on every sacrifice which is jointly

presented, while the waving is not practiced on every sacrifice which is jointly presented [before God]. If [the gentiles] are excluded from waving, which is less frequent, should I [not also] exclude them from the laying on of the hands, which is more frequent? Behold, because there is in the act of waving an element which is not in the act of the laying on of the hands, and [there is in] the act of the laying on of the hands an element which is not in the act of waving [so that the two acts are not analogous, Scripture] needs to say *Speak to the Children of Israel* [to teach us that] the Children of Israel practice the laying on of the hands but the gentiles may not practice the act of the laying on of the hands.

[*Speak to the Children (bny) of Israel* teaches us that] the sons (*bny*) of Israel lay their hands on the sacrifices but the daughters of Israel may not lay their hands on sacrifices.

Rabbi Yosi and Rabbi Simeon say: "The women's laying on of hands is an optional act."

Said Rabbi Yosi: "Abba Eleazar said to me that we [once] had a calf [as] a Peace-offering, and took it out to the woman's court [of the Temple], and the women laid hands on it, not because the laying on of the hands was [incumbent] on the women, but because of the satisfaction [given to the] women [who placed their hands on the offering]."

You might think that [the women could place their hands on the Peace-offering, but that] they should not [place their hands] on the Whole-burnt-offering; the waving of the breast is not [required] of the Whole-burnt-offering, for they laid their hands on the Peace-offering [only] because the waving of the breast [is required] of the Peace-offering; [however,] Scripture says, *And you shall say to them* (Lev. 1:2) to include all [the sacrifices] mentioned in this context: Just as they do not have to lay their hands on the Whole-burnt-offering, so also they do not have to lay their hands on the Peace-offering; [however, they may lay their hands on both offerings].

[*Speak to the Children of Israel and say to them: When] a man* (Lev. 1:2) [was said] to include the proselyte. *Among you* (Lev. 1:2) [was said] to exclude the apostates. And why do you say thusly? [Perhaps] *a man* was said to include the apostate [and] *among you* [was said] to exclude the proselyte. After Scripture expands [the application of a statement] it limits [its application]. Scripture says, [*Speak to] the Children of Israel.* Just as the Children of Israel are [those who] accept the Covenant, so also the proselytes [should be included, for they too] accept the Covenant. [But] this excludes the apostates, for they do not accept the Covenant. No, [your argument is incorrect]. Just as Israel are the children of those who accepted the Covenant, so also apostates are the children of those who accepted the Covenant; [therefore, we must] exclude the proselytes, for they are not the children of those who accepted the Covenant. [Therefore,] Scripture [must] say *among you* [to indicate that logic is unacceptable]. Now, [given this latter phrase] you can say that just as Israel are those who accept the Covenant, so also the proselytes are those who accept the Covenant. [And you could say that] this excludes the apostates, because they are not those who accept the Covenant, for behold, they broke the Covenant; and thus it says, *The offerings of the evil ones are an abomination* (Prov. 21:27).

COMMENTS

And YHWH called. The midrash attempts to explain why both the verb "call," *qr'*, and the verb "spoke," *dbr*, appear in the same verse. The midrash begins by stating that the two verbs teach us that God always "called" before He spoke.

But cannot [this be established]. The midrash raises the possibility that we do not need a verse to teach us that "calling" precedes "speaking," for we can learn this by means of a logical argument.

Just as with regard to the [holy] speech. The argument by analogy is based on Ex. 3:4–5, for with regard to the events at the burning bush we read that God called to Moses before He spoke to him. Thus, we could draw an analogy from God's calling and speaking to Moses at the burning bush to God's speaking to Moses in the Tent of Meeting. On the basis of this analogy we could reason that God called to Moses before He spoke to him in the Tent of Meeting; therefore, we do not need to learn this from the appearance of both "calling" and "speaking" in Lev. 1:1.

No, [these two instances are not analogous]. The midrash argues that the preceding logical argument is faulty because the two cases are not similar. The event at the burning bush was the first occasion on which God spoke to Moses; therefore, God needed first to call to Moses. This is not analagous to His speaking to him at the Tent of Meeting, for it was not the first time He had spoken with him. Because God had spoken to Moses before the Tent of Meeting, we need not reason that He would have "called" to him again in that instance. Logically, God simply could have spoken to Moses in the Tent; therefore, it was necessary for Lev. 1:1 to refer to both God's "calling" and His "speaking" to Moses. Without these specific references in Lev. 1:1, our reason could not have told us that God both "called" and "spoke" to Moses in the Tent of Meeting.

[Rather], the [holy] speech at Mount Sinai supports. Ex. 19:20–21 states, *And YHWH called to Moses on the top of the mountain and Moses went up and YHWH said to Moses.* This was not the first time that God spoke to Moses. Even so, here God "called" to Moses before He "spoke" to him. Thus, it appears as if we can deduce from the events at Mount Sinai that God always calls Moses before He speaks with him.

No, [these two instances are not analogous]. The midrash now rejects this analogy also, for the events at Mount Sinai are not comparable to the events in the Tent of Meeting. At Mount Sinai the holy speech was addressed to all of the Israelites, for the people stood at the foot of the mountain and saw the thunder and the lightning (Ex. 20:18). In the Tent of Meeting, however, God spoke to Moses alone, while the people waited outside of the Tent (Ex. 34:34).

Behold, you can argue by means of a prototype. Upon rejecting two arguments by analogy, the midrash now raises the possibility that another type of logical argument might work, an argument based on a prototype. In order to use an argument based on a prototype, one identifies a common element in two or more cases and argues that any other case which contains that element will be like the original cases in all respects.

The common element between them. Even though God's speaking to Moses at the burning bush is not exactly analogous to His speaking to Moses at Mount Sinai, the two events do have a similar element. In both instances we find that God spoke directly to Moses, and in both cases we learn that God called Moses before He spoke to him. We can now assume that in every case in which God spoke directly to Moses a "calling" preceded the "speaking." Therefore, because God spoke directly to Moses at the Tent of Meeting, we can conclude that a "calling" preceded the "speaking"; we need not learn this from Lev. 1:1.

Not necessarily. The midrash now suggests that we have focused on the incorrect common element. The common element between the burning bush and Mount Sinai is that in both cases God spoke to Moses through fire, Ex. 3:4–5 and Ex. 19:18. If this is the common element, we cannot use these verses to teach us about the events of the Tent of Meeting because we find no reference to God's speaking through fire at the Tent of Meeting. Thus, we need Lev. 1:1 to teach us that "calling" preceded God's speaking to Moses. Reason alone could not have brought us to this conclusion.

You might think that "calling." Having established that "calling" preceded "speaking" for the events mentioned in the opening of Leviticus, the midrash now raises the possibility that "calling" preceded "speaking" only in that one instance alone. The midrash now asks from where in the Bible can we learn that "calling" preceded all "speakings." The midrash answers that the end of the verse teaches us that every time God spoke to Moses in the Tent of Meeting "calling" preceded "speaking." Thus, the Bible's wording causes us to reject our original reasonable assumption. There is a problem with this section. The midrash asks how we know that "calling" preceded all "speakings" which were mentioned *in the Torah.* It responds by citing a verse which refers to only the Tent of Meeting. One commentator[7] has suggested that the midrash actually wanted to know how we know, each time we read in the Torah that God spoke to Moses in the Tent of Meeting, that He called to him before He spoke to him, for we would assume that God called to Moses only the first time that He spoke to him in the Tent. The key is that the prefix *mem,* "from," appears where the prefix *bet,* "in," would have been more appropriate; therefore, the appearance of the *mem* teaches us that every time God spoke to Moses in the Tent of Meeting He called him first.

You might think that "calling" preceded. The midrash has established that every time God spoke to Moses, He first called him. You could reason, therefore, that God called Moses only when He spoke, *dbr,* to him but not when He said, '*mr,* something to him or when He commanded him to do something. However, this logical conclusion will be shown to be incorrect.

Said Rabbi Simeon. Simeon's comment demonstrates that the Bible proves that God called Moses before He spoke to him, said anything to him, or commanded him to do something. There are two possible explanations of Simeon's comment. (1) His comment may be based on the repetition of the root *dbr* in Lev. 1:1; since the root was repeated, we can assume that it refers to the two other types of communication. (2) His comment could be based on the prefix *w* in *wydbr,* for the particle *w* is an "extending" particle which indicates that the word to which it is attached refers to more than just itself.[8]

You might think that calling indicates an interruption. The midrash raises the possibility that God's calling to Moses served as an interruption, perhaps as a respite between God's talking to Moses at the end of the Book of Exodus and the beginning of His talking to him at the opening of Leviticus. The midrash responds that the *w* before *wydbr* indicates that *qr'* and *dbr* are closely connected, for the *w* is a conjunction; therefore, we must conclude that the "calling" was done as a function of the speaking and that the two acts were intimately connected.

But is this really so? The midrash states that in fact there were interruptions in God's conversation with Moses. If the "calling" has nothing to do with those interruptions, they must have some other explanation. The midrash argues that these interruptions were necessary so that Moses would have time to contemplate God's words.

And behold, Moses' actions. The midrash argues that God's conversation with Moses should serve as the paradigmatic conversation among scholars. If Moses, who heard the divine word directly from God, needed time to reflect on what he heard, should we not conclude that a lesser man than Moses, who hears the divine word from a lesser speaker than God, also needs time to reflect on what he has heard while he is being taught?

And on what basis do we learn that all callings. The midrash answers this question by returning to Ex. 3:4. In that verse God called Moses *and said, wy'mr.* The midrash states that when God talks to Moses we do not normally find *wy'mr.* In fact, this claim is incorrect; however, such an incorrect generalization is often used in midrash in order to make a point. Here, the appearance of the "uncommon" phrase *and said* indicates that God always called to Moses by stating "Moses, Moses." Although the midrash's generalization is incorrect, it could be believed, for often when God speaks to Moses we find the word *wydr* instead of *wy'mr*.[9]

And on what basis do we learn that in response. Just as Ex. 3:4 supplied the paradigm for the language God used when He called to Moses, so the verse provides us with Moses' response to these "callings."

The repetition of the name. Because God merely could have called "Moses" and not repeated the name, the repetition must signify something. According to the midrash, God repeated the name of certain individuals to whom He called in order to signify His special love for them.[10]

Another matter. We find a similar discussion in Tosefta *Berakhot* 1:13–14. Tosefta tells us that Abram's name was changed to Abraham after God spoke with him, just as Sarai's name was changed to Sarah after God spoke to her. The *sugya* in Tosefta then discusses other names which were changed after God spoke with the person and ends by listing those names which were not changed as a result of conversations with God. Moses' name appears in this latter list.[11]

And YHWH called to Moses and spoke to him. The midrash demonstrates that Moses and Aaron are not equal. We shall see this topic raised elsewhere in this volume, for this was an issue of special concern to the rabbis. For the purposes of this discussion, we should read Moses as a code-word for "rabbi" and Aaron as a code-word for "priest." The subject was important to the rabbis, for by demonstrating that Moses was superior to Aaron, they could claim that they, who traced their teachings back to Moses, were superior to the priests, who traced their teachings back to Aaron.[12]

Said Rabbi Judah the son of Bathyra. Judah claims that thirteen times in the Torah Moses and Aaron are treated as equals; however, there are thirteen other passages in which Moses is pictured as superior to Aaron, for the former heard God's words directly from God, while Aaron heard them only from Moses.

And these are they. The important point is that we do not find thirteen verses or parts of verses. This is not unusual, for often when a rabbi claims that there are a specific number of items or references and then the text supplies these, the list does not have the same number of items as the introduction suggests there should be. It is probable that in such cases the list and the opening statements come from different sources, or at least from different hands.[13]

Rabbi Yosi the Galilean says. Yosi's statement is probably independent of Judah's comment. Yet it serves to strengthen it. Even though God did sometimes speak to Aaron, in the three important locations of revelation in the Torah—Egypt, Sinai, and the Tent of Meeting—God spoke directly to Moses alone. The three verses cited in Yosi's statement also appear in Judah's comment.

Rabbi Eleazar says. Although the content of the discussion which follows Eleazar's comment is in line with the subject discussed at this point, Eleazar's statement itself appears out of place, for it does not discuss a verse which has appeared in this context, nor does it appear to discuss an event which is relevant to our context. No one else has mentioned Aaron's consecration as a priest, Ex. 29:43, or the Children of Israel's witnessing or sanctifying God. I assume that Eleazar's comment was placed in this context along with the responses to it because the *whole unit* eventually demonstrates Moses' uniqueness.[14]

Or perhaps this means that only the honor of witnessing. Eleazar has stated that in the future Israel would be witnesses to God. The midrash now states that this does not mean that Israel will witness God's direct speaking, for Ex. 25:22 employs the singular, *lk,* when God states to whom He will speak in the residence the people are to build for Him.

Or perhaps it means that I should exclude Israel. The midrash now demonstrates that contrary to logic, which leads us to believe that Aaron was allowed to witness God's speech to Moses in the Tent of Meeting, God excluded not only Israel from witnessing His speaking in the Tent of Meeting but also the elders, who were fit to ascend Mount Sinai, the sons of Aaron, who were fit to be present when God spoke, and even Aaron himself, who on other occasions was fit to witness God's speaking to Moses. Ex. 30:6, which also contains a singular pronoun, *lk,* when discussing to whom God will speak *before the curtain,* supports this conclusion.

Or perhaps it means I should exclude them from witnessing. After showing that all but Moses were excluded from directly witnessing God's speaking in the Tent, the midrash excludes everyone but Moses from directly hearing God's words in the Tent.

You might think that they did not hear the speech. The midrash has demonstrated that Moses alone witnessed God's speaking and that he alone heard God's speech directly; now the midrash raises the possibility that perhaps those other than Moses at least were able to hear the sound of God's voice, even though they could not hear His speaking. The midrash concludes that, contrary to logic, Moses alone heard the sound of God's voice. Even the ministering angels did not hear Him. In a carefully designed passage, the midrash has demonstrated that Moses alone witnessed to God, heard God's speaking, and heard the sound of His voice. The midrash reached this point by carefully raising positions which were reasonable and logical and then demonstrating that a verse in Scripture proves that the "reasonable" possibility is untenable.

From the Tent of Meeting. One could read this to mean that YHWH's voice went forth from inside the Tent to the outside. However, the Bible and the midrash are clear that Moses alone heard God's voice when He spoke to Moses in the Tent of Meeting; therefore, we must conclude that God's voice was not heard outside the Tent where the people were waiting for Moses. Perhaps the exegesis is based on the particle *mem,* which is a limiting particle, for the text could have employed the preposition *bet,* "in," instead of the *mem,* "from".[15]

You might think that it did not leave the Tent. The midrash raises the logical possibility that God's voice was not heard outside the Tent because He spoke softly to Moses. The midrash rejects this "logical" possibility.

But Scripture does not normally say "the voice". The midrash claims that Scripture does not normally employ the phrase "the voice" when speaking of God's voice; therefore, the appearance of this phrase, which is only one word in Hebrew, in Num. 7:89 signifies something important. The midrash now employs a *gezarah shavah.* A *gezarah shavah* is an exegetical technique by which two passages are juxtaposed to each other because they contain the same word or phrase. In this case, Num. 7:89 is interpreted in light of Ps. 29:5–7 because the phrase "the voice" appears in both places. Because YHWH's voice is described as powerful in Ps. 29:5–7, we can conclude that any place in which the phrase "the voice" appears God's voice was also powerful there. For this reason, we know that God did not speak softly to Moses in the Tent of Meeting.

Similarly you say. The midrash notes that in another context we also learn about the limits of God's voice when He spoke. Ezek. 10:5 notes that when God spoke in the Temple from above the cherubim, His voice was heard only as far as the outer court. The same verse indicates, however, that this was the same voice with which God spoke at Sinai, Ex. 20:18–22. Because the passage in Exodus indicates the force with which God spoke at Sinai, we must conclude that God's voice was heard only as far as the outer court because He chose that His voice would not be heard any farther.

From the Tent of Meeting. This could mean that God's voice came from every place within the Tent; however, Ex. 25:22, which specifically mentions that God spoke to Moses from above the mercy seat, demonstrates that this "logical" possibility is untenable. In fact, by quoting Ex. 25:22, Aqiba is able to pinpoint the exact location from which God's voice proceeded within the Tent.

Said Rabbi Simeon the son of Azzai. Simeon states that he does not wish to contradict Aqiba; rather, he wishes to add to the latter's words. Simeon concludes that God's limiting Himself to the area above the mercy seat indicates how precious He considered Israel, for God was willing to limit Himself in order to communicate with Israel through Moses.

Rabbi Dosa says. I assume that Dosa's comment is here because Aqiba's comment follows it and Simeon responds to Aqiba's words with the same phrase which appears above. Probably this complex of Dosa-Aqiba-Simeon was a complete unit before it was placed here. Dosa states that according to Ex. 33:20, a man cannot see God and live. This means only that a man cannot see God during his lifetime. We know that a man can see God after he dies, for Ps. 22:30 states that those who have died bow before God.

Rabbi Aqiba says. Aqiba offers a second interpretation of Ex. 33:20.

According to Aqiba, even the holy beings, *ḥywt*, who carry God's throne do not see him. Aqiba's comment is a pun on *ḥy*, "live," and *ḥywt*, "beings." Aqiba's statement stresses the mystery of God and the greatness of His mystical throne.[16]

Said Rabbi Simeon. Simeon opens his statement with the same words attributed to Simeon the son of Azzai above. Simeon agrees with Aqiba that the angels do not see the Glory of God; however, the former stresses the eternity of the angels and that no angel will *ever* see God.

Saying. This word often introduces a direct quotation in the Bible, and it often appears to be a superfluous and meaningless word; therefore, it is often the subject of interpretation. Here, we learn that the extra gerund signifies that God told Moses to speak humbly before the Israelites, for it was because of their merits that God spoke to Moses.

Another matter. The extra word "saying" indicates that God told Moses to speak to the people and then to return and to speak to Him, relaying to Him the words of the Israelites. Ex. 34:34 and 19:8 are cited and taken literally.

Eleazar the son of Aḥwai says. Eleazar makes the point that God did not speak to Moses in order to fulfill a need within Himself; rather, He spoke to Israel because Israel needed to hear God's words. In other words, Eleazar teaches that God does not have "needs" in the way that humans do; therefore, we cannot assume that He *had* to speak to Israel.

Another matter. This is exactly the same as the "another matter" cited above. The repetition is probably the result of a scribal or editorial error.

The Children of Israel lay their hands on sacrifices. The midrash discusses two acts associated with sacrifices: the laying on of the hands and the waving of the sacrifice or its parts before YHWH. The act of placing one's hand on a sacrificial victim attests "that this victim comes from this particular individual who is laying his hands on it, that the sacrifice which is going to be presented to God by the priests is offered in his name, and the fruits of this sacrifice shall be his."[17] The act of laying one's hands on a sacrifice was obligatory for all sacrifices offered by individuals; it did not apply for the most part to communal sacrifices or to birds. The act had to be performed by the person for whom the sacrifice was offered and not by his agent or his proxy.[18]

The waving of a sacrifice was a method of showing the sacrifice to the deity in order to gain divine acceptance or rejection of the offering. Both grain and animal offerings were waved; however, in the case of animal sacrifices and some grain offerings, the waving was a preliminary to burning the sacrifices in the altar-fire. Waving was deemed a sufficient mode of sacrifice only for some fruits and grains. After the deity had viewed the sacrifice, it was removed and given to the priests for food.[19]

But gentiles may not lay their hands. The midrash presents a logical argument for the gentiles' not laying their hands on sacrifices. If this logical argument is accepted, we do not need the verse to teach us this fact. The midrash notes that the act of waving is more common than the act of the laying on of the hands, for the former is done for both animate and inanimate objects, while the latter applies only to animate offerings. Because gentiles may not wave sacrifices, the more common act, should we not conclude that they also cannot lay their hands on the sacrifices, the more unusual act?

Or, perhaps you say on the one hand. As the midrash has demonstrated above, one problem with logical arguments is that they can be turned upside down and proven to be just as convincing. Above, the midrash presented a line of reasoning which demonstrated that the gentiles may not lay their hands on sacrifices. Now, the midrash reverses the argument. Above, the gentile was excluded from laying hands on a sacrifice because it was a less frequent act than waving the offering before God, an act which gentiles do not perform. Here, the gentile is excluded from the laying on of hands because it is a more common act than the waving of the offering before God. In short, the midrash demonstrates that one can argue in entirely opposite ways and reach apparently logical conclusions. The implication is that reasoning alone is inconclusive and unreliable. Therefore, we need Lev. 1:2 to teach us that the gentiles may not lay their hands on sacrifices, for the biblical verse is conclusive and reliable.

Speak to the Children of Israel. The masculine plural *bny* means both "sons" and "children." Our midrash takes it in the former sense and concludes that only males may lay their hands on the sacrifices.

Rabbi Yosi and Rabbi Simeon say. Yosi and Simeon do not forbid the women from laying their hands on the offerings. They note, however, that it is an *optional* act for the women, implying that it is an *obligatory* act for the men. This means that God would reward the man for performing the act or punish him for not performing it. The implication is that the acceptance of a man's sacrifice depends on his performing this act. However, God's relationship to a woman is not dependent on this act related to the offering. If one had to lay hands on the sacrifice as part of the sacrificial ritual, the implication of this statement and the previous comment is that women did not participate in the sacrificial cult, or that they participated on a level different from men.[20]

Said Rabbi Yosi. In rabbinic thought, a rabbi's deed or action could serve as a legal precedent as much as his specific words; therefore, if one witnessed a rabbi's performing an act, one could assume that the *halakhah* supports that action. If the action was at variance with the *halakhah*, the former had to be justified. In this case, Abba Eleazar explains that even though the Peace-offering was brought into the women's court so that they could lay their hands on it, one should not conclude that women were required to lay their hands on the sacrifice. Rather, the women were allowed to place their hands on this offering because they derived personal satisfaction from performing the ritual.[21]

You might think. The midrash raises the possibility that Rabbi Yosi referred specifically to the calf of the Peace-offering because this was the only sacrifice on which the women were allowed to place their hands for any reason. Perhaps the women could place their hands on the Peace-offering, but not on the Whole-burnt-offering, because the two sacrifices involved different rituals? The midrash concludes that with respect to the women's laying their hands on the sacrifices, we learn that all the sacrifices mentioned in the present context are the same, and we learn this from Lev. 1:2. The exegesis seems to be based on the seemingly superfluous appearance of *to them.* This phrase is repetitious, for Moses has already been told to speak to the *Children of Israel.* The phrase *to them* implies that all the sacrifices are to be treated the same with regard to the obligations of males and females for the laying on of hands.

Speak to the Children of Israel and say to them: When a man. The midrash again focuses on the exact wording of Scripture: Why did the Bible qualify *a man* with the phrase *among you* after it had indicated that Moses' speech was directed to *the Children of Israel?* The midrash concludes that *a man* indicates that the laws apply to proselytes and that *among you* excludes the apostates, who are no longer counted among the Children of Israel.

And why do you say thusly? The midrash now raises the possibility that the phrases can be explained in the opposite fashion; that is, *a man* could imply the inclusion of the apostate, and *among you* could refer to the proselyte. The midrash answers by making a general observation: First the Bible includes things and then it excludes things. In this instance the Bible first includes the proselytes among its regulations and then it excludes the apostates from its concerns.

Just as the Children of Israel. The midrash now offers a logical argument to support the claim that the proselyte is included in the biblical injunctions while the apostate is not included. Because the Children of Israel and the proselyte both accept the Covenant between God and Abraham and Israel, the same regulations apply to both. These regulations do not apply to the apostate, who has rejected the Covenant by leaving the Jewish community.

No, your argument is incorrect. The midrash again demonstrates that logical arguments can be employed to support any conclusion. One could argue that the Children of Israel and the apostate should be treated the same, for they both had Jewish parents. On the other hand, the proselyte should not be treated the same as the Children of Israel, for the former did not have Jewish parents, while the latter did.

Therefore Scripture says among you. The midrash has demonstrated that logical arguments do not work, because both arguments appear logical. The solution to the dilemma can be found in Scripture. The phrase *among you* was needed to teach us that the former argument is the correct line of reasoning: The proselyte and the Children of Israel are treated the same because both of them accept the Covenant. The apostate is no longer among those who accept the Covenant; therefore he or she is not treated the same as the Children of Israel. Prov. 21:27 proves that the apostates should not lay their hands on sacrifices, for the sacrifices of evil ones are an abomination.

CONCLUSIONS

To refresh our memories, this section of Sifra is a commentary to the opening of Leviticus: *And YHWH called to Moses and spoke to him from the Tent of Meeting saying: "Speak to the Children of Israel and say to them, When a man among you . . ."* The midrash opens by asking the significance of the appearance of both "called" and "spoke" in Lev. 1:1. The midrash answers that Lev. 1:1 teaches us that "calling" precedes "speaking." An argument by analogy is brought which claims to prove the same point so that perhaps we do not need to learn that "calling" preceded "speaking" from Lev. 1:1. The argument by analogy is based on Ex. 3:4, for with regard to the events at the burning bush we also read that God "called" and then "spoke" to Moses. The midrash rejects this analogy, for it claims that the events at the burning bush are not comparable to the events in the Tent of Meeting: The burning bush was the first occasion on which God spoke to Moses; therefore, He had to call him before He spoke to him there.

After rejecting the comparison between the events at the burning bush and those referred to in Lev. 1:1, the midrash offers a second analogy, and it compares the events on Mount Sinai with those in the Tent of Meeting. However, the midrash also rejects this comparison, because at Mount Sinai God spoke to all of Israel, while in the Tent of Meeting He spoke only to Moses.

After rejecting these two arguments by analogy, the midrash now moves to another type of logical argument, an argument based on a prototype. The midrash argues that the events on Mount Sinai and the events at the burning bush have a common element: In both cases God spoke directly to Moses. Because in both of these instances God spoke directly to Moses, and in both cases "calling" preceded "speaking," we should conclude that every time God spoke to Moses, as He did in the Tent of Meeting, He called to him before He spoke to him. The midrash now rejects this argument by noting that the common element in the case of the burning bush and the case of Mount Sinai is that God spoke through fire. Therefore, from this prototype we can learn that God called to Moses before He spoke with him *only* in those cases where He spoke with him through fire. Because God did not speak to Moses through fire in the Tent of Meeting, we cannot learn about what happened in the Tent by means of this prototype. The midrash now concludes that both verbs had to appear in Lev. 1:1, for that is the only way we could know that in the Tent of Meeting God called to Moses before He spoke with him.

To this point the midrash has focused on the significance of the verbs "call" and "speak" in Lev. 1:1. It has concluded that they tell us that God called to Moses before He spoke to him in the Tent of Meeting, a fact we can learn only from the exact wording of Lev. 1:1. This is underscored by the midrash's rejection of two types of logical arguments which attempt to teach us the same thing. We are left with two impressions: (1) Everyword in the Bible is important, so that we must focus on each word in the text, and (2) the specific wording of the Bible is necessary to teach us things that we could not learn by using our reason alone. The authors of this section of the midrash clearly took every element of the Bible, that is every word of revelation, with the utmost seriousness.

The midrash has established that God called to Moses before He spoke to him during their first encounter in the Tent of Meeting. It now asks if this was the only occasion on which God called to Moses from the Tent of Meeting. In order to answer this question, the midrash cites the end of Lev. 1:1, *from the Tent of Meeting.* Because the verbs "calling" and "speaking" appear in Lev. 1:1 juxtaposed with the events of the Tent of Meeting without specifying any time element, the midrash concludes that God called to Moses every time He spoke with him in the Tent of Meeting.

The midrash now asks: Should we assume that God called to Moses only when He *spoke* with him but not when He *said* something to him or *commanded* him to do something? The midrash rejects this logical conclusion by quoting the end of Lev. 1:1, *Speak.* The double appearance of the verb "speak," *dbr,* indicates that God not only called to Moses, before He spoke with him, but also that He called to him before He said something to him or commanded him to act.

After having established that Lev. 1:1 teaches us that God called to Moses the first time He spoke with him from the Tent of Meeting, the midrash demonstrates that, in fact, God called to Moses every time He spoke with him in the Tent of Meeting. In addition, God also called to Moses when He said something to him or commanded him to do something. There is a logical progression in the midrash's thought. First, it established, on the basis of the opening of Lev. 1:1, that God called to Moses before He spoke with him the first time from the Tent of Meeting. Next, it demonstrated, from the next two Hebrew words in Lev. 1:1, that God called to Moses every time He spoke with him from the Tent. Then, the midrash proved, on the basis of the next Hebrew word in Lev. 1:1, that God called to Moses before He spoke with him, said anything to him, or commanded him to do anything. The progression of concerns is logical, and it is based on the consecutive word order of Lev. 1:1.

Up to this point the midrash has discussed the relationship of God's calling to Moses and His speaking to him. It now raises the possibility that the "callings" mark interruptions in the text. The midrash turns again to the opening of Lev. 1:1 and notes that the verb "calling" is joined to "spoke" by the conjunction "and." Therefore, we must assume that there was a close connection between God's calling to Moses and His speaking to him; that is, the biblical text indicates that there was no interruption after God called to Moses and before He spoke to him.

Because the midrash has raised the subject of interruptions in the biblical text, it now expands its discussion of this issue. The midrash assumes that there are marked interruptions in the Bible. I assume that these are the divisions between books, chapters, and subjects. In any case, Moses was given time to reflect on God's words. The midrash suggests that Moses' learning from God is a paradigmatic event, for it was the best student learning from the Perfect Teacher. If the best student needed time to reflect on the lessons given by the Perfect Teacher, should we not conclude that lesser students also need time to reflect on the lessons which they learn from less-than-perfect teachers?

This discussion of the interruptions is not directly based on the biblical text of Leviticus; however, it follows logically from the midrash's demonstration that Lev. 1:1 does not indicate that there were any interruptions between God's calling and speaking to Moses from the Tent of Meeting. Digressions of this sort—that is, expanding on subjects which are raised in the exegesis of a verse but which are not actually part of the exegesis itself—are common in rabbinic midrash. They underscore the fact that rabbinic midrash is much more than a mere commentary on the biblical text and is often a means of teaching important theological, social, or political points. Here we have an aside which is a message to the rabbis concerning the way in which they should teach their disciples.

After the aside concerning the interruptions, the midrash returns to its treatment of "calling." The midrash now discusses the exact language with which God called to Moses. It concludes, on the basis of Ex. 3:4–5, that every time God called to Moses He employed the words "Moses, Moses." The midrash claims that the "unusual" phrase *and said* in Ex. 3:4 proves that every time God called to Moses He called "Moses, Moses." In the commentary I noted that "and said" is not all that unusual. In addition, above, the midrash claimed that the events at the burning bush could not teach us about the events in the Tent of Meeting. Neither of these facts should bother us, for often the authors of the midrash employ arguments which are not wholly correct. Also, just because the events at the burning bush could not teach us about God's calling to Moses before He spoke with him in the Tent of Meeting, this does not mean that those events cannot tell us anything about what happened in the Tent. Notice that the midrash moves to a discussion of the content of God's call only after it has completed its treatment of the act of calling. Notice also that at this point the midrash is no longer providing an exegesis of Lev. 1:1; it is merely discussing the events about which Lev. 1:1 speaks according to its interpretation of those events.

After discussing the content of God's call, the midrash moves to the next logical issue, the content of Moses' response. Again the midrash focuses on Ex. 3:4–5. Just as it contained the contents of God's call, so also it contains the contents of Moses' response to that call. The argument about Moses' response corresponds to the argument about God's call; both focus on supposedly "unusual" phrases in the Bible.

The midrash now returns to the content of God's call, and it asks why God repeated Moses' name. It concludes that the repetition of the name indicates God's love for Moses or for anyone else whose name He repeated. The midrash then offers other instances in which God repeated the name of the person whom He addressed. Notice that this discussion has no direct relationship to Lev. 1:1. While it may serve as an exegesis of Ex. 3:4–5, it is not presented as a direct interpretation of those verses; rather, it is a discussion of the conclusion reached concerning the content of God's call to Moses.

The midrash now offers a second explanation of why God repeated Moses' name when He called to him: The repetition of the name indicates that Moses' name was not changed after God spoke with him. This explanation makes sense only in a larger context, a context which is fully worked out in other rabbinic texts. It is important to note that Moses' name was not changed because we know, for example, that Abram's name was changed to Abraham and Sarai's name to Sarah after Abraham was circumcised. We have two *different* and *unrelated* explanations of the repetition of Moses' name. This is also a common occurrence in rabbinic midrash. Often we find two or more interpretations of a verse or explanations of an issue. No judgment is made concerning their validity, and no choice is made as to which is preferred. Here, both explanations are presented to us as two possible reasons for the repetition of Moses' name.

To this point, the midrash has focused on God's calling to Moses; now, it raises a new issue. Lev. 1:1 states that YHWH called to Moses, and then it includes the phrase *to him*. The midrash discusses the significance of this seemingly unnecessary prepositional phrase. What follows is a long discussion which points to the special relationship which existed between God and Moses. The midrash emphasizes that Moses alone received much of the revelation from God. As I noted in my comments, this was an important statement for the rabbis to make, for by elevating Moses' reception of revelation, they devalued the priests' claim to have knowledge received from God. Thus, this discussion had important practical results for the fledgling rabbinic party's claim to be the sole reliable source of God's revelation to Israel.

The point where a live "political" issue is addressed in our midrash is also the place at which the comments are first assigned to named rabbis. To this point, the midrash has been almost totally anonymous. The discussion of Moses' importance vis-à-vis Aaron, the Israelites, the elders, and the sons of Aaron, that is, the priests, is assigned to Judah the son of Bathyra, Yosi the Galilean, and Eleazar. Although some of this discussion is anonymous, it is significant that three rabbis who flourished between 90 and 130 C.E., the exact period during which the character of the rabbinic movement was being established, are named.

Judah states that in thirteen places Moses and Aaron are equated with regard to God's speaking to them. However, he also cites "thirteen" verses in which God spoke directly to Moses alone. In my comments I noted that thirteen citations do not occur and that it is not uncommon for a given number of examples not to agree with the number found in the introduction to the examples. It is important to notice that the citations end by quoting Lev. 1:1; thus, the rather long and confused collection of texts end with the first verse of Leviticus, the verse upon which this whole passage is an exegesis. This literary form, citing several verses and ending with the opening verse of the section upon which the text comments, is fully developed in the *petihah*, which we shall discuss below in the contexts of Genesis Rabbah and Leviticus Rabbah.

Yosi now claims that with reference to the three places in which revelation took place, the Land of Egypt, Mount Sinai, and the Tent of Meeting, we find verses which specify that Moses alone received the revelation. Yosi and Judah make the same point; however, Yosi's comment more directly stresses Moses' special status with regard to revelation and indirectly emphasizes the rabbis' superiority over the priests.

Eleazar's comment is not really related to what has appeared to this point; however, it does introduce a rather large section which emphasizes Moses' superiority over the other Israelites, the elders, the sons of Aaron, and Aaron himself. Eleazar's comment was presumably included because of what was attached to it. Notice, therefore, that Eleazar does not discuss Lev. 1:1. In fact, the paragraphs which are related to Eleazar's comment and which follow it do not even cite Lev. 1:1. This phenomenon is common in rabbinic midrash, for a rather long discussion has been included because its subject-matter is the same as the exegesis of a particular verse even though the discussion itself does not cite the verse. Although this section does not interpret Lev. 1:1, it follows the pattern of Sifra, for the midrash raises logical possibilities which it rejects in favor of a citation of Scripture. In brief, in content and style this passage belongs at this point in Sifra; however, it is not an exegesis of Lev. 1:1, the subject of this section of the midrash.

The midrash now returns to Lev. 1:1 and discusses the meaning of *from the Tent of Meeting*. This portion of Lev. 1:1 teaches us that God's voice was not heard outside the Tent. This interpretation is probably based on the word "from." The midrash now raises the logical possibility that God's voice was not heard outside the Tent because He spoke softly to Moses. This is rejected because Num. 7:89, which also discusses God's speaking to Moses in the Tent of Meeting, states that Moses heard *the voice*. Again the midrash points to the "unusual" nature of this phrase, and it employs a *gezarah shavah* to juxtapose Num. 7:89 with Ps. 29:5–7. The *gezarah shavah* is a common rabbinic exegetical technique which the rabbis seem to have borrowed from the Greek rhetoricians of their age.[22] Again, Scripture teaches us that we must reject a logical possibility, that God's voice was not heard outside the Tent because He spoke softly to Moses, for God did not speak softly to Moses. Again we learn that logical arguments are to be rejected in favor of the exact words of Scripture.

This section contains several interesting phenomena. First, it interprets what Lev. 1:1 says about the events which occurred in the Tent of Meeting by means of the account of the events in the Tent of Meeting found in Num. 7:89. The midrash does not even raise the possibility that Num 7:89 and Lev. 1:1 deal with different events or with different periods of time. Such issues do not concern the authors of rabbinic midrash. Both verses discuss events in the Tent of Meeting; therefore, both verses can be juxtaposed and used to interpret each other. Second, the midrash employs an inner exegesis. The text reads: "But Scripture does not [normally] say *the voice*. Why did Scripture say *the voice* [here? It said this to indicate that it was] the [same] voice which was specified in the Writings. And to what [does] 'which was specified in the Writings' [refer]?" Thus the text interprets a reference contained within itself, "which was specified in the Writings." This phenomenon is common in rabbinic literature. Third, the text employs an exegetical technique, the *gezarah shavah*, without mentioning the technique. This is also a common feature of rabbinic midrash.

The midrash now continues its discussion of God's voice and the limits of its being heard. It does this on the basis of Ezek. 10:5. This section is introduced by "similarly," a sure sign that it is an editorial addition. This is underscored by the fact that it contains neither Lev. 1:1 nor the verses found in the previous treatment of this issue.

The midrash now returns to its discussion of Lev. 1:1 and the phrase *from the Tent of Meeting*. This section of the text is again assigned to known sages: Aqiba, Simeon the son of Azzai, and Dosa. Aqiba cites Ex. 25:22 to prove that God did not speak to Moses from the *whole* Tent of Meeting, as one might think from reading Lev. 1:1. Simeon states that God's contracting Himself, as if this were possible, demonstrates how much God loves Israel.

Dosa, Aqiba, and Simeon now interpret Ex. 33:20. This verse has not appeared to this point. In fact, the whole unit has been included probably because Simeon responds to Aqiba's comment with the same words he employed when he replied above to Aqiba's comment. Thus, this pericope seems to have been included not because it treats an issue found in the exegesis of Lev. 1:1 or because it discusses verses found in the previous sections, but rather because of a particular complex of sages, Aqiba-Simeon, and because of a specific phrase which appears immediately above, "I do not [speak] in order to refute the words of my teacher, but as one who adds glory to his words." Again we see that rabbinic midrash is much more than a mere commentary on a particular biblical book or a discussion of specific issues related to the verses of that biblical text. Notice that we have two different discussions of *from the Tent of Meeting.*

The midrash now returns to Lev. 1:1 and focuses on the next word of the text, *saying.* We have three different interpretations of this word: (1) Moses should speak to Israel humbly, (2) Moses should speak to Israel and bring their words back to God, (3) God spoke to Moses not because of His own needs but because of the needs of Israel. The last explanation is attributed to a named sage, Eleazar the son of Aḥwai. Again no choice is made among the three interpretations, even though only one of them is assigned to a named sage.

The first explanation suggests that God did not speak to Moses for the first thirty-eight years during which the Israelites wandered in the desert following their exodus from Egypt. The midrash makes its point by taking a verse out of context. It is clear from the account in Exodus that the events on Mount Sinai occurred shortly after Israel left Egypt. However, this section of our midrash claims that God spoke to Israel only after Israel was worthy; that is, after all those who had rebelled against God during the trip from Egypt to Israel had died. It makes its point by quoting the opening of Deut. 2:16–17, which states, that God spoke to Moses after all the "men of war had perished." In its biblical context the verse continues, *this day you are to pass over the boundary of Moab at Ar,* suggesting a time immediately prior to the Isralites' entering Canaan. In the context of the midrash this verse is supposed to mean that God did not reveal His will to Moses until those who were to die had died. This phenomenon, the midrash's taking a verse out of its biblical context and interpreting it in light of its own needs, is common in the rabbinic texts. The original context of a biblical verse *need not* be considered when it is employed by the rabbis.

This section of the text contains the same paragraph twice. This is probably the result of a scribal error, a common occurrence in these documents.

The midrash now returns to a discussion of Lev. 1:2, the next portion of the biblical text, and it focuses on the phrase *Children of Israel.* It undertakes this discussion by joining Lev. 1:2 with Lev. 24:14. Although this verse is cited, the reference should probably be to Lev. 1:4. The difference between the two verses is that the verb is in the singular in the latter verse, while it is in the plural in the former. In any case, the discussion of the laying on of hands is placed here because this is part of the message God told Moses to deliver to the Children of Israel at the opening of Leviticus.

The first interpretation takes *Children of Israel* as a reference to Jews and notes that Jews lay their hands on sacrifices, but that non-Jews may not lay their hands on any sacrifices they bring to the Temple in Jerusalem. The section follows the form we have seen above: Logical arguments are advanced and then rejected. In this case, the arguments are rejected because one can argue two opposing positions with equal force. The midrash concludes by stating that we need Lev. 1:2 to teach us that non-Jews may not lay their hands on sacrifices because we cannot establish this point by means of logical arguments.

The next section takes *Children of Israel* as referring to males, for the word for "children" in Hebrew is the same as the word for "sons." An anonymous statement claims that the reference to males means that women may not lay their hands on sacrifices. Yosi and Simeon state that the verse means that women are not *required* to lay their hands on sacrifices; however, they *may* do so if they wish. Yosi then states that Abba Eleazar told him that they used to take the calf of the Peace-offering into the women's court of the Temple and that the women would place their hands on the calf.

The next section focuses on what Abba Eleazar told Yosi. Because Abba Eleazar referred to a specific sacrifice, should we conclude that the women could place their hands only on the sacrifice that Eleazar mentioned? The midrash rejects this logical conclusion by referring to Lev. 1:2. Note that this section is occasioned by Abba Eleazar's comment and not by Lev. 1:2; however, it does bring the verse to answer its question.

The midrash now moves to the last section of Lev. 1:2 with which we shall deal, and it asks why the Bible had to say both *a man* and *among you*, since Moses was to speak to the *Children of Israel*. Following a pattern which we have seen many times above, the midrash raises logical possibilities and rejects them because reason does not allow us to reach a definite conclusion. We again learn that the Bible had to be written the way it was so that we could learn things which we could not learn if we had to rely on our reason alone.

We have seen that this section of Sifra interprets virtually every element of Lev. 1:1–2 and takes the *exact* wording of the Bible seriously. Sifra's message is clear: The Bible had to be written in the way that it was in order to teach us things which we could not learn by use of our fallible human reason. This point is made over and over again. It is common for Sifra to state a position, present one or several logical arguments for its acceptance or rejection, reject these arguments, and reach its final conclusion by citing Scripture.

The midrash deals with several types of issues.

1. It discusses, in detail, the way in which God communicated with Moses in the Tent of Meeting, the content of God's call and Moses' response, and the importance of the exact wording of God's call.

2. It uses the conversation between God and Moses as a paradigm for the way in which a rabbi should teach his students.
3. It emphasizes the importance of the rabbis' teachings vis-à-vis those of the priests, written in code as a discussion of the way in which Moses and Aaron received revelation from God.
4. It deals with the nature of God's voice when He spoke with Moses and the way in which His speaking to Moses demonstrated His love for Israel.
5. It contains a digression on who may see the glory of God and when.
6. It tells us of the need of Moses (read, of rabbis) to speak to Israel humbly.
7. It discusses certain sacrificial laws and their application to men, gentiles, women, converts, and apostates.

All of these topics seem to be of importance primarily to rabbis and to have been chosen by them. Some may have been of interest to the population in general, but it is doubtful that most Jews of the time would have been very concerned with many of the issues addressed in this text.

We have seen that this midrash is much more than a commentary to Lev. 1:1. In several places we found sections inserted on the basis of several principles: (1) logical progression of topics, (2) expansion of previous comments, (3) repetition of a series of names, (4) repetition of similar phrases, and the like. We have seen sections which interpret portions of the Bible from books other than Leviticus. We also have seen that several methods of exegesis and logical argumentation appear in our text. The methods of argumentation are those which the Greek rhetoricians of the period also employed. In brief, we have before us much more than a mere commentary on Leviticus, for our authors were not limited by the text to which the commentary is juxtaposed or to the issues raised in that document, even though Sifra is arranged according to the structure of Leviticus. We have a rabbinic text which is not appreciably different from other examples of rabbinic literature. Furthermore, this is not a legal exegesis; much of what is contained in our text has no practical legal implications at all. We do not appear to have sermons, for much of what is contained in our text seems to be addressed to the rabbinic class, and not to the common people. We have discovered theological statements, practical statements, legal statements, theoretical statements, and political statements. We have discovered here much more than we probably expected to find. However, all is logically arranged and argued, and everything is presented *as if* it were merely a commentary to Leviticus.

NOTES

1. D. Hoffmann, *Zur Einleitung in die halachischen Midraschim* (Berlin, 1886–87), 20.

2. Maimonides (1113–1204) claimed that Rav (mid-third century C.E.) was the editor of our Sifra, and I. H. Weiss attempted to support this contention. The MaLBiM (1807–1879) claimed that Rabbi Ḥiyya (early 2 cent. C.E.) edited Sifra, and D. Hoffmann attempted to prove the truth of this suggestion. J. N. Epstein argued that Ḥiyya might have compiled a midrash to Leviticus that was similar in many points to our present text; however, he was not convinced that Ḥiyya was the final editor of Sifra. Epstein claimed that the midrash in its original form was known in Rav's school and that Rav himself taught it to his students; however, the text which Rav knew was enlarged by his students, and its final editor is yet unknown to us. M. D. Herr, s.v. "Sifra," *Encyclopaedia Judaica* XIV, 1518–1519. M. Friedman, *Mekhilta deRabbi Ishmael* (Vienna, 1870), xvii–xix. J. N. Epstein, *Prolegomena ad Litteras Tannaiticas*, E. Z. Melamed (ed.), (Jerusalem, 1958), 552–566. Moses ben Maimon, *Introduction to Yad HaHazakah* (Jerusalem, 1974), 4. I. H. Weiss, *Sifra debe Rav* (Vienna, 1862), iv. M. Loeb, *Sifra debe Rav* (Bucharest, 1860), introduction. C. M. H. (?), s.v. "Sifra," *Jewish Encyclopedia*, II, 30. Hoffmann, 20 ff.

3. Herr, 1517–1518. H. L. Strack, *Introduction to the Talmud and Midrash* (New York, 1959), 206–207.

4. Herr, 1518–1519.

5. J. Neusner, *History of the Mishnaic Laws of Purities, VII: Negaim Sifra* (Leiden, 1975), i–ii.

6. This translation is based on I. H. Weiss, *Sifra debe Rav* (Vienna, 1862), 3c–4c.

7. See the comment of Qorban Aaron on 1:6; *Sefer Qorban Aaron* (Dessau, 1742), 38a.

8. L. Jacobs, "Hermeneutics," *EJ*, VIII, 370–371. Although the *w* is not normally included among the "extending" particles, my own work on the traditions of Rabbi Ishmael suggests that the *w* was such a particle.

9. See the entries under *wy'mr* and *wydr* in S. Mandelkern, *Veteris Testamenti Concordantiae Hebraicae Antque Chaldaicae* (Tel Aviv, 1974), 119–126, 281.

10. Compare this passage with a much longer version in Tosefta

Berakhot 1:12–14. Our passage is virtually the same as Tosefta *Berakhot* 1:14. See also Exodus Rabbah 2:6, Numbers Rabbah 14:21, Midrash Samuel (Buber), 9:8.

11. From the opening of the passage until this point, the section is paralleled in Numbers Rabbah 14:21.

12. On the issue of the priests, rabbis, and Pharisees, see J. Neusner, *A Life of Rabban Yohanan ben Zakkai* (Leiden, 1970), 61–65, 70–73, 86–89. J. Neusner, *Development of a Legend* (Leiden, 1970). J. Neusner, *There We Sat Down* (Nashville, 1972), 72–128. J. Neusner, *Judaism: The Evidence of Mishnah* (Chicago, 1982), 233–234, 248–250. J. Neusner, "Priestly Views of Yohanan ben Zakkai, *Kairos*, II (1969), 306–312. G. Allon, "On the History of the High Priesthood in the Days of the Second Temple," *Tarbiz*, XXII, 1–24. J. Neusner, *The Rabbinic Traditions about the Pharisees before 70* (Leiden, 1971), III, 142–179, 282–319. A. J. Peck, *The Priestly Gift in Mishnah* (Chico, Calif., 1981), 1–7. G. G. Porton, "Midrash: Palestinian Jews and the Bible in the Greco-Roman Period," in *Aufstieg und Niedergang der römischen Welt*, ed. H. Temporini and W. Haase (Berlin, 1979), II.19.2, 113–115. It is my view that the most important result of the Maccabean wars for the history of Judaism was the disruption and eventual disintegration of the priesthood. From the time that Onias III was exiled until Herod's appointment of a Babylonian teenager as high priest, the prestige of the priesthood decreased, as did its right and authority to interpret Scripture. This was a major reason behind the rise of the Pharisees and the eventual success of the rabbis.

13. The Hebrew text is corrupt in places, and it is not at all clear to which verses the midrash refers. I have tried to identify the "thirteen" passages as best I could.

14. From "Rabbi Eleazar" until "did not hear the voice" is also found in Numbers Rabbah 14:21. The interesting point of comparison between Sifra and Numbers Rabbah is that much of Sifra to this point appears in Numbers Rabbah but in a different order.

15. Again we find a different version of this section of Sifra in Numbers Rabbah 14:21.

16. On the mystery of God's throne, see G. Scholem, *Kabbalah* (New York, 1974), 377–381. Neusner, *Life*, 139–141. Neusner, *Development*, 24, 66–67, 84–85, 96–98. D. J. Halperin, *Merkabah in Rabbinic Tradition* (New Haven, 1980).

17. R. deVaux, *Ancient Israel* (New York, 1965), II, 416.

18. A. Rothkoff, s.v. "Semikhah: Of Sacrifices," *Encyclopaedia Judaica*, XIV, 1140.

19. B. Levine, s.v. "Cult: Grain Offerings," *Encyclopaedia Judaica*, V, 1161; Mishnah *Menahot* 9:6–9.

20. Compare Babylonian Talmud, *Hagigah* 16b.

21. Ibid.

22. For a discussion of the relationship between the rabbinic exegetical techniques and the techniques employed by the Greek rhetoricians, see D. Daube, "Rabbinic Methods of Interpretation and Hellenistic Rhetoric," *Hebrew Union College Annual*, XXII (1949), 239–264. S. Lieberman, *Hellenism in Jewish Palestine*, 2 ed. (New York, 1962).

3 Mekhilta

The earliest midrashic collection to the Book of Exodus is entitled Mekhilta. In amoraic (3rd–7th cent.) and early geonic times (9th cent.), the tannaitic midrash to Exodus formed part of Sifre or Sifre debe Rav.[1] Saadya Gaon (882–942) is the first to mention the Mekhilta, and Nissim (11th cent.) was the first to apply the designation Mekhilta deRabbi Ishmael to our text.[2] The name Mekhilta deRabbi Ishmael was commonly used from the time of Samuel b. Hofni (d. 1013) and onward.[3]

The exact meaning of the term Mekhilta is unclear. Some have argued that it means "tractate" and was applied to our text because it is divided into nine tractates.[4] Still others have suggested that Mekhilta means "law" and was placed on our text because it is a legal midrash, a set of rules, *middot*.[5]

Although the text has commonly been ascribed to the school of Rabbi Ishmael,[6] there is little clear evidence to support the claim that Ishmael or his students composed it.[7] Jacob Z. Lauterbach, who compiled a modern edition and translation of Mekhilta, has written:

> The original draft of Mekhilta, most likely had its origins in the school of Rabbi Ishmael, or at least was based for the greater part upon some collected teachings of his disciples. . . . But, it would be unwarranted to assume that this earlier work was known to the Amoraim as a work of the school of Rabbi Ishmael exclusively, as contrasted with or distinguished from, a similar work of the school of Rabbi Aqiba. The Amoraim would not hesitate to incorporate teachings originating in the one school in a collection consisting, in the main, of teachings from the other school, as they were, in the collection, given the name of the respective authors.[8]

Lauterbach seems to be saying that the text comes and does not come from Ishmael's school. In brief, we simply do not know the originators of our midrash or the date of its final compilation.[9]

Mekhilta does not comment upon the whole of Exodus, and most agree that as far as we know, the text began with Ex. 12:1 and ended with Ex. 35:3.[10] In the words of Lauterbach, Mekhilta deals "with practically all of the laws contained in Exodus as well as with some of its most important narrative portions."[11]

Because there is an excellent and readily available English translation of Mekhilta, I have included a comparatively short passage in this anthology.[12] Our selection is the next-to-the-last chapter of the midrash; it interprets Ex. 31:12–17.

> *And YHWH said to Moses saying: "And you shall speak to the Children of Israel saying, 'Indeed you shall keep My Sabbaths, for it is a sign between Me and you throughout your generations, in order to know that I, YHWH, sanctify you. And you shall keep the Sabbath, for it is holy to you. One who desecrates her shall surely be put to death, for any who performs work on her, that soul shall be cut off from among her people. Six days work shall be done. But the Seventh Day is a Sabbath of rest. It is holy to YHWH. Any one who does work on the Sabbath-day shall surely be put to death. And the Children of Israel shall keep the Sabbath throughout their generations. It is an eternal covenant. It is a sign forever between Me and the Children of Israel, for in six days YHWH made the heavens and the earth, but on the seventh day He rested and was ensouled.' "*

We assume that the Sabbath was an important day in the ritual life of the Jew in late antiquity, and everything we read in this section of Mekhilta supports that assumption. The midrash tells us over and over again, and in several different ways, to observe the Sabbath according to the rabbinic injunctions. Several times our passage tells us that the Sabbath is the sign of the special relationship which exists between God and Israel. In order to keep this sign valid, the text explains what it means to work on the Sabbath, what it means to rest on the Sabbath, and when it is permissible not to rest on the Sabbath. In fact these are the main topics of the passage: sign, work, rest. The passage ends with a short "homily" on the topic of justice in the world.

Our section from Mekhilta deals with virtually every phrase in Ex. 31:12– 17. The most commonly encountered pattern in this section from Mekhilta is that Ex. 31:12–17 was written in the way it was in order to modify verses found elsewhere in the Bible. The major point of this section of Mekhilta is that the whole Bible is interrelated and that every verse modifies every other verse. While Sifra's main lesson seems to be that revelation was needed to

counter fallible human reason, Mekhilta's main point seems to be that the whole Bible is interrelated.

While some portions of our selection from Mekhilta do not focus on the verses from Ex. 31:12–17, this phenomenon is not as common as it was in Sifra. In fact, Mekhilta seems much more tied to the text of Exodus than Sifra was to the verses from Leviticus. Furthermore, the editor(s) of Mekhilta were concerned with presenting a sequential exegesis of virtually every phrase in Ex. 31:12–17. So much so, that some comments appear more than once, both in their proper place and, as well, elsewhere in the text. Also, obvious, literal interpretations of verses appear, so that the midrash will include a comment on every phrase in the section. All of this suggests that the text before us has been carefully edited and compiled.

And YHWH said to Moses (Ex. 31:12). [This teaches us that YHWH spoke to Moses directly and] not through an angel or an agent.[13]

Indeed you shall keep My Sabbaths (Ex. 31:12). Why was this said? [It was said] because it says [in Ex. 20:10:] *You shall not do any type of work.* [From Ex. 20:10] I [can learn] only [about] acts which are [considered] a type of work. On what basis [can I learn about] acts which [merely detract from one's] resting [on the Sabbath]? Scripture says: *Indeed you shall keep My Sabbaths* to include actions which [merely detract from one's] resting [on the Sabbath].

One time Rabbi Ishmael, Rabbi Eleazar the son of Azariah, and Rabbi Aqiba were walking on the road, and Levi the net-maker and Rabbi Ishmael the son of Rabbi Eleazar the son of Azariah were walking on the road after them, and this question was asked before [the former by the latter]: "On what basis [do we learn that] saving a life supersedes [the commandment of not working on] the Sabbath?" Rabbi Ishmael answered and said: "Behold it says, *If a thief is found breaking in [and is struck so that he dies, there shall be no bloodguilt on account of him; but if the sun has risen upon him, there shall be bloodguilt on account of him]* (Ex. 22:1–2). And what [type of case] is this? [The verse refers to a case in which] there is uncertainty about whether [the intruder] came to steal or to murder. Now, behold [this] case [forms the basis of] an *a fortiori* argument: Now, if the spilling of blood, which renders the Land [of Israel] unclean, and which causes the Holy Presence to remove Herself [from the Land], supersedes [the commandment not to work on the Sabbath], how much the more the saving of a life, [which does not render the Land unclean and which does not cause the Holy Pres-

ence to remove Herself from the Land], should supersede [the commandment not to work on the] Sabbath." Rabbi Eleazar the son of Azariah answered and said: "Just as circumcision, which affects [positively] only one limb of a man's body, supersedes [the commandment not to work on the] Sabbath, [for one may be circumcised on the Sabbath], how much the more [may one engage in an act which affects positively] the rest of a man's body [on the Sabbath]." They said to him: "From the case which you bring [us we can learn only that one may violate the commandment not to work on the Sabbath only when there is certainty.] Just as there [in your example] it is certain [that the Sabbath is the eighth day after the male's birth, so that he must be circumcised on that day or be subject to the penalty of being 'cut off' from among his people], so also here [in the case of saving a life on the Sabbath there must be] certainty [that if we do not violate the Sabbath the person will die]." Rabbi Aqiba says: "If the [execution of] a murderer supersedes the performance of the worship service, [for we read in Ex. 21:14 that *if a man willfully attacks another to kill him treacherously, you shall take him from My altar, that me may die,*] and [the worship service] supersedes the [commandment not to work on the] Sabbath, [for the regular sacrifice is offered before the special Sabbath sacrifice,] how much the more does the saving of a life supersede [the commandment not to work on the] Sabbath."

Rabbi Yosi the Galilean says: "When it says, *Indeed you shall keep My Sabbaths* [the particle] *indeed*, *'k*, [indicates that there are] distinctions [among the Sabbaths; for instance], there are Sabbaths which you may supersede, and there are Sabbaths [which you may] not supersede."

Rabbi Simeon the son of Menasyah says: "Behold it says, *And you shall keep the Sabbath, for it is holy to you* (Ex. 31:14). [This means that the] Sabbath is given to you, and you are not given to the Sabbath; [therefore, you may work on the Sabbath in order to save a life]."

Rabbi Nathan says: "Behold it says: *And the Children of Israel shall keep the Sabbath throughout their generations* (Ex. 31:16) [which means that one may] desecrate one Sabbath so [that the one whose life is saved] may keep many [future] Sabbaths."

For it is a sign between Me and you (Ex. 31:13), and [it is] not [a sign] between Me and the [rest] of the nations of the world.

Throughout your generations (Ex. 31:13) [means] that the thing should be observed throughout [your] generations.

In order to know that I, YHWH, sanctify you (Ex. 31:13). Why was this said? [This was said] because it says [in Ex. 31:16], *And the Children of Israel shall keep the Sabbath.* [If I had only Ex. 31:16], I might think that even a deaf person, an intellectually incompetent person, or a minor [is obligated to keep the Sabbath; therefore,] Scripture says, *In order to know that I, YHWH . . .* [which means] I said this [to place the obligation of observing the Sabbath] only upon [those] who possess the [ability to] know [how to observe it].

That I, YHWH, sanctify you [refers to the sanctification] for the world-to-come, which is like the sanctification of the Sabbath in this world. We learn that [the sanctification of the Sabbath in this world is like] the sanctification of the world-to-come; and thus it says, *A Psalm, a song of the Sabbath day* (Ps. 92:1), [which refers] to the world which is entirely [like] the Sabbath.

And you shall keep the Sabbath (Ex. 31:14). This is what Rabbi Simeon the son of Menasyah used to say: "The Sabbath is given to you, and you are not given to the Sabbath."

For it is holy to you (Ex. 31:14) indicates that the Sabbath adds holiness to Israel. Why is so-and-so's shop closed [on the Sabbath? The shop is closed] because he keeps the Sabbath. Why does so-and-so stop his labors? [He stops his labors] because he observes the Sabbath. [And not only these people but all who observe the Sabbath] testify [to the existence of] the One who spoke and the world was [created], for He created His world in six days, and He rested on the seventh day; and thus it says, "*And you are My witnesses," says YHWH, "that I am God"* (Isa. 43:12).

"*One who desecrates her shall surely be put to death* (Ex. 31:14). Why was this said? [It was said because it says in Ex. 31:15 that] *Any one who performs work on the Sabbath day shall surely be put to death.* [From here] we learn the punishment [for one who performs work on the Sabbath, but] we do not learn the warning [that one should not work on the Sabbath. Therefore,] Scripture says, *And the seventh day is the Sabbath for YHWH, your God, you shall not do any manner of work* (Ex. 20:10). [So far,] I [can learn] only [about] the punishment and the warning concerning work [done] during the daytime. On what basis [can I learn about the punishment and the warning concerning work done] during the night [of the Sabbath]? Scripture says, *One who desecrates her shall surely be put to death.* We learn [about the] punishment, [but] we do not learn [about the] warning; [therefore,] Scripture says, *And the seventh day is the Sabbath for YHWH, your God* (Ex. 20:10).

[But, there is] no [need for the word] *Sabbath* [to be mentioned in Ex. 20:10; therefore,] why does Scripture say *Sabbath* [in this verse? It used the word *Sabbath* here] only to include the night [of the Sabbath] in the general warning"—the words of Rabb Aḥai the son of Rabbi Yoshiah.

Rabbi Judah the son of Bathyra says: "Behold [if] the gentiles surrounded the cities of Israel, and [the] Israel[ites] had to] profane the Sabbath [for a short time in order to defend the cities, the] Israel[ites] should not say, 'Because we have profaned a part of her, we [may] profane all of her'; [therefore,] Scripture says, *One who desecrates her shall surely be put to death* [which indicates that] even [one who profanes the Sabbath unnecessarily for only the time that it takes] to wink an eye [falls under the injunction stated in Ex. 31:14; that is,] *One who desecrates her shall surely be put to death.*"

For any who performs work on her, that soul shall be cut off (Ex. 31:14). [This verse does not apply] until one does a complete act of work on her. Behold, [if] one wrote one letter [of a word in the] morning and one letter [of the same word at] dusk, or [if] one wove one thread in the morning and one thread at dusk, I might think that he is culpable [for the punishment of "cutting off" for each letter or for each act of weaving; however,] Scripture says: *And you shall keep the Sabbath, for it is holy to you. One who desecrates her shall surely be put to death, for any who performs work on her, that soul shall be cut off* [which means that the punishment does not apply] until he does a complete act of work on her.

That soul shall be cut off from among her people (Ex. 31:14). Why was this said? [It was said because the verse also states:] *One who desecrates her shall surely be put to death.* [From this latter part of the verse] I [can learn] only [about] one who willfully violates [the Sabbath] in spite of the warning of witnesses. On what basis [can I learn about the punishment for] one who willfully violates [the Sabbath] when he is alone? Scripture says, *Shall be cut off (wnkrth)* to include one who willfully violates [the Sabbath] while he is alone.

Shall be cut off [was said because] "cutting off" means "ceasing [to exist]."

"*That soul* [refers to] one who willfully violates [the Sabbath]"—the words of Rabbi Aqiba.

From among her people [indicates that] her people shall be at peace [after that soul is removed].

Six days work shall be done (Ex. 31:15). One verse says, *Six days work shall be done* (Ex. 31:15), and one verse says, *Six days you shall labor and do all your work* (Ex. 20:4). How shall these two verses be reconciled? Now, when Israel does the will of the Omnipresent, [*six days work shall be done,* which indicates that] their work is done by others, and thus it says, *Strangers shall stand and feed your flocks, and the children of foreigners shall be your plowmen and vinedressers* (Isa. 61:5). But when Israel does not do the will of the Omnipresent, *six days you shall labor and do all of your work,* [which indicates that] their work shall be done by them, and not only this but even the work of others shall be done by them, for it is said, *Therefore, you shall serve your enemies whom YHWH will send against you* (Deut. 28:48).

But the seventh day is a Sabbath of rest. It is holy to YHWH (Ex. 31:15). Why was this said? [It was said] because [in Lev. 23:4] it says, *These are the appointed feasts of YHWH, holy convocations which you shall proclaim [at the time appointed for them.* On the basis of this latter verse] one might think that just as the [declaration of the] sanctification of the appointed feasts is dependent on the court, so also the [declaration of the] sanctification of the Sabbath should be dependent on the court; [however,] Scripture says, *But the seventh day is a Sabbath of rest. It is holy to YHWH.* [This indicates that the sanctification and declaration of the Sabbath] is dependent upon itself and is not dependent on the [proclamation] of the court; and thus it says, *And you shall keep the Sabbath* (Ex. 31:14).

And the Children of Israel shall keep the Sabbath (Ex. 31:16). This is what Rabbi Nathan used to say: "One may profane one Sabbath so that he might observe many [future] Sabbaths."

Rabbi Eliezer says: [*And the Children of Israel shall keep the Sabbath,]* to observe the Sabbath throughout their generations, it is an eternal covenant* (Ex. 31:16) [refers to] a thing whose covenant is cut upon an individual. And which [thing] is this? This is circumcision; [therefore, the act of circumcision supersedes the commandment not to work on the Sabbath]."

Rabbi Eleazar the son of Parta says: "All who keep the Sabbath, it is as if they observed the Sabbath, for it is said, *And the Children of Israel shall keep the Sabbath, to observe the Sabbath.*"

Rabbi says: "How do you know that, as for anyone who keeps [just] one Sabbath [exactly] according to [the rabbinic] statute[s], it is accounted to him as if he kept all the Sabbaths from the time that the Holy One, blessed be He, created His world until [the day when] He will revive the dead? [We know this from Ex. 31:16], for it is said: *And the Children of Israel shall keep the Sabbath, to observe the Sabbath throughout their generations; it is an eternal covenant."*

Between Me and the Children of Israel (Ex. 31:17), and not between Me and the [rest] of the nations of the world.

It is an eternal sign (Ex. 31:17) tells [us] that the Sabbath will never be removed from Israel. And thus you find that everything for which [the] Israel[ites] sacrificed themselves has been established in their midst [forever]; but anything for which [the] Israel[ites] did not sacrifice themselves was not established in their midst [forever]. For example, the Sabbath, circumcision, the study of the Torah, and ritual immersion, for which [the] Israel[ites] did sacrifice themselves, were established in their midst [forever]. Conversely, the Temple, the courts, the sabbatical years, and the jubilee years, for which [the] Israel[ites] did not sacrifice themselves, were not established in their midst [forever].

For in six days YHWH made the heavens and the earth, but on the seventh day He rested [and was ensouled] (Ex. 31:17). From what did He rest? Did [He rest only] from work, or [did He rest] also from [administering] justice? Scripture says, *And was ensouled,* [which] tells [us] that justice never ceases from before Him. And thus it says, *Righteousness and justice are the foundation of Your throne; steadfast love and truth go before Your face* (Ps. 89:15); and it is written, *Clouds and thick darkness surround Him, righteousness and justice are the foundation of His throne* (Ps. 97:2); and it says, *The Rock, His work is perfect, for all His ways are justice* (Deut. 32:4).

COMMENTS

And YHWH said to Moses. The midrash claims that this indicates that God conversed directly with Moses. This underscores the accuracy of what Moses received and transmitted, an important issue for the rabbis, who claimed that their teachings could be traced directly back to Moses, who heard them directly from God.[14]

Indeed you shall keep My Sabbaths. The rabbis believed that every word in the Torah was significant; furthermore, the word-choice was meant to teach us something special. In this instance, the midrash asks why the verb "keep," *tšmrw,* was employed. The word "remember" (Ex. 20:8) appears elsewhere; why does it not occur here?

You shall not do any type of work. The word "keep" must be included in Ex. 31:12, for without it we might conclude that Ex. 20:10 tells us all we need to know about resting on the Sabbath. However, the latter verse tells us only that we may not work on the Sabbath; it does not discuss those acts which are not actually considered work but which do interrupt one's resting on the Sabbath, such as, riding on a donkey or climbing a tree.[15] The injunction to "keep" the Sabbath teaches us not only that we may not engage in work on the Sabbath but also that we may not engage in any activity which interrupts our resting on the Sabbath.[16]

One time Rabbi Ishmael. The interesting point here is that we have a narrative context for the rabbis' statements. Although this is not totally unique, it is uncommon for the comments of rabbinic masters to be set in a specific narrative setting. Tannaitic literature shows little interest in placing rabbinic statements in specific contexts. The lack of such settings gives the content of the remarks a transcendent quality.[17]

On what basis do we learn. This question serves as the introduction for the exegetical comments which follow. The question presupposes that one may violate the Sabbath in order to save a life; it asks only for the scriptural support for this activity. The section is not an exegesis of Exodus 31; in fact, this chapter is not even cited in the pericope. Presumably it was included here because the activity which one may perform while saving a life on the Sabbath may not be strictly classified as work, but may be an activity which only interrupts one's rest on the Sabbath.

Rabbi Ishmael answered and said. Ex. 22:1–2 states that if a thief breaks into your house while it is dark and you strike him so that he dies, you are not guilty of killing an innocent person. Ishmael implies that

61

although the thief broke into your house, the darkness prevented you from ascertaining whether he broke into your house for the purpose of killing you or merely with the intention of stealing some items from the house. Even though you are uncertain about the thief's intentions, you are permitted to kill him because he *may* have intended to kill you. The assumption is that if the thief merely intended to steal from you, killing him is an unjustified act; however, if the intruder intended to kill you, you were justified in killing him first. Ishmael also assumes that the thief entered your house and that you killed him on the Sabbath.

Now, behold, this case forms the basis. If one can spill blood on the Sabbath, even though the spilling of blood may be too harsh a response to the intruder's planned actions and is a vile act which defiles the Holy Land and causes the Holy Presence to remove Herself from the world, should we not conclude that one may prevent the death of someone on the Sabbath?

Rabbi Eleazar the son of Azariah answered. Eleazar notes that one may be circumcised on the Sabbath, even though circumcision involves certain types of work.[18] He further notes that circumcision affects only one part of the body, the male genital organ; therefore, should not saving a life, which affects a dying person's entire body, also be performed on the Sabbath?[19]

They said to him. We do not know who "they" are. Perhaps they are the two who asked the original question. We often find the clause "they said to him" in rabbinic texts even though we have no clue to the identity of "they." In any case, this interrupts the flow of the story, for the opinions of the other two rabbis are not questioned. Furthermore, we notice that Eleazar's comment is different from those of Aqiba and Ishmael, for the other sages base their comments on an interpretation of Scripture, just as the question "on what basis can we learn?" demands. Therefore, it is possible that both Eleazar's comment and the statement which "they" made originally were set in another context. They were brought here as a unit because Eleazar dealt with the subject of our passage.

From the case which you bring us. "They" suggest that Eleazar's example is unique and we cannot learn from it the general principle that one may save a life on the Sabbath.

Just as there it is certain. I have followed Lauterbach's explanation of the passage.[20] He suggests that a child may be circumcised on the Sabbath only if it is certain that the Sabbath is the eighth day after his birth. If the child was born at dusk, so that it is not certain whether the Sabbath is the eighth day after his birth, the child may not be circumcised on the Sabbath.

Also here. "They" argue that if one may circumcise a male only if there is certainty that the Sabbath is the eighth day after the birth, we may act to save a life on the Sabbath *only if* we are certain that our act will indeed save the person's life, and that without our acting, the person would die. If we accept this line of reasoning, we must restrict our actions on the Sabbath only to those cases in which we are certain that we must act to save a person's life; therefore, we do not have a general principle that one may always violate the Sabbath in order to save a person's life. Notice that Eleazar does not respond to the objection "they" raised, nor is their point taken up in the rest of the pericope. Also, "they" have not rejected the principle that one may save a life on the Sabbath; "they" have only qualified what "saving a life" means.

Rabbi Aqiba says. Aqiba argues that Ex. 21:14 teaches us that we may interrupt the sacrificial service in order to remove a murderer and execute him. We know that the performance of the sacrificial ritual takes precedence over the commandment not to work on the Sabbath, for the sacrificial service is performed on the Sabbath and the daily offering is sacrificed before the Sabbath offering. We also know that the sacrificial ritual may be suspended in order to remove and execute a murderer. Therefore, if something more important than the Sabbath may be suspended in order to remove a murderer and execute him, should we not conclude that the Sabbath itself may be suspended in order to save a life?[21]

Rabbi Yosi the Galilean says. Yosi bases his comment on the particle 'k, "indeed." One school of rabbinic exegesis based its interpretations on conjunctions, adverbs, and similar particles. According to this school, 'k was a "limiting" particle, that is, it limited the phrase it introduced to only certain cases. In this example, Yosi argues that the 'k indicates that the injunction to keep the Sabbath applies only to certain Sabbaths.[22]

There are Sabbaths which you may supersede. In the present context, this suggests that one may supersede the commandment not to work on the Sabbath in order to save a life.

There are Sabbaths which you may not supersede. The traditional commentators suggest that the building of the Tent of Meeting was stopped on the Sabbath so that the Hebrews could rest on that day.[23]

Rabbi Simeon the son of Menasyah says. Simeon bases his comment on the phrase *it is holy to you;* the prepositional phrase, *to you,* indicates that the Sabbath was given for the benefit of humans. For this reason, the comment may be read in this context to mean that one may violate the commandment not to work on the Sabbath in order to save a life, for people are primary and the Sabbath is secondary. Simeon's comment is virtually the same as Jesus' statement in Mark 2:27, "The Sabbath was made for man, not man for the Sabbath." Although the two are similar, it is impossible to argue dependence of one upon the other.[24]

Rabbi Nathan says. Nathan argues that the phrase *throughout your generations* means that one should have the opportunity to celebrate the Sabbath throughout one's lifetime. In this context, Nathan's comment means that you may save a person's life on the Sabbath so that he can celebrate subsequent Sabbaths.[25]

For it is a sign between Me and you. The midrash takes this verse literally. The Sabbath is a sign of the special relationship between YHWH and Israel, a relationship which God does not have with the rest of the nations of the world.

Throughout your generations. The midrash also takes this portion of the verse literally. The Jews are obligated to celebrate the Sabbath forever.

Why was this said? We need Ex. 31:13 to modify Ex. 31:16. The latter verse states that *the Children of Israel shall keep the Sabbath.* If we had only this verse, we would conclude that every Jew, regardless of his or her abilities, is obligated to keep the Sabbath. However, the phrase *in order to know* in Ex. 31:13 limits the application of Ex. 31:16 to those Jews who are able to know that YHWH sanctifies Israel. This excludes the deaf person, the intellectually incompetent person, and the minor, for they do not have the ability to know how God relates to Israel through the Sabbath or to know the correct manner in which to observe the Sabbath.

That I, YHWH, sanctify you. The midrash draws an analogy between the Sabbath and the world-to-come. In a much later document, the Letters of Rabbi Aqiba, ca. 700 C.E., we find the following story, which illustrates the point our midrash makes: "At the time of the giving of the Torah, the Holy One, blessed be He, called to [the] Israel[ites] and said to them: 'My children, I have a good object in this world, and I shall give it to you forever if you accept My Torah and keep My commandments.' [The] Israel[ites] answered and said before the Master of the World, 'What is this good object which you are giving us if we keep Your Torah?' The Holy One, blessed be He, answered them, '[This good object] is the world-to-come.' [The] Israel[ites] answered and said: 'Master of the World, show us an example of the world-to-come.' The Holy One, blessed be He, answered and said to them: 'This is the Sabbath [which is an example of what you shall experience in the world-to-come].' "26

A Psalm, a song of the Sabbath day. The content of Psalm 92 deals with the psalmist's and God's victory over their enemies: *For lo, Your enemies, O YHWH, for lo, Your enemies shall perish; all evildoers shall be scattered. . . . My eyes have seen the downfall of my enemies, my ears have heard the doom of my evil assailants. The righteous flourish like the palm tree, and grow like a cedar in Lebanon. They are planted in YHWH's house, they flourish in the courts of our God.* This easily could be seen as a reference to the eschatological situation in which Israel will stand justified before God, and her enemies will be completely defeated. Thus, one could claim that this eschatological situation, which is called the Sabbath, is a time of peace and justification as well as of rest and fulfillment. Therefore, the psalm speaks of a time when all reality will conform to the situation on the ideal Sabbath.

And you shall keep the Sabbath. Above we found Simeon's comment on this verse; however, it was out of sequence. It is repeated here, in sequence, with an introduction, "this is what Rabbi Simeon the son of Menasyah used to say," which indicates that it is either well known or said elsewhere.27

Notice that the earlier context in which Simeon's remark occurred allowed us to give it a specific interpretation; however, here, with no interpretive context, Simeon's comment is much more ambiguous.

For it is holy to you. The midrash interprets this verse to mean that the Sabbath is holy to Israel because it is a means by which Israel adds holiness to herself. That holiness is evidenced by the fact that the Jews do not engage in their normal daily activities on the Sabbath. The Jews' rest testifies to God's existence because the Jews rest from their everyday work on the Sabbath just as God rested on the Sabbath from His work at the time He created the world.

Why was this said. The rabbis believed in God's absolute justice and fairness. They concluded not only that God specified the punishment for violating certain injunctions, but also that He supplied, in a different place, a warning that one would be punished for violating the specific commandment. For this reason, the midrash is here concerned with establishing the warning against working on the Sabbath as well as the punishment for one who commits this transgression.

Ex. 31:15 tells us that anyone who works on the Sabbath *shall be put to death;* this verse supplies the punishment for one who works on the Sabbath. Ex. 20:10, which commands us not to work on the Sabbath, supplies the warning not to work on the Sabbath, for it does not specify the punishment one who works on the Sabbath will receive. Because Ex. 20:10 explicitly mentions the *seventh day,* the midrash concludes that the verse warns us only that we cannot work on the *day* of the Sabbath, while Ex. 31:15, which refers to the *Sabbath day,* provides the punishment only for one who works during the day. The midrash now attempts to find the verse which contains the warning against working during the night of the Sabbath and the punishment for one who does work at that time. Ex. 31:14 states that *one who desecrates her shall surely be put to death.* Because this verse does not specify the Sabbath *day,* Ahai states that it refers to the Sabbath *night;* therefore, Ex. 31:14 provides the punishment for one who works during that time. Ex. 20:10 mentions both the *seventh day* and the *Sabbath.* Because the appearance of the word "Sabbath" seems to be superfluous and the verse contains a specific reference to day, Ahai concludes that the seemingly superfluous reference to the "Sabbath" is meant to include the night in the warning contained in the verse.

Rabbi Judah the son of Bathyra says. Judah raises the possibility that after the Jews had fought a defensive battle during a few hours of the Sabbath, they might conclude that since they had violated part of that particular Sabbath they need not abstain from activity during the remainder of that day. Judah concludes that Ex. 31:14 teaches that anyone who desecrates unnecessarily even a split second of the Sabbath deserves the punishment of death. According to Judah, one may violate the Sabbath if it is absolutely necessary; however, one may violate her only for the exact time it takes to respond to the emergency. For the remainder of that Sabbath, the Jews must observe the commandments relating to the Sabbath.[28]

For any who performs work on her. The midrash states that one violates the Sabbath only by performing a complete act of work on that day. Thus, one who writes a single letter of a word but does not complete the word has not violated the Sabbath; similarly, weaving only one thread is not a violation of the Sabbath, but weaving two threads is. The implication of our text is that these acts constitute complete acts of work. Mishnah *Shabbat* 7:2 states that one who weaves two threads violates the Sabbath, and Mishnah *Shabbat* 12:3–4 rules that one is guilty for writing two letters on the Sabbath even if the letters do not constitute a word. What our text seems to add is that writing two letters at different times during the day or weaving the threads at different times during the Sabbath is a violation of the Sabbath. This conclusion is based on the phrase *on her, bh,* which the midrash interprets as "any time on her, the Sabbath."[29]

Why was this said. Rabbinic law generally assumes that there must be two witnesses to an act before a person can be punished;[30] Num. 35:30 specifically states that *no person shall be put to death on the testimony of one witness.* In addition, rabbinic law assumes that one is not normally liable for a transgression unless forewarned by others, Mishnah *Sanhedrin* 5:1. Our midrash argues, on the basis of the phrase *shall be cut off,* that people are culpable for violating the Sabbath even if they did so in private so that witnesses did not see them or warn them about the punishment they would incur. The punishment of "cutting off" is taken as referring to God's acting directly on a person.[31] The punishment is generally interpreted to mean that a person's life is "cut short" by God; therefore, the general rules of the court, such as those concerning the number of witnesses and their forewarning of an individual, do not apply. For this reason, we learn that a person who violates the Sabbath in private, so that the matter will probably never be adjudicated by the rabbis, will be punished directly by God.

Shall be cut off. The midrash states that "cutting off" refers to one's ceasing to exist; that is, the person's life will be cut short directly by God.

That soul. Aqiba states that the verse refers to one who intentionally violates the Sabbath. In short, Aqiba's interpretation of the verse is the same as the anonymous comment which immediately precedes it. One commentator suggests that the word "that" indicates that it is a specific soul, the one who willfully violates the Sabbath. The word "that" is important, for the text could have merely stated "the" soul.[32]

From among her people. The midrash suggests that the reference to *her people* indicates that the people of Israel will benefit when a Sabbath violator is removed from their midst, for then they can live in peace.[33]

Six days work shall be done. Every element of the biblical verse was important to the rabbis. In this case, the midrash focuses on the voice of the verb. In Ex. 31:15 the verb is in the passive voice, *work shall be done,* but in Ex. 20:9 we find an active verb, *you shall do all your work.* The midrash asks why the statement is found in both the active and the passive voices. The text concludes that each verse teaches something different. The passive voice suggests that when Israel is faithful to God, her *work shall be done* by others; however, if she is not faithful to God, she *shall do* all her work as well as the work of her enemies. Deut. 28:48, which states that the Hebrews shall serve their enemies when they do not obey God, supplies proof for the latter interpretation of Ex. 20:9.[34]

Why was this said. The midrash argues that Ex. 31:15, which mentions that the Sabbath *is holy to YHWH,* was needed to modify what one might deduce from Lev. 23:4, which states that *you,* the people, *shall proclaim* the date of the holy convocations. During the rabbinic period, the court in Jerusalem, and later in Babylonia, declared the appearance of the new moon, Mishnah *Rosh Hashanah* 1:1–3:1.[35] Because the festivals were on specific days of given months, declaring the new moon also serves to declare the date of the festivals. Therefore, the proclaiming of the festivals was dependent on the rabbinic courts. From Lev. 23:4, we could conclude that the proclamation of the Sabbath should also be made by the courts; however, Ex. 31:15 states that the Sabbath is holy to YHWH. Our midrash takes this to mean that the Sabbaths are holy for YHWH; therefore, He alone declares when the Sabbath should occur, so that its appearance is not dependent on a proclamation by the courts.[36]

This is what Rabbi Nathan used to say. We saw Nathan's comment earlier. Here it is introduced by the phrase "used to say," which perhaps indicates that it was well known or a statement which he often said.[37] It is interesting to note that both of the attributed statements which appear twice in this section of Mekhilta are introduced by "used to say" the second time they occur, but not the first. I have translated the comment differently the second time from the first time because the context in which it appears first defines the remark as a reference to saving one's life on the Sabbath. Because that implication is dependent on its context, I have not included it here, where the context is different.

Rabbi Eliezer says. Eliezer focuses on the word *covenant,* which appears in the context of the Sabbath and also in the context of God's commanding Abraham to circumcise himself and his household and His commanding the Hebrews to circumcise all of their males, Gen. 17:9–14. In Gen. 17:13, circumcision, like the Sabbath in Ex. 31:16, is called *an eternal covenant.* From this fact, Eliezer concludes that the commandment to circumcise a male on the Sabbath overrides the commandment not to work on the Sabbath. This agrees with the opinion attributed to Eleazar the son of Azariah near the opening of our passage and the anonymous statement in Mishnah *Shabbat* 18:3.

Rabbi Eleazar the son of Parta says. Eleazar is concerned with the appearance of two different verbs, "keep," *šmr,* and "observe," *ʿśh,* in our verse. It is unclear exactly to what Eleazar thought the two verbs referred. It is possible that he read *keep* to mean "resting," while he read *observe* to mean "doing something positive." Or perhaps the word translated here as "observed" should be rendered instead as "created, making." Therefore, "keeping" the Sabbath is comparable to creating the holy day of rest.[38]

Rabbi says. Rabbi states that one who observes all of the appropriate *taqqanot*,[39] rabbinic injunctions, on just one Sabbath is the same as one who kept every Sabbath from the creation of the world until the messianic period. Presumably Rabbi based his interpretation on the word *eternal.* In any case, Rabbi states that one must observe the Sabbath according to its rabbinic interpretation.

Between Me and the Children of Israel. This comment appeared above, where it was also appropriate.

It is an eternal sign. The midrash makes an interesting point: Those things which are important to Israel last forever, because Israel takes care that they should be maintained. However, those things for which Israel did not exercise care were removed from her. The midrash implies that the Temple was destroyed and the sabbatical and jubilee years were brought to an end because Israel did not take them seriously enough to preserve, or to deserve, them. The Temple was destroyed in 70 C.E. by the Romans, and the sabbatical and jubilee years probably ended shortly after the end of the Bar-Kokhba Revolt in 135 C.E.[40] It is interesting that all of these things came to an end as the result of the Jews' fighting the Romans. Perhaps we have here a message similar to Jeremiah's: The Israelites should not put their trust in arms; they should place their trust only in God.

But on the seventh day He rested. Unlike Gen. 2:3, which specifies that *God rested from all the work which He had done in creating,* Ex. 31:17 does not specify from what God rested. Our midrash asks if God completely rested on the Sabbath, so that He ceased even from administering justice in the world. The clause *and was ensouled* teaches us that even on the Sabbath God still administers justice. The midrash demonstrates that the rabbis could not imagine that God ever ceased from assuring there would be justice in the world. This may be related to the previous point that the Temple was destroyed and the sabbatical and jubilee years were brought to an end because Israel was not worthy for them to continue.

CONCLUSIONS

To refresh our memories, this section of Mekhilta is a commentary to Ex. 31:12–17.

And YHWH said to Moses saying: "And you shall speak to the Children of Israel saying, 'Indeed you shall keep My Sabbaths, for it is a sign between Me and you throughout your generations, in order to know that I, YHWH, sanctify you. And you shall keep the Sabbath, for it is holy to you. One who desecrates her shall surely be put to death, for any who performs work on her, that soul shall be cut off from among her people. Six days work shall be done. But the seventh day is a Sabbath of rest. It is holy to YHWH. Any one who does work on the Sabbath day shall surely be put to death. And the Children of Israel shall keep the Sabbath throughout their generations. It is an eternal covenant. It is a sign forever between Me and the Children of Israel, for in six days YHWH made the heavens and the earth, but on the seventh day He rested and was ensouled.' "

The topic of this section of Exodus is the Sabbath. But it is only one of several biblical passages which concentrated on this holy day. As we shall see, one of Mekhilta's main concerns is to determine why this section was composed in these exact words while other sections of the Bible which also discuss the Sabbath employ other words.

The midrash opens by stating that Ex. 31:12 means that God, alone, spoke directly to Moses. Thus, the following discussion of the Sabbath is the correct and authoritative discussion of the Seventh Day. The importance of Moses' receiving revelation directly from God was a major point of the section of Sifra we have included in this collection. Again we learn that Moses (read, rabbis) communicated God's message to the Israelites.

The midrash continues its discussion of Ex. 31:12 and asks why we are told to *indeed keep* the Sabbath when we have been told to remember the Sabbath in Ex. 20:8–11. The midrash states that Ex. 31:12, *you shall keep my Sabbaths*, modifies Ex. 20:10, *you shall not do any type of work*. The latter verse teaches us only that we must refrain from acts of work. We learn from Ex. 31:12 that we should not engage in activities which interfere with our rest on the Sabbath. This point is not obvious from the verse, and this

69

creative exegesis seems to be an attempt to juxtapose with a biblical text the principle that one should not engage in any type of activity on the Sabbath.

At this point the midrash includes a narrative which seeks the biblical basis for the principle that one may violate the Sabbath in order to save a life. This section does not interpret our passage from Exodus. As I suggested above, it may have been included here because the activity in which one might engage in order to save a life may not be classified as a type of work. However, this "reason" is determined by the context in which the story appears; it is not inherent in the story itself. The story *assumes* that one may save a life on the Sabbath; it asks only for the biblical texts from which one may deduce this fact. In the commentary, I noted that the story has some awkward portions; however, it does circulate as a whole unit.

Yosi returns to the verse at hand and concentrates on the particle *'k*, *indeed*. This again points to the fact that the above narrative is an insertion into the exegesis of Ex. 31:12 ff. Yosi's exegesis derives from the assumption by some rabbis that certain particles within the biblical text "extend" or "limit" the application of the contents of the verse in which they occur. Yosi offers our second interpretation of Ex. 31:12; however, his focus on the issue of "superseding" the Sabbath reflects the story inserted above his comment.

Simeon's comment is out of sequence, for it is an exegesis of Ex. 31:14; it will appear again below in its proper place. The statement is a folk-maxim which circulated not only in rabbinic circles but also within the circles of those who created the Gospels. The remark appears here because it could be read to mean that humans control the Sabbath and thus may violate it in order to save another human's life. Notice, however, that in another context, this statement might have entirely different implications.

Nathan's comment, which is also out of sequence but which also will appear later in sequence, is another folk-maxim. In this context the remark means that one should save a life on the Sabbath so that the person whose life has been saved may observe future Sabbaths. In another context, the statement might mean that one could act on the Sabbath so that he himself could observe future Sabbaths. We have two statements, both offered as exegeses of Exodus, which depend on the context for their specific meanings. They were included at this point, even though they do not interpret the particular verses under consideration, because they interpret a verse of this section of Exodus and because they deal with the Sabbath and could be read as relevant to the present discussion.

The midrash returns to the proper sequence of verses and takes Ex. 31:13 literally: the Sabbath is a sign of the special relationship between YHWH and the Jews. Therefore, the Sabbath shall be eternal, for this relationship is eternal.

The anonymous midrash focuses on the next element of Ex. 31:13. When the verb "to know" in Ex. 31:15 modifies Ex. 31:16, we learn that only those who have the ability to know how to celebrate correctly the Sabbath or how YHWH sanctifies Israel are obligated to celebrate the Sabbath. There are two interesting points here. First, both verses appear in Exodus 31. Second, Ex. 31:16 modifies Ex. 31:13 in the same way in which the latter modifies the former. According to the latter, one should celebrate the Sabbath in order to know and so on, while the former tells us that it is the Children of Israel who must know that YHWH, and so on.

The midrash now interprets the next section of Ex. 31:13. I see no feature inherent in the verse itself which obviously points to the midrash's claim that the sanctification referred to in Ex. 31:13 is related to the sanctification of the world-to-come. This position is supported by Psalm 92; however, there is no clear feature of Ps. 92 which connects it with the world-to-come. This seems to be a case in which a commonly held view concerning the relationship between resting on the Sabbath and living in the messianic age is juxtaposed with a biblical passage even though the text itself makes no obvious reference to this view.

Simeon's comment appears here in sequence, and it is introduced by the phrase "used to say." I have translated the remark differently in each place to underscore that its meaning is dependent upon its context.

The midrash continues with its exegesis of Ex. 31:14. In this paragraph we find, for the first time, an illustration of the midrash's interpretation. The illustrations are independent of the exegesis of Ex. 31:14, and Isa. 43:12 serves as the climax of this section.

The midrash continues with its exegesis of Ex. 31:14 and returns to its pattern of demonstrating how one verse modifies another. However, this is a rather complex passage. Although it opens by citing Ex. 31:14, it deals extensively with Ex. 20:10. The midrash first notes that Ex. 20:10 provides the warning and Ex. 31:15 supplies the punishment for one who works during the daytime on the Sabbath. The midrash next states that Ex. 20:10 provides the warning and Ex. 31:14 provides the punishment for one who works during the evenings of the Sabbath. This rather complex discussion is attributed to Aḥai.

Judah offers a theoretical situation to which one can apply the message of Ex. 31:14. Judah's point is that one cannot unnecessarily violate the Sabbath; however, one may supersede her in an emergency. Judah's interpretation is an alternative to the one presented in the previous paragraph.

The midrash continues with Ex. 31:14 and focuses on an important point of law. The fact that the point is not obvious from the verse suggests that the legal position was well known and that we have here an attempt to juxtapose it with "its" biblical basis. The exegesis is based on a literal understanding of the phrase *on her*, one Hebrew word.

The form of the next exegesis of Ex. 31:14 is familiar to us. What is unusual is that one part of the verse modifies a second portion of the same verse. Until this point, we have been told that one verse modifies another verse. The practical implication of this paragraph is essential for the rabbis' attempt to assure that the population observe the Sabbath even in private. Obviously, one who violates the Sabbath while alone is not subject to punishment by the court because the court would have no way of knowing that the individual had violated the Sabbath. Therefore, it was necessary for the rabbis to demonstrate that one would be punished for violating the Sabbath in private. The only possible being to administer the punishment is God.

Now we are presented with three short comments which interpret the same phrases of Ex. 31:14 which were just interpreted. The first two short interpretations seem to be alternate forms of the point made in the paragraph which preceded them. The third interpretation implies that Sabbath violators disrupt the life of all Jews.

The next section moves to Ex. 31:15 and focuses on the voices of the main verbs in Ex. 31:15 and Ex. 20:9. Neither position seems to be obvious from Ex. 31:15 or from Ex. 20:9. In fact, had the midrash not told us that the verses needed to be reconciled, we probably would not have realized it.

The form of the next section of the midrash is familiar: Ex. 31:15 modifies Lev. 23:4. Because it must have been obvious that the courts do not declare the onset of the Sabbath, again we have a case in which a well-established custom is tied to a biblical text.

Nathan's statement now appears in its proper sequence. As was the case with Simeon's remark, Nathan's statement also depends on its context for its exact meaning.

Eliezer's remark is totally off our subject, and my interpolation depends on the context in which the statement appears. Eliezer discusses circumcision; in its simplest meaning, it has nothing to do with the Sabbath.

Eleazar offers a third interpretation of Ex. 31:16. It attempts to explain why two different verbs appear in the verse, a concern with which Sifra opened. However, the exact meaning and implication of Eleazar's interpretation are unclear to me.

Rabbi does not open with the verse; however, Ex. 31:16 does form the climax of his remarks. Rabbi makes the point that observing one Sabbath correctly is the same as observing all the Sabbaths which ever were and ever shall be. Rabbi offers us our fourth interpretation of Ex. 31:16. The interpretations are different, and no choice is made concerning the validity of the several exegetical remarks.

The next remark is the same which occurred earlier as an interpretation of a similar passage in the Bible.

The midrash now makes an important theological point and connects it with Ex. 31:17: Those things which the Israelites take to heart last; those things which the Jews do not take seriously are not maintained. There is justice in the world, and the Jews' actions, implicit and explicit, are responsible for the realities of their world.

This same point is made at the end of this section of Mekhilta: God always acts justly, and justice never ceases from the world. The juxtaposition of this point with the previous paragraphs underscores the point made above. The connection of this point with Ex. 31:17 is tenuous. It is clear that the midrash wanted to end this section with a small "homily" on justice.

This section of Mekhilta presents us with a virtual line-by-line, even word-by-word, interpretation of the relevant section of Exodus. The section has brought us a number of different types of comments. Some remarks simply follow the obvious, literal meaning of the verse. Other interpretations seem to be rather far from the "plain" meaning of the biblical text. Often, it seemed that a well-known practice, custom, belief, or comment was juxtaposed with a particular verse even though the point made by the midrash was not obvious in the verse. We have found rabbinic comments, one narrative portion, one theoretical case in which the verse might be applied, and a short "homily." Most of the content of this section of the midrash deals with proper action on the Sabbath or activity connected with the observance of the Sabbath; that is, much of this section of midrash deals with halakhah.

The underlying assumption of this section of Mekhilta is that there are no unnecessary repetitions in the Bible. Each time the Bible states something, it states it in order to teach something specific. Furthermore, the midrash assumes that the whole Bible is interrelated. Verses in one part of the Bible modify other verses; in fact, one part of a verse might even modify another phrase in the same verse. One must interpret a statement in the Bible in light of statements which appear elsewhere in Scripture.

We see that this passage is considerably different from the selection we included from Sifra. Sifra's underlying assumption was that Scripture needed to be written the way it was in order to counteract fallible human reason. In addition, Sifra presented us with a long introduction on Moses' special status. Although the same point is made in our passage from Mekhilta, it was much more prominent in Sifra than it is here in Mekhilta. In addition, Sifra often spent much more time on its issues than did Mekhilta. Our section of Mekhilta contains many more short, independent comments then did the section from Sifra included above. We have also seen that the way in which the two texts phrased their questions and the way in which their comments were related to the actual biblical texts were different. These differences may be a result of the content of the biblical verses on which they comment. After all, the section from Mekhilta focuses on the Sabbath, while the section from Sifra dealt with the opening lines of Leviticus, which contain no real content. However, the features of each midrashic collection do seem to be typical of the two texts as a whole.

The discussions in Mekhilta, because they deal with the Sabbath, which was probably observed by the masses, could have been directed at the common people. However, the way in which the comments are designed, and the frequent absence of a clear relationship between the interpretations and the biblical text, suggests that these comments were clearly created by rabbis. Surely, Sabbath law was not taught to the people on the basis of Mekhilta; however, the grounding in the biblical text of accepted ways in which to observe the Sabbath could have been directed to the public at large. While we clearly do not have sermons, we do have a good deal of raw data which would have been useful to anyone who wanted to relate the keeping of the Sabbath to chapter 31 of Exodus.

NOTES

1. J. Z. Lauterbach, "The Two Mekhiltas," *Proceedings of the American Academy of Jewish Research*, IV (1932–33), 113, *[PAAJR]*.

2. L. Finkelstein, "The Mekhilta and Its Text," *PAAJR*, V (1933–34), 547.

3. Ibid., 548.

4. Lauterbach, 114.

5. M. Friedman, *Mekhilta deRabbi Ismael and Sefer Shemot 'im Tosafot Me'ir Ayyin* (Vienna, 1870), xxxii.

6. D. Hoffmann, *Zur Einleitung in die halachischen Midraschim* (Berlin: 1886–87), 36–45. H. Strack, *Introduction to the Talmud and Midrash* (New York, 1959), 207.

7. J. N. Epstein, *Prolegomena ad Litteras Tannaiticas*, ed. E. Z. Melamed (Jerusalem, 1958), 550. Lauterbach, 115. Ch. Albeck, *Untersuchungen über die halakhischen Midraschim* (Berlin, 1927), 87–120.

8. J. Z. Lauterbach, *Mekhilta deRabbi Ishmael* (Philadelphia, 1976), I, xxiv–xxvi.

9. Compare M. Friedman, *Mekhilta deRabbi Ismael and Sefer Shemot 'im Tosafot Me'ir Ayyin* (Vienna, 1870), xiv–xxx. B. Z. Wacholder, "The Date of the Mekilta de-Rabbi Ishmael," *Hebrew Union College Annual* XXXIX (1968), 117–144. J. Neusner, *Development of a Legend* (Leiden, 1970), xiii–xiv, note 2.

10. Lauterbach, "Two Mekhiltas," 115–116; Epstein, 548.

11. Lauterbach, *Mekhilta*, xvii–xix.

12. Lauterbach's Mekhilta is now available in paperback.

13. The translation is based on H. S. Horovitz and J. A. Rabin, *Mechilta d'Rabbi Ismael* (Jerusalem, 1960), 340–344.

14. J. Neusner, *The Rabbinic Traditions about the Pharisees before 70* (Leiden, 1971), I, 15–23, III, 143–179, 282–291; A. Saldarini, "The End of the Rabbinic Chain of Tradition," *Journal of Biblical Literature*, XLIII, 1 (March 1974), 97–106.

15. See comment of David Moses Abraham on Mekhilta Bo' 9:6, *dbrym*, and the comment of *Zeh Yenahamu* on the same word.

16. This is part of a longer passage in Mekhilta Bo' 9:6.

17. G. Porton, *The Traditions of Rabbi Ishmael [Ishmael]* (Leiden, 1976–1982), III, 136–137. There is an error on 137, for Ishmael does appear on Babylonian Talmud *Yoma* 85a.

18. See Mishnah *Shabbat* 19:1–6, especially 19:2.

19. T. Zahavy, *The Traditions of Eleazar ben Azariah* (Missoula, 1977), 45–48.

20. Lauterbach, *Mekhilta*, III, 198, note 3.

21. See comment of M. Friedman, *Mekhilta*, 103b, note 7.

22. Strack, 96. On Babylonian Talmud *Yoma* 85 we find this comment attributed to Yosi the son of Judah.

23. See comment of David Moses Abraham on ʾk.

24. On Babylonian Talmud *Yoma* 85b this is attributed to Rabbi Yonatan the son of Joseph.

25. On Babylonian Talmud *Yoma* 85b this is attributed to Simeon the son of Menashia.

26. Quoted by *Zeh Yenaḥamu* in his comment on mʿyn.

27. On the use of hyh + participle see M. H. Segal, *A Grammar of Mishnaic Hebrew* (Oxford, 1958), 156. E. Y. Kutscher, s.v. "Hebrew Language: Mishnah," *Encyclopedia Judaica*, XIV, 1600. Porton, IV, 24–25.

28. On Babylonian Talmud *Zebaḥim* 63a Rabbi Yohanan the son of Bathyra states this; on Babylonian Talmud *Menaḥot* 8b this is attributed to Judah the son of Bathyra. See M. D. Herr, "On the Question of the Laws of War on the Sabbath during the Period of the Second Temple and the Talmud," *Tarbiẓ*, XXX, 243–256, 341–356.

29. See the discussions on Babylonian Talmud *Shabbat* 105a and Babylonian Talmud *Keritot* 16b.

30. On the issue of witnesses in rabbinic law, see H. H. Cohn, s.v. "Witness: The Two Witness Rule," *Encyclopaedia Judaica*,XVI, 585.

31. On the problem of "cutting off," see H. H. Cohn, s.v. "Divine Punishment," *Encyclopaedia Judaica*, VI, 121.

32. See *Zeh Yenaḥamu* on hhyʾ.

33. The passage form "shall be cut off" to "peace" is found also in Sifre Numbers 112.

34. For a similar discussion see Porton, II, 187–188.

35. On the declaring of the New Moon, see Mishnah *Rosh Hashanah* 1:5–3:1.

36. On the importance of the court's declaring the new moon, see J. Neusner, *A History of the Jews in Babylonia: I The Parthian Period*, 2 printing, rev. (Leiden, 1969), 122–177.

37. See note 27 above.

38. This interpretation was suggested by Professor Alan Avery-Peck.

39. On the meaning of *taqqanot*, see Nathan son of Yaheil, *Aruch Completum sive Lexicon*, ed. A. Kohut, V, 265.

40. On the end of the sabbatical years, see M. Avi-Yonah, *The Jews of Palestine: A Political History from the Bar Kokhba War to the Arab Conquest* (New York, 1976), 108–109. D. Sperber, *Roman Palestine: 200–400: The Land* (Ramat-Gan, 1978), 91–93.

4 Sifre Numbers

Although Sifre Numbers and Sifre Deuteronomy are often printed together as one work,[1] it was demonstrated in the last century that the two collections do not form a unified whole.[2] Because there is general agreement among scholars that our midrash was unknown to the compilers of the Babylonian and Palestinian Talmuds, the general consensus of scholarly opinion is that Sifre was edited after the fourth century of the common era.[3] However, the exact date of its compilation and the name(s) of its compiler(s) are unknown to us.

Sifre Numbers does not contain interpretations of the whole of Numbers. It expounds Numbers 5–12, 15, 18–19, 25:1–13, 26:52–31:24, and 35: 9–34.[4] Many scholars agree that some of the sections of Sifre Numbers derive from sources different from those from which the main body of the text was composed.

The selection from Sifre Numbers which follows is decidedly halakhic, that is, legal, exegesis. It is an interpretation of Numbers 18:1–14.

And YWHW said to Aaron: "You, and your sons and your father's household with you shall bear the sin of the sanctuary. And you and your sons with you shall bear the sin of your priesthood. And also your brothers, the tribe of Levi, the tribe of your father, bring near with you to accompany you and serve you, and you and your sons with you before the Tent of Testimony. And they shall attend to you and to the service of the whole Tent. But they shall not draw near to the holy vessels nor to the altar so that they shall not die, neither they nor you. They shall accompany you and perform the service of the Tent of Meeting, all the service of the Tent. But a stranger shall not draw near to you. And you shall perform the duties of the altar so that there shall not again be wrath against the Children of Israel. For I, behold, I took your brothers the Levites from among the Children of Israel for you, a gift given to YHWH to perform the service of the Tent of Meeting. But you and your sons with you shall guard your priesthood concerning all the things of the altar and that which is within the curtain, and you shall serve. I give the service as a gift, your priesthood. For the stranger who draws near shall be put to death."

And YHWH spoke to Aaron: "For I, behold, I have given you what is kept of My offerings. All the holy things of the Children of Israel I have given to you as a portion, and to your sons as an eternal statute. This shall be yours from the most holy things from the fire: Each one of their offerings, each of their Cereal-offerings, each of their Sin-offerings, each of their Guilt-offerings which they return to Me is a most holy thing to Me and to you and to your sons. In a most holy place you shall eat it. Every male may eat it; it is holy to you. And this shall be yours: The offering of their gift; every Wave-offering of the Children of Israel I have given to you and to your sons and to your daughters with you for an eternal statute. Anyone who is clean in your house may eat it. All the best of the oil, and all the best of the wine and of the grain, the first fruits of what they give to YHWH I have given to you. The first fruits of everything in their land which they bring to YHWH shall be yours. Anyone clean in your house may eat it.

This section from Numbers has two parts, and our midrash can also be divided into two distinct portions. The first unit, Num. 18:1–7, speaks of the relationship between the priests and the Levites and the duties each should perform before the altar. The second section, Num. 18:8–14, lists the offerings which are given to the priests.

The midrash is divided into two logical sections, as are the verses from Numbers which it interprets, and each section opens with an exegesis of Numbers which introduces what follows. An important issue in Sifre Numbers is that revelation was necessary to counter fallible human reason. The same point appeared in our selection from Sifra, and the sections of the texts which deal with the subject are formulated in much the same way. In addition, our editor(s) included several narrative sections to illustrate the exegetical remarks. We encounter the same phenomenon in Mekhilta. Furthermore, the text summarizes longer arguments which appear elsewhere and repeats verses in sequence which had appeared out of sequence as part of larger arguments. This feature also occurred in Mekhilta.

Each of the two sections focuses on one theme. The first section focuses on the priestly duties. It demonstrates that the priests and the Levites each have their own tasks and that no one may engage in an activity different from the one in which he is normally active. Secondarily, the midrash stresses that these activities must be performed in their proper manner. The second unit deals with the priestly gifts and demonstrates that the priestly portions were given to Aaron and to his sons, the priests who served after him, because they deserved them. Furthermore, some of these gifts are given to the priests throughout all time. The only gifts which the priests may receive, however, are those which the rabbis have ordained should be given to them. Finally, the midrash demonstrates that all of the gifts which the rabbis ordained that the priests should receive are based on Num. 18 even though they are not specifically mentioned there.

And YHWH said to Aaron: "You and your sons and your father's household with you shall bear the sin of the sanctuary. [And you and your sons with you shall bear the sin of your priesthood] (Num. 18:1). Rabbi Ishmael says: "To whom was this matter transmitted? [It was transmitted] to him whom they forewarned."[5]

Rabbi Yoshiah says: "On what basis [can] you say that if [a priest] correctly sprinkles the blood [on the altar] but does not know for the sake of whom he sprinkled it, or [if] he burns the fat correctly [on the altar] but does not know for the sake of whom he burned it, the priests bear iniquity for [acting in] this manner? Scripture says: *You and your sons and your father's household with you shall bear the sin of the sanctuary."*

Rabbi Yonatan says: "On what basis [can] you say that if [a priest] took possession of the flesh [of an offering] before the sprinkling of the blood [was performed or if he took possession] of the breast and the thigh before he burned the fat, the priests bear the iniquity for [his acting] in this way? Scripture says: *And you and your sons with you shall bear the sin of your priesthood."*

And thus we find that He decreed a judgment on the sons of Eli only because they treated the holy things disrespectfully; and thus it says: *Moreover, before the fat was burned [the priest's servant would come and say to the man who was sacrificing, "Give meat for the priest to roast; for he will not accept boiled meat from you, but raw."] And if the man said to him, "Let them burn the fat first, [and then take as much as you wish," he would say, "No, you must give it now; and if not I will take it by force."] Thus the sin of the young men was very great [in the sight of YHWH; for the men treated YHWH's offering with contempt]* (I Sam. 2:15–17).

And thus we find that He decreed a judgment on the men of Jerusalem only because they treated the holy things disrespectfully, for it is said, *You have despised My holy things* (Ezek. 22:8).

And you and your sons with you shall bear the sin of your priesthood (Num. 18:1). This [refers to] the iniquity [resulting from] a thing which was under the priesthood's jurisdiction. You might say [that] this [refers to] the iniquity [resulting from] a thing under the priesthood's jurisdiction, or [perhaps, rather, it refers to] the iniquity [resulting from] a thing under the court's jurisdiction. When it says, *But you and your sons with you shall guard your priesthood concerning all the things of the altar* (Num. 18:7), [it can be argued that this] was said [with reference to] the iniquity [resulting from] a thing under the court's jurisdiction. Why, then, did Scripture say, *You shall bear the sin of your priesthood?* [This proves that the verse refers to] the iniquity [resulting from] a thing under the priesthood's jurisdiction. You might say [that] Israel does not bear the iniquity of the priests, but [that] the Levites do bear the iniquity of the priests; [however], Scripture says, *But the Levites shall do the service of the Tent of Meeting, and they shall bear their iniquity* (Num. 18:23) [which proves that the Levites bear their own iniquity and not the iniquity of the priests].

And also your brothers (Num. 18:2). I might understand this to imply that [all] Israel [is included in this admonition; however,] Scripture says, *The tribe of Levi* (Num. 18:2). I might understand this to imply that even women [are included in this admonition; however,] Scripture says, *Your brothers* to exclude women.

Bring near with you (Num. 18:2). Rabbi Aqiba says: "*With you* is said here [in Num. 18:2], and *with you* is said elsewhere [in Num. 18:1]. Just as [with the phrase] *with you* which is said there, Scripture refers to the Levites, so also here [in Num. 18:2 the phrase] *with you* which is said [indicates that] Scripture speaks of the Levites in order to warn the Levites concerning the songs [they sung] on their platform [during the worship service]."

To accompany you and serve you (Num. 18:2). [This refers to] their doing their own duties. And [the priest] should select the treasurers and the officers from them. [Therefore,] you might indeed say [that] *serve you* [means] in their service, for [the priest] selected the treasurers and the officers from them. Or [perhaps] *serve you* [means that they helped] in [the priest's] service. [However,] Scripture says, *And they shall attend you and to the service of the whole Tent* (Num. 18:3) [which means that Num. 18:2 refers to their own duties].

Still, I might say [that both interpretations are possible, and that] *serve you* [means] "in your service," and *serve you* [means] "in their service"; [however,] Scripture says, *And I, behold, I took your brothers the Levites from among the Children of Israel for you, a gift given to YHWH* (Num. 18:6). [This verse indicates] that they have been given to [the One with the holy] name and not to the priests. Behold, you cannot teach according to the last interpretation; rather, [you must teach] according to the first interpretation. [That is,] *serve you* [means they will minister] in their service [by doing their own duties, and that the priest should select the treasurers and the officers from them.

And you and your sons with you before the Tent of Testimony (Num. 18:2) [means] the priests [minister] from within and the Levites [minister] from without. Or, [perhaps it means] that these and those [all minister] from within. [However,] Scripture says, *And they shall accompany you and perform the service of the Tent of Meeting* (Num. 18:4). [Because Num. 18:4 clearly states that the Levites shall join the priests], behold, why did Scripture [also] say, *And you and your sons with you before the Tent of Testimony?* [It said this to teach you that] the priests [minister] from within and the Levites [minister] from without.

And they shall attend to you and to the service of the whole Tent (Num. 18:3). This is the verse [from] which we said [that] they shall serve you in their service. And [the priest] should select the treasurers and the officers from them.

But, they shall not draw near to the holy vessels (Num. 18:3). This [refers to] the ark and the portion containing the ark, [for it is said,] *But they shall not go in to look upon the dismantling of the holy things even for a moment [lest they die]* (Num. 4:20). Rabbi Nathan says: "Here [we find] a hint in the Torah concerning the Levites' singing; but it was specifically mentioned [only] by Ezra." Rabbi Hananyah the son of Rabbi Joshua's brother says: "There is no need [for Rabbi Nathan's interpretation], for behold, already it was said, *Moses spoke and God answered him in a voice* (Ex. 19:19). Here we have a hint in the Torah concerning the [Levites'] singing."

But they shall not draw near to the holy vessels nor to the altar (Num. 18:3) is the warning; *So that they shall not die* is the punishment. [From here] I [can learn] only [about the] Levites who are punished and warned concerning the priestly service. From where [can I learn about the punishment and the warning for the] priests concerning the levitical service? Scripture says, *[So that they shall not die,] neither they nor you* (Num. 18:3). [From where can I learn about the punishment for one who moves] from [his own] service to its associate [service]? Scripture says, *Nor you.* One time Rabbi Joshua the son of Hananyah sought to assist Rabbi Yohanan the son of Godgadah. [The latter] said to him, "Turn back, for already you have rendered your soul culpable, for I am from the [line of the] gatekeepers, but you are from the [line of the] singers."

Rabbi says: "There is no need [for this argument], for behold already it was said: *Let not the tribe of the families of the Kohathites be destroyed from among the Levites; but deal with them, that they may live [and not die when they come near to the most holy things]* (Num. 4:18–19). [From here] I [can learn] only [about] the sons of Kohat; from where [can I learn about] the sons of Gershom and the sons of Merari? Scripture says: *[And you shall appoint] Aaron and his sons, and they shall attend to the priesthood; but if any stranger comes near, he shall be put to death* (Num. 3:10). *And they shall attend the priesthood.* [From here] I [can learn] only [about the] Levites who are punished and warned concerning the priestly service. From where [can I learn about the warning and the punishment of the] priests concerning the levitical service? Scripture says: *When the Tabernacle sets out, the Levites shall take it down; and when the Tabernacle is set up, the Levites shall set it up. [And if a stranger comes near, he shall be put to death]* (Num. 1:51). From where [can I learn about one who moves from his own] service to its associate [service]? Scripture says: *And those to encamp before the Tabernacle on the east, before the Tent of Meeting toward the sunrise, were Moses and Aaron and his sons, having charge of the tribes within the sanctuary, whatever had to be done for the Children of Israel; and any stranger who comes near shall be put to death* (Num. 3:38). And why does Scripture say, *Neither they nor you* (Num. 18:3)? [It says this] because Korah came and complained against Aaron, and [here] Scripture warned [Aaron] about him and the whole incident.

They shall accompany you (Num. 18:4). This is [the verse from] which we said [that] the priests [minister] from within and the Levites [minister] from without.

But a stranger shall not draw near to you (Num. 18:4). Why was this said? [It was said] because it says [in Num. 3:38], *But the stranger who comes near shall be put to death*. [From this verse] we hear [about] the punishment; from where [do we learn the] warning? Scripture says, *But a stranger shall not draw near to you* (Num. 18:4).

And you shall perform the duties of the sanctuary and the duties of the altar (Num. 18:5). Behold, this is a warning to the courts of Israel to warn the priests that the Temple service should be done exactly according to the ordinance[s], for when the Temple service is done exactly according to the ordinance[s, the priests] prevent divine punishment from coming into the world.

So that there shall not again be wrath against the Children of Israel (Num. 18:5). Scripture says *again* only because previously [God's] wrath was [directed against the Children of Israel]. Similarly, you say, *And not again shall there be a flood* (Gen. 9:11); however, Scripture does not [usually] say *again*. And why does Scripture say *again* [here? It says this] only [because] previously there was [a flood]. Similarly, you say, *And they shall not again sacrifice their offerings to satyrs* (Lev. 17:6); however, Scripture does not [usually] say *again*. And why does Scripture say *again* [here? It says this] only [because] previously they had sacrificed [to satyrs]. Similarly, you say, *And the Children of Israel shall not again come near the Tent of Meeting* (Num. 18:22); however, Scripture says *again* only because previously they had drawn near [to the Tent of Meeting].

Also here you say, *So that there shall not be again wrath against the Children of Israel;* however, Scripture says *again* only because previously [God's] wrath was [directed] against the Children of Israel, for it is said: *For wrath has gone forth [from YHWH]* (Num. 17:11).

And I, behold, I took your brothers the Levites from among the Children of Israel for you, a gift given to YHWH (Num. 18:6). To the [One whose] name [is holy] they were given; they were not given to the priests.

But you and your sons with you shall guard your priesthood concerning all the things of the altar (Num. 18:7). On the basis [of this verse] Rabbi Eleazar HaQappar Berebbi [a title] used to say: "*All the things of the altar* [refers to] only [those things which] shall be [done] by you and your sons."

And that which is within the curtain (Num. 18:7). On the basis [of this verse] they said that there was a place behind the curtain where they [would] examine the [purity] of the priests' genealogies.

And you shall serve (Num. 18:7). I might think [that everyone] was mixed together [so that there were no assigned tasks; however,] Scripture says, *I give the service as a gift* (Num. 18:7). Just as a gift [is given] according to an allotment [to a specific person,] so also the Temple service is [divided up and assigned] by allotment [to specific individuals].

I give the service as a gift, your priesthood (Num. 18:7) [tells you] to perform the eating of the holy things within the borders [of the

Land of Israel, but outside the Temple precincts], just as [you would perform] the Temple service within the Temple precincts. Just as [with regard to] the Temple service, [which was done] within the Temple precincts, [the priest first] sanctifies his hands [by washing them], and after that he performs the Temple service, so also [with regard to] the eating of the holy things within the borders [of the Land, but outside of the Temple precincts, the priest first] sanctifies his hands, and after that he eats.

One time Rabbi Ṭarfon had not been present in the schoolhouse [the previous evening]. Rabban Gamliel said to him: "Why did you fail [to be present in the schoolhouse last evening]?" He said to him: "[I was not present] because I was performing the Temple service." [Gamliel] said to him: "Your words surprise [me]. Is there really a Temple service [now that the Temple has been destroyed]?" [Ṭarfon] said to him: "Behold it says, *I give the service as a gift, your priesthood* [which tells us] to perform the eating of the holy things within the borders [of the Land, but outside the Temple precincts], just as [we would perform] the Temple service within the Temple precincts."

Rabbi says: "[Numbers 18:7 means that the priests shall] eat the holy things within the borders [of the Land, but outside the Temple precincts,] just as the Temple service [was performed] within the Temple precincts. Just as [with regard to] the Temple service [the priest first] sanctifies his hands and afterwards performs the Temple service, so also [with regard to] the eating of the holy things within the borders [of the Land, but outside the Temple precincts, the priest] sanctifies his hands and afterwards he eats. If so, just as elsewhere, [with regard to the Temple service, the priest first sanctifies] his hands and his feet, so also here, [with regard to his eating the holy things within the borders of the Land, but outside the Temple precincts, should not the priest sanctify] his hands and his feet [and afterwards eat]? You say [in] an instance [in] which he must [make use of] his hands and his feet, he sanctifies his hands and his feet. [But in] an instance [in] which he only needs to make use of his hands, he sanctifies only his hands. [Thus,] we find [that] we learn [the requirement for the priests'] washing [their] hands [before eating the holy things within the borders of the Land, but outside the Temple precincts] from the Torah."

For the stranger who draws near shall be put to death (Num. 18:7). [This verse refers to a stranger who comes near to perform] the Temple service. You say [this verse refers to a stranger who comes near to] perform the Temple service. Or [perhaps] you say [it refers both to one who comes near to perform] the Temple service and [to one who comes near but] not [to perform] the Temple service? Now, just as [a priest] who has a defect, and who, [should he offer a sacrifice,] is not punished by death, is not punished [at all] unless [he comes near to perform] the Temple service, so also a stranger, [that is, a nonpriest,] who, [should he offer a sacrifice,] is punished by death, how much the more should he not be punished [under the rule of Num. 18:7] unless [he comes near to perform] the Temple service. Behold, what does Scripture say? *For a stranger who draws near shall be put to death.* [This applies only if he comes near to perform] the Temple service.

For the stranger who draws near shall be put to death even if he performs the Temple service while he is pure. Or perhaps it refers to only a case in which he performed the Temple service while he was impure. You may reason: If the one who enters [the Temple precincts] while impure is [still] culpable even though [he did not perform] the Temple service, how much the more [should he be culpable if he drew near] to perform the Temple service [while he was impure]. Behold, why did Scripture say, *For the stranger who draws near shall be put to death?* [This was said to teach us that contrary to reason the stranger who comes near is put to death] even if he performs the Temple service while he is pure.

Shall be put to death (Num. 18:7). Rabbi Ishmael says: "*Shall be put to death* is said here and *shall be put to death* is said elsewhere [in Deut. 13:6, *And that prophet or that dreamer of dreams shall be put to death*]. Just as *shall be put to death* which is said elsewhere [refers to death by] stoning, so also *shall be put to death* which is said here [refers to death by] stoning." Rabbi Yoḥanan the son of Nuri says: "*Shall be put to death* is said here, and *shall be put to death* is said elsewhere. Just as *shall be put to death* which is said elsewhere [refers to death by] strangulation, so also *shall be put to death* which is said here [refers to death] by strangulation."

For the stranger who draws near shall be put to death. [In this verse] we learn [about] the punishment. But the warning we have not [yet] learned; [therefore, we need Num. 18:4, for] Scripture says: *A stranger shall not draw near to you.*

And YHWH spoke to Aaron (Num. 18:8). I might think that this statement was [spoken by God directly] to Aaron; [however,] Scripture says, *To be a reminder to the Children of Israel, so that no stranger shall come near* (Num. 17:5). Here we learn that the statement [was spoken by God] to Moses, who then would speak with Aaron.

"*And I* (Num. 18:8) [means] with desire. *Behold* (Num. 18:8) [means] with joy"—the words of Rabbi Ishmael. His students said to him: "Our teacher, because it says, *And behold, I will bring a flood of water upon the earth* (Gen. 6:17), might I think that there was joy before the Omnipresent [in this event]?" He said to them: "[Yes,] there is joy before the Omnipresent when those who anger Him are destroyed from the world. And thus it says, *When it goes well with the righteous, the city rejoices; and when the wicked perish there are shouts of gladness* (Prov. 11:10). And it says, *The teeth of the wicked are broken* (Ps. 3:8). And it says, *Deliverance belongs to YHWH; Your blessings be upon Your people* (Ps. 3:9). And it says, *YHWH is king for ever and ever; the nations shall perish from His land* (Ps. 10:16). And it says, *Let the sinners be consumed from the earth and let the wicked be no more! Bless YHWH, O my soul! Praise YHWH* (Ps. 104:35)."

Rabbi Nathan says: "*And I* [means I will] add on to their service. *Behold* [means] with joy. And thus it says: *And also behold, he is coming out to meet you, and when he sees you he will be glad in his heart* (Ex. 4:14)."

All the holy things of the Children of Israel (Num. 18:8). Scripture makes a covenant with Aaron concerning all the most holy things to decree and to make a covenant about them because Korah came and complained against Aaron on account of his priesthood. It is a parable: To what can this thing be compared? [It can be compared] to a king of flesh and blood who had a member of his household to whom he gave a field as a gift, but he did not write, sign, and deliver [a document] to the archives. One [other member of his household] came and complained against him because of the field. The king said to him: "Let all who wish to come and to complain against you because of this field come, and I will write, sign, and deliver for you [a document] to the archives." Thus, Korah came and complained against him because of his priesthood. The Omnipresent said to him [Aaron]: "Let all who wish to come and to complain against you because of the priesthood come, and I shall write, sign, and deliver for you [a document] to the archives"; therefore, this section is said close to [the section about] Korah.

A reminder to the Children of Israel (Num. 17:5). Behold we learn [from here] that Korah was both among those who were swallowed up and those who were burned.

I have given you (Num. 18:8) because of your merit. *As a portion (lmšḥ). Mšḥ* means [to elevate] to greatness, for it is said, *This is the elevation (mšḥt) of Aaron and of his sons* (Lev. 7:35).

Rabbi Isaac says: "*Mšḥ* [refers to] the ordination oil, for it is said, *It is like the precious oil upon the head, running down upon the beard, upon the beard of Aaron* (Ps. 133:2)."

And to your sons (Num. 18:8) [means] because of your sons' merit. *As an eternal statute* (Num. 18:8) [means] the matter [discussed at Num. 18:8] shall apply throughout your generations.

This shall be yours from the most holy things from the fire (Num. 18:9). You say, "Go and see which of the most holy things are entirely offered up in the fire, and you have from them what remains." You [will] discover that [this applies] to only the Burnt-offering to the beasts.

Each one of their offerings (Num. 18:9). These are the two loaves and the Bread of the Presence. *Each of their Cereal-offerings* (Num. 18:9). This is the Cereal-offering of the one who sins and the Cereal-offering of the Freewill-offering. *Each of their Sin-offerings* (Num. 18:9). This is the Sin-offering of the individual, the Sin-offering of the community, the Sin-offering [offered] from the birds, and the Sin-offering [offered] from the beasts. *Each of their Guilt-offerings* (Num. 18:9). This is the Guilt-offering for a known transgression, the Guilt-offering for one in doubt as to whether or not he transgressed, the Guilt-offering of the Nazirite, and the Guilt-offering of the leper. *Which they return to Me* (Num. 18:9). This is [the penalty and the added fifth levied against one] who steals from a proselyte [and denies the theft but later confesses]. *Is a most holy thing* (Num. 18:9). This is the *log* of the leper's oil. *And to you and to your sons* (Num. 18:9). [This means that these things were given to you and to your sons] because of your merit and your sons' merit.

In a most holy place you shall eat it (Num. 18:10). Scripture made a covenant with Aaron concerning the most holy things that they should be eaten only in a holy place.

Rabbi Judah the son of Bathyra says: "Behold, [if] gentiles surround the Temple court, from where [do we learn] that the most holy things may be eaten even in the Temple? Scripture says: *In a most holy place you shall eat it.*"

Every male may eat it (Num. 18:10). Scripture makes a covenant with Aaron concerning the most holy things that they should be eaten only by the males of the priest[ly families].

It is holy to you (Num. 18:10). Why does Scripture say [*It is holy to you?* It said this] because I might think that [the verse applies to] only a thing which is fit for eating, that it [alone] should be treated as holy. From where [can I learn about a thing] that is not fit for eating [that it also should be treated as holy]? Scripture says, *It shall be holy to you*, whatever [it is].

And this shall be yours: The offering of their gift (Num. 18:11). Scripture tells [you here] that just as Scripture included the most holy things to make decrees and to make a covenant concerning them, so also it included the lesser holy things to make decrees and to make a covenant concerning them. *Every Wave-offering of the Children of Israel* (Num. 18:11) [is said] to include a thing which must be waved. *I have given to you and to your sons and to your daughters with you for an eternal statute* (Num. 18:11) [means] the thing shall be practiced throughout the generations. *Anyone who is clean in your house may eat it* (Num. 18:11). [Here] Scripture makes a covenant with Aaron concerning the lesser holy things, that they can be eaten only by those who are ritually clean.

All the best of the oil, and all the best of the wine and of the grain (Num. 18:12). [Here] Scripture tells [you] that just as Scripture included the most holy things to make a decree concerning them and to make a covenant concerning them, so also Scripture included the lesser holy things consumed within the border[s of the Land of Israel, but outside the Temple precincts], to decree and to make a covenant concerning them. *All the best of the oil, and all the best of the wine and of the grain.* This [refers to] the Heave-offering and the Heave-offering of the tithe. *The first fruits* (Num. 18:12). This is the first shorn wool. *Of what they give* (Num. 18:12). This is the shoulder, the jaw, and the maw. *To YHWH* (Num. 18:12). This is the Dough-offering.

The first fruits of everything in their land (Num. 18:13). Scripture comes and teaches about the first fruits that they attain a status of sanctity while they are [yet unpicked and still] attached to the ground, for one might make an argument by analogy: Because a status of sanctity applies to the Heave-offering, and [in the same way] sanctity applies to the first fruits [they are comparable offerings; therefore, I could reason that] because I have learned about the

Heave-offering that it does not attain a status of sanctity while it is attached to the ground, so also the first fruits should not attain a status of sanctity while they are attached to the ground. [However,] Scripture says, *The first fruits of everything in their land.* Scripture comes and teaches [you] concerning the first fruits that a status of sanctity applies to them while they [as yet] are attached to the ground.

Which they bring to YHWH shall be yours (Num. 18:13). Scripture comes and teaches [you] about the first fruits that they should be given to a priest.

Anyone clean in your house may eat it (Num. 18:13). Why was this said? Was it not already said [that] *anyone who is clean in your house may eat it* (Num. 18:11)? And why does Scripture [again] say, *Anyone clean in your house may eat it* [in Num. 18:13? It said this] in order to include the Israelite who is engaged to a priest [and to teach] that she may eat the Heave-offering. Or [perhaps, you might argue that Scripture] speaks [of] only [an Israelite] who is married [to a priest]. When it says, *Anyone who is clean in your house may eat it* (Num. 18:11), behold, one who is married [to a priest] is spoken of. Here, why does Scripture say, *Anyone clean in your house may eat it* (Num. 18:13)? [This was said] in order to include an Israelite who is engaged to a priest [to teach you] that she may eat the Heave-offering.

Logically, it includes [the Israelite] who is engaged [to a priest], and it includes the sojourner and the hired hand [who are part of the priest's household]. But [if this is so,] how [can] I understand [Ex. 12:45, which says] *A sojourner or a hired hand may not eat it?* [This verse applies to] a sojourner and a hired hand who are not under your power. But a sojourner and a hired hand who are under your power may eat it. Or [perhaps], logically it excludes the sojourner and the hired hand but includes the Israelite] engaged [to a priest]. But [if this is so,] how [can] I understand [Num. 18:11, which says,] *Anyone who is clean in your house may eat it?* [This means] every clean one in your house may eat it except for a sojourner and a hired hand. Or [perhaps it] even [includes] the sojourner and a hired hand. [However,] Scripture says again in another place: *The sojourner of a priest and a hired hand shall not eat a holy thing* (Lev. 22:10), [which means] whether or not he is under your power [he may not eat it].

And one time Rabbi Yoḥanan the son of Bag Bag sent to Rabbi

Judah in Nisibis [in Babylonia]. He said to him: "I heard about you that you would say concerning an Israelite who was engaged to a priest that she [could] eat the Heave-offering." [Judah] sent to him: "And you, don't you [also] say thus? I know about you that you are an expert in the mysteries of the Torah and argue by means of an *a fortiori* argument. Don't you know that if [with regard to] a Canaanite handmaiden, for whom intercourse [with a priest] does not [constitute an act of] acquisition, [for a priest cannot marry a non-Jew, so that intercourse does not allow her] to eat the Heave-offering, but [the priest's paying her] money for her work [does constitute an act of] acquisition [as a member of his household, so that she may] eat the Heave-offering, so [with regard to] an Israelite woman, [for whom] intercourse [with a priest does constitute an act of] acquisition, [for a priest may marry an Israelite, so that she may] eat the Heave-offering, how much the more does [the priest's giving her] money [as a sign of their engagement constitute] acquisition so that she may eat the Heave-offering." [Yoḥanan replied]: "But what shall I do? For behold [the] sages said: 'An Israelite woman engaged [to a priest] does not eat the Heave-offering until she has entered under the bridal canopy [during the marriage ceremony.' If] she has entered under the bridal canopy [during the marriage ceremony], even though she has not had intercourse [with her new husband], she may eat the Heave-offering. And [even] if she dies [before they have had intercourse] her husband inherits [from her].

COMMENTS

Rabbi Ishmael says. Rabbinic tradition pictured Moses as a unique individual. Among his most important achievements was his conversing, face
to face, with God, Deut. 34:10. Here, Ishmael asks if we are to take Num.
18:1 literally: Did YHWH actually speak directly to Aaron or through Moses?
Ishmael states that God did speak directly to those to whom the chapter
applies; that is, in this instance, God did speak directly to Aaron. We have
noted elsewhere that Aaron should be read as a code-word for the priesthood, and Moses should be seen as a symbol for the rabbis. In the first
centuries of the common era, the rabbis were attempting to establish their
power as the new leaders of the Jewish people. Their major competitors
would have been the former leaders, the priests. Thus, the debate concerning with whom God conversed, Moses or Aaron, was really a discussion
about the relative validity of the priestly and rabbinic traditions.[6]

Rabbi Yoshiah says. The Whole-burnt-offerings, one of the Most Holy
Things, were first slaughtered by the person who offered the sacrifice. Next,
the priest collected the blood and sprinkled it on the altar and/or poured it
out at the altar's base. After this, the priest placed the animal's fat on the
altar and burned it.[7] Yoshiah asks what happens if the priest performs the
sprinkling of the blood or the burning of the fat but does not know for
whose sake he has performed these rituals. The exact meaning of Yoshiah's
comment is unclear. According to Mishnah *Zebaḥim* 3:6, the priest must
be aware of six things while offering the sacrifice: the offerings, the one
making the offering, God, the altar-fires, the odor, the sweet savor. If it is a
Sin-offering or a Guilt-offering, the priest must also be cognizant of the sin
for which the offering is being presented to YHWH. It appears that Yoshiah
could refer to the priest's not knowing the name of the person who brought
the sacrifice or to the name of the deity to whom the sacrifice is presented.
The traditional commentators assume that a legitimate priest is sprinkling
the blood and offering the fat; therefore, he would know the correct name of
the deity before whom the offering was being made. For this reason, they
assume that the issue is whether or not the priest correctly named the
person who brought the animal to be offered.[8]

Rabbi Yonatan says. Yonatan does not actually discuss the ritual of the
sacrifice; rather, he is concerned with the priest's taking possession at the
correct time of the animal's portions which are due him. The order of the

instructions concerning the offering, for example, Lev. 7:1–5, clearly implies that the priest receives his due only after the sacrificial ritual has been performed. Thus, Yonatan explains that a priest who removes his portion before he has performed his part of the ritual is culpable. Yonatan is concerned with the priest's taking his portion of the sacrifice; therefore, he cites the end of Num. 18:1, which mentions the *sin of your priesthood*. Yoshiah, on the other hand, cites the opening of Num. 18:1, which refers to the *sin of the sanctuary*, because he is interested in the ritual performed in the sanctuary.

And thus we find. The story of Eli's sons perfectly illustrates Yonatan's point. Eli was the priest at Shiloh during the time of Samuel. I Sam. 2:12–36 contains the story of Eli's sons. I Sam. 2:15–17 states that Eli's sons did exactly that with which Yonatan was concerned: They demanded the priestly portion before the sacrificial ritual was completed. The Bible states, *Thus the sin of the young men was very great in YHWH's sight, for the men treated YHWH's offering with contempt.* In I Sam. 2:33, YHWH tells Eli that his sons *shall die by the sword of men.* In I Sam. 4:11 we read, *And the ark of God was captured; and the two sons of Eli, Hophni and Phinehas, were slain.*

And thus we find. This discussion of the "men of Jerusalem" does not belong here, for our section focuses on the priests and their actions. It is here because it opens with the same phrase with which the section on Eli's sons opened, "And thus we find that He decreed a judgment on . . . because they treated the holy things disrespectfully." The passage notes that Jerusalem and the Temple were destroyed because the Jews of Jerusalem did not act properly with regard to the sacrifices and the sacrificial ritual.

And you and your sons with you shall bear the sin of your priesthood. The style of this section appears frequently in this volume. The midrash raises two possible *logical* interpretations of the verse. It then demonstrates that reason could lead us to an incorrect interpretation. In this case, our reason suggests that this verse could refer either to matters under the control of the court or to matters under the control of the priesthood. The midrash argues, however, that Num. 18:7 refers to those items under the court's control; therefore, Num. 18:1 must refer to those matters under the priests' jurisdiction. We learn that everything in the Bible has a purpose and that each phrase teaches something unique. In addition, we discover that the Bible must be interpreted as a whole; each section must be read in light of every other portion. We also are told that reason can lead to faulty conclusions.

This section of the midrash presupposes that there were two authorities over the priesthood: the priesthood itself and the courts. I assume that this refers to the rabbinic courts and thus reflects the period after 70 C.E., when the Pharisees/rabbis attempted to control the priesthood.[9] In fact, the rabbinic tradition claimed that the priests always followed the teachings of the Pharisees, those whom the rabbis claimed were the precursors of the rabbinic movement. *Toledot Adam* (19th cent.) suggests that the matters under the court's jurisdiction concerned the purity of the priestly families;[10] this issue appears below. On the other hand, below we are told that the priesthood must perform the sacrifices according to the correct statutes, which I take to refer to the rabbinic ordinances. In any case, our text specifies only that there were two authorities over the priesthood; unfortunately, it does not make clear over what these two authorities had jurisdiction or which matters were controlled by which authority.

Concerning all the things of the altar. The midrash states that this refers to the items under the court's control. *Toledot Adam* argues that this verse cannot refer to the items under the priests' control because it discusses those males who were disqualified from the priesthood but who approached the altar. Because they are technically not priests, they would not bear the sin of the priesthood. Because it was the court which determined the purity of a person's genealogy, according to *Toledot Adam*, and thus whether or not he was fit to serve as a priest at the altar, an unqualified priest who approached the altar came under the court's jurisdiction.

Bear the sin of your priesthood. Again following *Toledot Adam*, this refers to those who were qualified priests. Because the court's jurisdiction was limited to determining the fitness of a priest, the priests were concerned with all other issues affecting themselves.

You might say that. Again, the midrash demonstrates that logic alone could lead to an erroneous conclusion, for one might think that the Levites, who assisted the priests, could bear the iniquity of the priests. However, Num. 18:23 specifically states that the Levites shall bear their *own* iniquity; therefore, the priests alone bear their own sin.

And also your brother. At this point the midrash explains why we find an apparently superfluous phrase in Num. 18:2. The midrash asks why Num. 18:2 refers to both *your brothers* and to *the tribe of Levi*. The midrash concludes that if we had only the former phrase, we might reason that the Israelites are included in the admonition; however, the second phrase, *the tribe of Levi*, qualifies the first and teaches us that Num. 18:1–2 refers to only the Levites and not to all Israel. The phrase *your brothers* is needed so that we would not conclude that women as well as men are included in the verses' admonitions. Therefore, this seemingly redundant phrasing is in reality neither repetitious nor superfluous.

Rabbi Aqiba says. Aqiba employs a *gezarah shavah*. This technique juxtaposes two verses which contain the same word or phrase. According to this principle, what applies in one verse also applies in the other because the two contain the same word or phrase. In this instance, the phrase *with you* allows Aqiba to connect Num. 18:2 and Num. 18:1. Num. 18:1 speaks of the Levites and contains the phrase *with you*; therefore, Num. 18:2, which also contains the phrase *with you*, also refers to the Levites.

Concerning the songs they sung. I. Chron. 23:30 states that the Levites *shall stand every morning, thanking and praising YHWH, and likewise at evening.* I Chron. 23:31 adds that they should do this *whenever Burnt-offerings are offered to YHWH on Sabbaths, new moons, and feast days.* I Chron. 5:16 states that *David also commanded the chiefs of the Levites to appoint their brothers as the singers who should play loudly on musical instruments, on harps, and lyres, and cymbals, to raise sounds of joy.* In the Babylonian Talmud, *Arakhin* 11b, we read that the sacrifices cannot be offered unless the Levites sing.[11]

To accompany you and serve you. Once more the midrash demonstrates that reason unaided by Scripture leads to incorrect conclusions. The issue here is whether Num. 18:2 refers to the Levites' assisting the priests or to the Levites' own duties. The midrash opens by stating that Num. 18:2 refers to the Levites' own service; however, it suggests that the priests appointed the appropriate levitical officials. The midrash raises the possibility that the verse is ambiguous and that one could reason that it refers either to the Levites' own service or to their assisting the priests. Num. 18:6 demonstrates that the Levites were given to YHWH and not to the priests; therefore, they were selected to perform their own duties and not those of the priests.[12]

And you and your sons with you. The midrash suggests that decisions should be made on the basis of biblical interpretation and not on the basis of logic. The key word here is *before.* This teaches that the priests served directly before the ark; that is, within the Temple's innermost precincts. Mishnah *Tamid* 1:1 states that the priests kept watch at three places in the Temple: the chamber of Abtinas, the chamber of the flame, and the chamber of the hearth. According to the Mishnah, the "elders of the father's house used to sleep in the chamber of the hearth with the keys of the Temple court, and they would open the gates." Thus, the authors of this section of Mishnah believed that the priests were always inside while the Levites were outside. In his commentary to Mishnah, Bartinoro (15th cent.) suggests that because the priests were primary and the Levites were secondary, the former served inside the Temple, while the latter ministered without.

The midrash next raises the possibility that Num. 18:2 does not specifically state where the Levites and the priests should minister; therefore, one could conclude that both of these ministered inside the Temple. However, Num. 18:4 specifically says that the Levites shall accompany the priests and perform the service of the Tent of Meeting. If Num 18:4 tells us that the priests and the Levites serve together, why did Num. 18:2 specify that the priests are *before* the Tent of Meeting? Num. 18:2 said this to indicate that although the Levites and the priests do serve together at the Tent of Meeting, as Num. 18:4 indicates, they serve in different places.

And they shall serve you. This is a summary of the longer argument, which we found above, which discussed whether the Levites performed their own duties or those of the priests.

But they shall not draw near. Because the Levites were specifically commanded to carry the Tabernacle, Num. 1–2, to what does this verse refer? The midrash concludes that it refers specifically to the ark and to the portion containing the ark.

Rabbi Nathan says. In the Babylonian Talmud, *Arakhin* 11b, Nathan's opinion is attributed to Yonatan. In the *gemara*, we find that Yonatan's comment is based on Num. 18:3, *that they not die, neither they nor you.* *Toledot Adam* assumes that Nathan's reasoning is the same as Yonatan's in the Talmud, as interpreted by Rashi (11–12th cent.). According to Rashi, Num. 18:3 equates the Levites and the priests and means that each group must do only that service which is appropriate to it. Because singing is the only part of the sacrificial ritual which is assigned to the Levites, Num. 18:3 serves as an indirect indication that the Levites are supposed to sing during the sacrificial ritual of the Temple service. The circular form of this argument need not detain us here. Rather, we must focus on its appropriateness to Nathan's comment. We cannot assign this line of reasoning to Nathan with any confidence, for it is an eleventh-century explanation of the statement attributed to Yonatan in a document edited somewhere between the sixth and the eighth centuries of the common era.[13]

But it was specifically mentioned only by Ezra. Ezra 3:10–11 states: *And when the builders laid the foundation of the Temple of YHWH, the priests in their vestments came forward with trumpets, and the Levites, the sons of Asaph, with cymbals, to praise YHWH according to the directions of David king of Israel; and they sang responsively, praising, and giving thanks to YHWH.* Earlier, in Ezra 2:14, the sons of Asaph are identified as the singers.

Rabbi Ḥananyah the son of Rabbi Joshua's brother says. Ḥananyah's comment also appears in the Babylonian Talmud, *Arakhin* 11b. Ḥananyah argues that we do not need to accept Nathan's claim that the only reference in the Torah to the Levites' singing is this rather indirect reference in Num. 18:3; rather, we find a more "explicit" reference in Ex. 19:19. According to the Talmud, Ḥananyah meant that in Ex. 19:19 God spoke to Moses concerning matters of the voice. Rashi (11–12th cent.) says that God commanded Moses to sing because he was a Levite, Ex. 2:1.[14] Rashi offers us an eleventh-century explanation of a comment by a second-century master.

But they shall not draw near. The rabbis believed that for every offense for which God mentioned a punishment in the Bible, He also stated elsewhere a warning not to commit the deed. In the opening of Num. 18:3, we find the warning that the Levites should not draw near to the holy vessels; at the end of the verse, we find the punishment for those who ignore the warning.

From where can I learn the punishment. The midrash makes the obvious point that Num. 18:3 refers to only the Levites who draw near to the holy vessels like a priest. It now asks about the basis for claiming that the priests cannot engage in those activities reserved for the Levites. The midrash concludes that the phrase *neither they nor you* indicates that what applies to the Levites, *they*, also applies to the priests, *you*; therefore, the verse supplies the warning and the punishment for both priests and Levites who engage in activities reserved for the other class.

From where can I learn the punishment. The midrash assumes not only that the priests may not perform the levitical tasks nor the Levites the priestly duties, but also that each priest and each Levite may perform only those duties assigned to him or to his family. The midrash answers that the phrase *nor you* teaches us about one who moves from his traditionally assigned activity to another task. I assume that this explanation is based on the appearance of the words *gm . . . gm, neither . . . nor.* Some rabbis considered *gm* an inclusive particle;[15] that is, its appearance in a verse meant that the meaning of the verse could be extended to include items not appearing in the biblical text. In this case, the appearance of *gm* suggests the two additional prohibitions mentioned in our midrash.

One time Rabbi Joshua the son of Ḥananyah. This story illustrates the point which the midrash has just made. Joshua, who was from the clan of the singers, sought to help Yoḥanan, who was a gatekeeper. The latter would not allow the former to help him, because it was not Joshua's proper task to deal with the gates. Yoḥanan states specifically that Joshua has put his soul in danger by attempting to help him by seeking to engage in an activity not assigned to him or to his family.[16]

Rabbi says. Rabbi suggests that one need not rely on Num. 18:3 alone in order to demonstrate that a priest and a Levite may do only those tasks which are assigned to their respective groups or to prove that one may not do a job other than the one normally performed by his family. Rabbi cites Num 4:18–19 as proof that at least one levitical family's tasks were limited, for they were forbidden to approach the most holy things. One might argue that Num. 4:18–19 applies to only the sons of Kohat, for they are specifically mentioned in the verses; Rabbi cites, however, Num. 3:10, which forbids *any stranger*, that is, any nonpriest, from attending to the duties of the priesthood. Therefore, Num. 3:10 warns everyone, including the Levites, not to act like priests. One could argue that this applies only to the Levites, who have the opportunity to act like priests; therefore, Rabbi cites Num. 1:15, which defines the Levites' duties and then states that *any stranger,* that is, non-Levite, who performs a levitical task *shall be put to death.* From here we learn that just as the Levites may not perform the priestly tasks, so also the priests may not engage in activities assigned to the Levites. The last prohibition which was derived from Num. 18:3 was the warning not to engage in an activity not assigned to one's family. Rabbi cites Num. 3:38 as the biblical source for this prohibition. The verse mentions *whatever had to be done,* which Rabbi seems to take as a reference to the individual tasks assigned to *Moses, Aaron, and his sons.*

This verse also ends by stating that *any stranger who comes near shall be put to death*. Rabbi seems to have believed that this meant that any stranger to a particular task would be put to death if he attempted to perform that task.

And why does Scripture say. Rabbi has now demonstrated that all of the things which the midrash previously had stated were derived from Num. 18:3 can be based on other biblical verses. He now must explain the meaning of Num. 18:3. Rabbi concludes that Num. 18:3 was stated as a warning to Aaron concerning the future rebellion of Korah. *Toledot Adam* notes that Rabbi's interpretation is awkward, for Num. 18:3 refers to *their* punishment and to *your* punishment. He suggests that Rabbi meant that Num. 18:3 refers to a lesser priest's attempt to take over the high priesthood.[17]

They shall accompany you. This is a summary of the longer argument which appeared above.

But a stranger shall not draw near to you. Here the midrash deals with an apparently superfluous verse. Num. 3:38 states that *a stranger who comes near shall be put to death;* therefore, why must the same thing appear in Num. 18:4? The midrash concludes that Num. 18:4, which does not include the punishment for one who does draw near, is the warning, while Num. 3:38, which does state the punishment, supplies the punishment for one who violates the warning given in Num. 18:4. Again we learn that every verse and word in the Bible is necessary and that nothing is mere repetition.

And you shall perform the duties of the sanctuary. Exactly why this verse refers to the Israelite's court is unclear; perhaps it is based on the fact that the punishment mentioned at the end of the verse falls upon the Children of Israel and not just on the priests and the Levites. In any case, the midrash states that Num. 18:5 establishes the principle that the priests must perform their duties according to the regulations laid down by the courts. Unfortunately, we do not know who composed the courts; we do not know how many priests and nonpriests dealt with the issues discussed. This is a matter of scholarly debate and need not detain us here.[18] I would assume, however, that the author(s) of our midrash believed that there were nonpriests on the court, for this is a rabbinic document, and this passage probably contains the message that the priests should perform the sacrificial ritual according to rabbinic law.

So that there shall not be again wrath. At first glance, the midrash's point seems obvious; of course the word *again* means that previously God's wrath had been against the Children of Israel. Similarly, the list of biblical passages in which the word *again* refers to a thing which had also occurred previously seems to be obvious. We may then ask ourselves why the midrash made this point at all. I assume that the author(s) of the midrash felt something had to be said because the word *again* was not necessary; it could be read as a superfluous word. The midrash teaches, therefore, that the word *again* appeared *specifically* to teach us that God's wrath had already been directed against Israel and that if the priests did not follow the court's instructions concerning the sacrificial ritual, the Israelites would suffer in the same manner in which they had suffered earlier.

A gift given to YHWH. The verse is ambiguous, for it states that the Levites were taken from among the Israelites *for you*, the priests, and it says, *a gift given to YHWH*. The question arises concerning who has control of the Levites; were they to be under the priests' control or not? The midrash answers that the Levites were appointed to perform their own duties and not the priests' tasks, for the former were *a gift given* directly *to YHWH*. This agrees with the conclusion reached above, *viz.,* the Levites were to perform their own service and not the priestly duties.

Rabbi Eleazar HaQappar in the name of Rabbi. Eleazer gives a nonspecific interpretation of *all the things of the altar*; it refers to all the things done by the priests. *Toledot Adam* states that this includes the removal of the ashes from the altar. His explanation is based on Levi's interpretation, which appears in the Babylonian Talmud, *Yoma* 24a; therefore, it may not be relevant to Eleazar's interpretation cited here. In fact, *Toledot Adam* includes in his comments all of the interpretations found in the *gemara*; however, neither Eleazar nor Rabbi appears in the Talmud's discussion of this verse.[19]

And that which is within the curtain. The midrash claims that there was a place behind the curtain in the Temple where a court met and investigated the family purity of the priests. Mishnah *Middot* 5:4 states that the investigation of the purity of the priestly families took place in the Chamber of Hewn Stones. These were not the same places, for the Chamber of Hewn Stones was to the south in the Temple court, Mishnah *Middot* 5:4. Apparently, there was not a clear tradition concerning where the priestly genealogies were examined.

And you shall serve. The midrash attempts to prove a point assumed above; *viz.,* each family was assigned a specific task so that the priestly duties were ordered and carefully arranged. The midrash finds proof for this from the end of the verse, which calls the service a gift. The priestly service, like a gift, is given to a specific person; therefore, there were assigned duties for each priestly and levitical family. *Toledot Adam*[20] and Horovitz[21] draw attention to Mishnah *Shabbat* 23:2, which states that a person may cast lots at a dinner in order to determine who receives which portion. The Mishnah ends by stating, "they may cast lots on a festival day for the holy things [offered on the festival day] but not for the portions." Our midrash, however, seems to deal with the priestly service, ᶜbdh, and not with the offerings.

I give the service as a gift, your priesthood. With the destruction of the Second Temple in 70 C.E. a problem arose: What are the priestly duties and prerogatives if there is no Temple? Our midrash answers that the service was given to the priesthood as a gift; therefore, it assumes that the holy things were given to the priests even though there was no Temple. Furthermore, the midrash argues that the priests must eat these holy things just as if the Temple were standing. The midrash opens by stating that just as the priest washed before he conducted his part of the sacrificial service, so also he must wash before he eats the holy things even though they were not actually part of the sacrificial service.

One time Rabbi Tarfon. According to tradition, Tarfon was from a priestly family.[22] One time he failed to attend the meeting in the schoolhouse. Gamliel asks why he had missed the session, and Tarfon answers that he was performing the sacrificial service. Gamliel is surprised, for the Temple is no longer standing. Tarfon answers that with the Temple in ruins, the priests' eating of their portions now constitutes the sacrificial service, for the priests now eat their food in the same way that they performed the sacrificial ritual. Thus, this story illustrates the conclusion reached above.[23]

Rabbi says. Rabbi begins by stating that the priests eat their portions now just as what they did when the Temple stood; that is, they wash before they eat just as they did in the Temple precincts. He then notes that if what the priests do now is supposed to be the same as what they did when the Temple stood, they should wash their hands *and* their feet. He argues that just as the priests washed their hands and their feet before they engaged in the Temple ritual, so also now they must wash their hands and their feet before they eat their portions. He concludes, however, that this is not the case, for while the Temple was standing they had to wash their hands and their feet before they approached the holy precinct of the altar and walked around the altar while sprinkling the blood on it with their hands; now, they do not need to wash their hands *and* their feet, for they do not approach any holy space and do not walk around while they eat. In fact, the priests wash their hands now not because they are to replicate the acts which encompassed the sacrificial ritual; they must wash their hands before they eat their portion because the Bible, Num. 18:7, states that they must do so. Again we learn that reason unaided by Scripture can lead one to an incorrect conclusion.

For the stranger who draws near. The midrash opens with an obvious interpretation of the verse: A stranger, nonpriest, who draws near to the altar in order to perform the priestly duties shall be put to death. The midrash raises the possibility that this is not the correct interpretation. Perhaps the verse means that any nonpriest who approaches the altar should be executed, whether or not he performs the Temple ritual. The midrash now presents an *a fortiori* argument which establishes the original interpretation. If a priest with a physical blemish is not told to stop until he actually begins to perform the sacrificial ritual, how much the more should a nonpriest not be subject to death until he has begun to perform the sacrificial ritual. The argument is as follows: If the lesser penalty is not imposed unless the guilty party begins to perform the sacrificial ritual, is it not reasonable to assume that the more stringent penalty also is not assessed until the guilty party begins to perform the Temple ritual?

Behold, why does Scripture say. The problem with this unit as it now stands is that Scripture proves only what logic already said. We have seen in this selection and in the passages from Mekhilta and Sifra that Scripture usually establishes a point which is in opposition to that based on logic.

For the stranger who draws near. The midrash now opens by stating that even if the nonpriest is ritually pure he still may not perform the priestly ritual. Next, it raises the logical possibility that the verse means that only an unclean nonpriest is subject to the death penalty. It bases this on an *a fortiori* argument: If one is not punished for entering the Temple precincts unless he is unclean, how much the more should one not be punished for performing the Temple ritual unless he is unclean, for should not the same condition apply for the major misdeed, performing the sacrificial ritual, which applies to the lesser violation, entering the Temple precincts? The midrash refutes this argument by quoting the verse. True, reason might lead one to conclude that the punishment of death applies only to an unclean nonpriest who performed the Temple ritual; therefore, we need Num. 18:7 to teach us that a nonpriest, even if he is clean, cannot perform the Temple ritual.

Rabbi Ishmael says. Ishmael employs a *gezarah shavah.* According to this exegetical technique, two verses are juxtaposed when they contain the same word or phrase. When the two verses are connected in this fashion, what applies in one verse also applies in the other. In this case, Num. 18:7 is connected with Deut. 13:6 because they both contain the phrase *shall be put to death;* therefore, the manner of death for the person named in Deut. 13:6 is the same as for the one named in Num. 18:7. Ishmael states that the punishment in both cases is stoning.[24]

Rabbi Yoḥanan the son of Nuri says. Yoḥanan, like Ishmael, employs a *gezarah shavah;* however, the former states that in both cases the punishment is strangulation.

And YHWH spoke to Aaron. We have seen this issue discussed several times in this volume.[25] Did God speak directly to Aaron, or did He speak directly to Moses alone? At the opening of this selection, Ishmael said that God spoke to Aaron; here, the anonymous midrash states that God spoke directly to Moses, alone. Again, remember that Moses is a code-word for rabbi and that Aaron is a code-word for priest. The issue here is the relative importance of the rabbinic and the priestly traditions.

To be a reminder to the Children of Israel. It is unclear to me how Num. 17:5 serves as proof for the fact that Num. 18:8 was spoken to Moses and not to Aaron. *Toledot Adam* states that just as Num. 17:5, which served as a warning to the priesthood, was spoken by God to Moses, so also everything which served as a warning to the priests was spoken by God to Moses.[26] Rabbenu Hillel (12th cent.) states that just as Num. 17:5, whose context speaks of things placed on the fire, was spoken by God to Moses, so also all the passages which mention things offered on the fire were spoken by God to Moses.[27] It is clear that no one is certain exactly how Num. 17:5 was supposed to illuminate Num. 18:8.

The words of Rabbi Ishmael. Ishmael states that the word *behold* indicates that God acted with joy. His students respond that if this is so, we must assume that when God brought the flood upon the earth at the time of Noah He also acted with joy, for the word *behold* also appears in that context. This is troublesome to Ishmael's students because it suggests that God was happy when He destroyed everything except those on Noah's ark. Ishmael responds that in fact this was the case, for God is happy when the wicked are destroyed. He quotes several verses which support his point of view.[28]

Rabbi Nathan says. Nathan seems to base his interpretation on the particle *w, and,* which some rabbis took as an extending particle.[29] Nathan suggests that the particle means that God added onto the priests' service with joy. I assume that Nathan means that God acted with joy when He gave the priests the portions which are listed in Num. 18:8 ff.

And also behold. Nathan quotes Ex. 4:14 to demonstrate that the idea of gladness and joy appears in the same context as the word *behold.*

All the holy things of the Children of Israel. The midrash indicates that here God specifically promises that Aaron and his sons shall receive a portion from all of the holy things which the Children of Israel shall offer. This had to be explicitly stated so that no one could claim that Aaron was appropriating things which did not belong to him. The midrash specifically refers to Korah's objection to Aaron's claims to the high priesthood, Num. 16.

It is a parable. The rabbis often used parables to demonstrate why God acted in the way in which He did.[30] Often, these parables compare God's actions to those of human kings. In this instance, just as an earthly king had to sign and deliver to the public archives a document which specified the gift he had given to a member of his household, so also God had to specify in a document, the Torah, what He had given to Aaron. In both instances, the publicly recorded document was designed to prevent others from coming and complaining about the gifts given to the person mentioned in the document.

A reminder to the Children of Israel. This section is out of place, for it interrupts the continuous exegesis of Num. 18. It might better be placed above, where Num. 17:5 was used by the anonymous midrash. It was probably placed here because the passage which immediately precedes it discusses Korah's rebellion. Num. 26:10 states that *the earth opened its mouth and swallowed them up together with Korah;* therefore, the Torah states specifically that Korah was swallowed up by the earth. However, the Bible does not explicitly state that Korah was burned with the fire that *came forth from YHWH,* Num. 16:35. Our midrash states that Num. 17:5 teaches us that Korah was burned by this fire. Apparently we learn that Korah was burned by the fire by analogy with the censers which Eleazar took *out of the blaze,* Num 17:2, for these censers were to be a reminder to the Children of Israel not to be like Korah and his sons.[31]

I have given to you. The point of the midrash is that God gave the priestly portions to Aaron because he deserved them; therefore, others, who do not deserve them, should not be jealous of Aaron.

As a portion (lmšḥ). The midrash explains the meaning of *mšḥ.* First, it states that the root means "to be elevated," as it does in Lev. 7:35.

Rabbi Isaac says. Isaac takes *mšḥ* in its more common sense, "ordination" or "ordination oil."[32] However, Isaac's exegesis is awkward because the verse does not contain the word *mšḥ.* The Wilna Gaon (18th cent.) emended the text as follows: "To elevate to greatness only refers to the oil of ordination, for it is said, '. . .'." I don't find the Gaon's emendation especially helpful, for it completely changes Isaac's comment; however, clearly there is something wrong with the text he way that it now stands.[33]

And to your sons. At this point the midrash makes it clear that the priests received the priestly portions because they deserved them. Not only should one not complain about Aaron's receiving the priestly portions, but also one should not complain that any priest receives the priestly gifts.

As an eternal statute. The midrash makes it clear that not only did Aaron and his sons deserve the priestly portions, but also all the priests at all times deserve to receive these gifts. As before, one should not complain against the priests because they receive the priestly portions.

From the fire. The midrash explains that the priests receive items from the Burnt-offerings of the beasts, for these are the only offerings which are completely offered up in the fire. Lev. 6:3 mentions that the Burnt-offering was totally consumed by the fire, and Lev. 1:3–9 indicates that the Whole-offering, except for its entrails and legs, was burnt on the altar.

Each one of their offerings. The midrash now lists the specific offerings to which Num. 18:8–9 refers. Lev. 23:17 mentions two loaves which were to be waved on Shevuot; Lev. 23:20 states that the priests waved these and that *they shall be holy to YHWH for the priest,* and Ex. 25:30 mentions that twelve cakes which were set in order every Sabbath *shall be for Aaron and his sons, and they shall eat it in a holy place. Toledot Adam* suggests that we need Num. 18:9 to teach us that these were given to the priests because Ex. 28:33 states that only those things with which atonement was made are given to the priests for food. Because the breads do not effect atonement, we might conclude that they were not given to the priests for food.[34]

Each of their Cereal-offerings. Lev. 5:14 specifically states that the

Cereal-offering along with the remainder of the offering of the one who sins is the priest's. Lev. 2:3 states that what remains of the Freewill-cereal-offering also belongs to the priest. *Toledot Adam* again refers to Ex. 29:33 and states that we need Num. 18:9 because these do not effect atonement.[35] Rabbenu Hillel adds that Num. 18:9 includes the Cereal-offering of the 'Omer.[36]

Each of their Sin-offerings. Lev. 4:1–12 discusses the Sin-offerings of an individual, and Lev. 4:13–21 discusses the Sin-offering of the congregation. Lev. 6:18 f. discusses *the law of the Sin-offering.* Lev 6:19 states that the priest who makes the offering may eat it. According to Rabbenu Hillel this covers both the Sin-offering of the individual and the Sin-offering of the community.[37] However, Lev. 6:30 states that *no Sin-offering from which blood is brought into the Tent of Meeting to make atonement in the holy place shall be eaten.* Thus, Num. 18:9 was needed to teach us that the priest may eat the Sin-offering of the individual and the Sin-offering of the community. Num. 18:9 teaches about the Sin-offering of the bird because one could assume that the bird was unfit for the priest because it was not slaughtered in the normal manner.[38] The Sin-offering of the bird was killed by wringing the bird's neck, while other animals were slaughtered by cutting their windpipes and gullets, Lev. 1:14–15. In the Babylonian Talmud, *Zebaḥim* 44a and *Menaḥot* 73b, the Sin-offering of the beast does not appear. Because Lev. 7:7 specifically states that this Sin-offering belongs to the priest, the reference to the Sin-offering of the beasts appears superfluous. However, it may be included here to emphasize that all the Sin-offerings from which blood was not taken into the Tent of Meeting were given to the priests for food.

Each of their Guilt-offerings. Lev. 7:6–7 states that the Guilt-offering is like the Sin-offering and that they both belong to the priests. Every male among the priests may eat both of them. Lev. 14:11–14 states that the Guilt-offering of the leper is like the Sin-offering, for both belong to the priests. Thus, the Bible specifically states that these Guilt-offerings belong to the priests. However, the Torah does not say that the Guilt-offering of the Nazirite belongs to the priest, and I assume that the point of our midrash is to teach that this Guilt-offering is also given to the priest for food. Num. 6:9–12 discusses the Nazirite who becomes unclean because *a man dies very suddenly beside him.* On the eighth day after this has occurred, the Nazirite brings a Sin-offering, and the priest makes atonement for him. On that same day, the Nazirite should *separate himself to YHWH for the days of his separation, and bring a male lamb, a year old for a Guilt-offering.* Again, *Toledot Adam* suggests that we might reason that because this offering does not effect atonement it is not given as food to the priests; therefore, we need Num. 18:9 to teach us that in fact it is given to the priest for food.[39]

Which they return to Me. Mishnah *Baba Qama* 9:11 states that if a man stole from a proselyte and swore falsely about the theft, and the proselyte died, the man pays the value of the object stolen plus the added fifth to the priest. This seems to be derived from Num. 5:7–8, *He shall confess his sin which he has committed; and he shall make full restitution for his wrong, adding a fifth to it, and giving it to whom he did wrong. But if the man has no kinsman to whom restitution may be made for the wrong, the restitution for wrong shall go to the priest.* We need Num. 18:9 to teach us that this belongs to the priest because the priest normally receives only things which are placed on the altar and not money. This part of Num. 18:9 refers to Num. 5:7–8 because the causative form of the root *šwb* appears in both verses.[40]

Is a most holy thing. Lev. 14:10 ff. describes the ritual the priest performs when cleansing a leper. Lev. 14:10 states that *on the eighth day he shall take two male lambs without blemish, and one ewe lamb a year old without blemish, and a Cereal-offering of three tenths of an ephah of fine flour mixed with oil and one log of oil.* The *log* of oil was waved before YHWH with the other items. Eventually, some of the oil is poured on the leper. We need Num. 18:9 to teach us about the oil, because we might assume that the priest may receive only those items which remain from the fire, and the oil was never placed on the fire.[41]

And to you and to your sons. The midrash restates the point that these items were given to the priests because they merited them.

In a most holy place. The midrash states that the priests may eat the items listed above only in a holy place; that is, they may be eaten only within the Temple precincts. From this text, we must conclude that the only things given to the priests after the Temple was destroyed were items *not* mentioned above. Earlier, we read that the priests were supposed to eat their portions in the same manner they did when the Temple was standing. Here we learn that the priestly portions mentioned above must have been things like the tithes and the other offerings which were not placed on the altar.

Rabbi Judah the son of Bathyra says. Normally the priests would eat these portions in the Temple courts; however, if the priests are unable to enter the Temple courts, they may move into the Temple itself in order to eat their food.

Every male may eat it. The midrash takes the verse literally: Only males may eat the items listed above.

It is holy to you. The biblical text appears to be repetitious, for Num. 18:9 already stated that *this shall be yours from the most holy things.* Why does it state in Num. 18:10 that *it is holy to you?* The midrash answers that while the first reference tells us to treat as holy only those things which may be eaten, the latter verse teaches us that even things which are not eaten should be treated as holy. Therefore, we again learn that the Bible does not needlessly repeat itself.

The offering of their gift. Midrash Zebaḥim 5:1–5 lists the following as

Most Holy Things: The bull and the he-goat of the Day of Atonement, the Sin-offering of the individual, the Sin-offering of the congregation, the Whole-offering, the Peace-offering of the congregation, and the Guilt-offerings. Mishnah *Zebaḥim* 5:6–9 names the following as the Lesser Holy Things: The Thank-offering, the ram of the Nazirite (Num. 6:14), the Peace-offerings (excluding those of the congregation), the firstling, the tithe of the cattle, and the Passover-offering. According to the midrash, the phrase *the offering of their gift* refers to the Lesser Holy Things.

Every Wave-offering of the Children of Israel. Lev. 10:15 mentions the thigh and the breast, which serve as Wave-offerings. The midrash states that the reference in Num. 18:11 includes anything which was waved before YHWH.

Anyone who is clean. Unlike the Most Holy Things, which the midrash states could be eaten only by males, here it states that anyone who is clean, male or female, may eat the Lesser Holy Things.

All the best of the oil. Here the midrash is specific concerning those items which the priests received and consumed after the Temple was destroyed. As we argued above, those things would have been *other than* the Most Holy Things.

All the best of the oil. The Pharisees/rabbis decreed that the Israelites were required to make several agricultural gifts: First Tithe given to the Levite, Second Tithe which the Israelite eats in Jerusalem, the Poorman's Tithe given to the poor, the First Fruits waved before the altar in Jerusalem, the Dough-offering for the priest, the Heave-offering for the priest, and the Heave-offering of the tithe which the Levites give the priest from their tithe.[42] As our midrash states, the biblical basis for the last two gifts is Num. 18:12. With regard to the Heave-offering, Peck states: "It is difficult to determine the number and nature of the offerings listed in vss. [Lev. 18:]11–13. 'The offering of their gift,' vs. 11, appears to be a general term referring to all agricultural gifts which are eaten by the priests, and including wave offerings (vs. 11), the best of the oil, wine, and grain (vs. 12) and first fruits (vs. 13). People who stand behind Mishnah, however, have read 'the offering of their gifts' in conjunction with vs. 12's 'best of the oil, wine, and grain, the first of them.' In this manner they identify a single agricultural gift, distinct from the 'first fruits' of vs. 13. In Mishnaic parlance, this gift is called 'heave-offering' *(trwmh),* although it is also known by the term 'first,' suggested by vs. 12."[43]

The first fruits. Deut. 18:4 states that *the first fruits of your grain, of your wine, and of your oil, and the first wool of your sheep you shall give to him* [the priest]. I assume that the midrash wants to indicate that the verses in Numbers and Deuteronomy actually contain the same priestly gifts.

Of what they give. Deut. 18:3 states: *And this shall be the priests' portion from the people, from those offering a sacrifice, whether it be an ox or a sheep; they shall give to the priests the shoulder, the jaw, and the maw.* Again the midrash implies that Deuteronomy and Numbers contain the same list of priestly gifts. In this case, it is possible to connect Deut. 18:3 with Num. 18:12 by means of a *gezarah shavah*, for both verses contain the root *ntn.* As we mentioned above, a *gezarah shavah* is an exegetical principle by which two verses are juxtaposed because they contain the same word or phrase. According to this principle, what applies to one verse also applies to the other.

To YHWH. Num. 15:21 states: *Of the first of your coarse meal you shall give to YHWH, an offering throughout your generations.* I assume that the midrash has juxtaposed Num. 15:21 with this portion of Num. 18:12 because they both contain the phrase *to YHWH.* Although not all of the major agricultural gifts are specifically mentioned in Num. 18:12–13, the midrash has demonstrated that in fact these gifts are implied in these verses. Thus, all of the major agricultural gifts given to the priests are grounded in Num. 18:12–13 even though they may be specifically mentioned elsewhere.

The first fruits of everything in their land. Mishnah *Bikkurim* 3:1 states that a man sets apart his first fruits as follows: When he goes down to his field and sees a ripe fig, or a ripe cluster of grapes, or a ripe pomegranate for the first time, he binds them with reed grass and says: "Behold, these are first fruits"; that is, he sets apart his first fruits before he harvests them, while they still are attached to the ground. On the other hand, the Heave-offering may be separated only from produce after it has been harvested; see, for example, Mishnah *Terumot* 1:8–9. Our midrash argues that we need Num. 18:13 to teach us that one must dedicate the first fruits while they are still attached to the ground, for without this verse, our reason could lead us to an erroneous conclusion: We might draw an incorrect analogy between the first fruits and the Heave-offering, and we might conclude that both of them may be dedicated only after the produce has been detached from the earth. *Toledot Adam* suggests that the phrase *b'rṣ* teaches us that the first fruits must be dedicated while the fruit is still attached to the ground because the particle *b* means "in" or "on" the land.[44]

Which they bring to YHWH shall be yours. Although the first fruits are sanctified for YHWH, they are given to the priests. The midrash takes the verse literally.

Anyone clean in your household may eat it. The midrash again explains that the Bible does not needlessly repeat itself. It finds a special meaning in Num. 18:13 because Num. 18:11 seems to have said the same thing. The midrash argues that Num. 18:13 teaches that an Israelite woman who is engaged to a priest may eat the Heave-offering as though she already were a member of his household. Num. 18:11 teaches that an Israelite woman married to a priest may eat the Heave-offering, and Num. 18:13 teaches that an Israelite woman engaged to a priest may eat the Heave-offering.

Logically it includes. Num. 18:13 mentions *anyone clean in your house;*

therefore, if this may refer to a woman engaged to a priest, should it not also include the sojourner and the hired hand who are also part of the priest's household? However, Ex. 12:45 specifically states that the sojourner and the hired hand may not eat any of the Lesser Holy Things, for the Passover sacrifice is one of the Lesser Holy Things. The midrash states that Ex. 12:45 applies only to the sojourner and the hired hand who are not actually part of the priest's household, for they are not under his power. If this is so, the sojourner and the hired hand who are under the priest's power and thus part of his household may eat the Lesser Holy Things, and we learn this from Num. 18:13.

Or perhaps logically it excludes the sojourner. The midrash now raises the possibility that in fact Num. 18:13 refers only to the woman engaged to a priest. If this is the correct interpretation of Num. 18:13, what does Num. 18:11 mean, for it also mentions that *anyone who is clean* in the priest's household may eat the Lesser Holy Things? Surely, this must include the sojourner and the hired hand. In fact, one could logically deduce that this verse does include these servants or one could deduce that it does not include these servants. In short, we simply cannot determine what the verse means with regard to the sojourner and the hired hand. The problem is solved by Lev. 22:10, which specifies that *the sojourner of a priest and a hired hand shall not eat a holy thing.* This verse makes it clear that under no condition may a sojourner or a hired hand eat any of the holy things; that is, it makes no difference whether or not they are under the priest's power or whether it is a Most Holy Thing or a Lesser Holy Thing. Under no circumstances may a sojourner or a hired hand eat any holy thing. We must conclude, therefore, that Num. 18:13 was meant to teach us about an Israelite woman who was engaged to a priest, and Num. 18:11 was meant to teach us about an Israelite woman married to a priest, for both of these may eat the Lesser Holy Things, which could be eaten only by the members of the priestly household. Only after the Israelite woman had joined her husband's household could she partake of the Lesser Holy Things, and she joined his household by her engagement to him.

And one time Rabbi Yoḥanan the son of Bag Bag. Yoḥanan sent to Judah and determined that the latter ruled that an Israelite woman engaged to a priest could eat the Heave-offering. Judah replied that he assumed that Yoḥanan taught the same thing, for he was expert in the use of the *a fortiori* argument, and one could easily prove by such an argument that an Israelite woman engaged to a priest could eat the Heave-offering. If a non-Jewish handmaiden cannot eat the Heave-offering if she has had intercourse with a priest, but may eat the Heave-offering if she is hired by a priest, should we not conclude that an Israelite woman, who can marry a priest and eat the Heave-offering if he has intercourse with her, can also eat the Heave-offering if she has been engaged to the priest through his giving her money? Yoḥanan responds that he was forced to rule according to the sages who stated that an engaged Israelite woman could not eat the Heave-offering until she had married the priest under the bridal canopy. She may eat the Heave-offering even if she has not had intercourse with her husband as long as she has gone through the marriage ceremony. Yoḥanan has been forced to follow the practice as established by "sages," whoever they were, even though he could prove by logical argument that their ruling was incorrect.[45]

CONCLUSIONS

This section of Sifre Numbers interprets a portion from the Book of Numbers which discusses the priestly service, its relationship to the Levites, and the various priestly gifts. As I mentioned above, this section would have been important to the rabbis. Since they believed that the Temple would eventually be rebuilt and that the sacrificial ritual would be reinstituted at that time, they felt that it was crucial to study the biblical descriptions of the sacrificial ritual so that they would be ready to reestablish the sacrificial cult when the need arose. In addition, through their exegeses of the biblical descriptions of the sacrifices and the priestly duties and prerogatives, the rabbis were able to establish their control over and superiority to the priests.

The midrash opens by Ishmael's stating that this section of Numbers was transmitted directly to the priests. As we have seen many times, the issue of who received God's revelation, Moses or Aaron, that is, the rabbis or the priests, was an important issue for the authors of our midrashic texts. In this instance, Ishmael comes down on the side of the priests.

Yoshiah next explains the meaning of the phrase *the sin of the sanctuary.* He concludes that this refers to a priest's offering a sacrifice but not knowing for the sake of whom he offered it. In my comments, I noted the ambiguous nature of Yoshiah's remarks. Yonatan takes up the next phrase of Num. 18:1 and concludes that if a priest took possession of the flesh before sprinkling the blood, or of the breast and thigh before burning the fat, he is guilty of *the sin of your priesthood.*

The midrash next brings a discussion of Eli's sons. The section is included here because Eli's sons were guilty of acting in the way which Yonatan described. They sought to take possession of their portions before they had burned the fat. As the Bible states, Eli's sons died at the hands of man because they treated the sacrifices disrespectfully.

The next section of the midrash, which discusses the men of Jerusalem, is included here because it opens with the same phrase as the section of Eli's sons. The reference to the "men of Jerusalem" is inappropriate, even though it does discuss those who were disrespectful of the sacrifices, because the Bible and the midrash focus on the priests and the Levites, not on the men of Jerusalem.

The midrash returns to Num. 18:1 and offers an anonymous interpretation of the phrase *the sin of your priesthood.* The midrash concludes that this refers to the things which were under the priesthood's jurisdiction; however, it does not specify exactly what these things were. Like so many passages we have seen to this point, the midrash next offers a logical alternative to its opening interpretation: Perhaps this phrase refers to things under the court's jurisdiction. The midrash cites Num. 18:7, which it claims refers to the things under the court's jurisdiction, without ever explaining what these things are or why Num. 18:7 refers to them. Because Num. 18:7 refers to the things under the court's jurisdiction, we must conclude that Num. 18:1 refers to things under the priesthood's jurisdiction. Again we learn that reason unaided by reference to Scripture can lead to incorrect conclusions.

The midrash next raises the possibility that although the Israelites do not bear the priest's iniquities, the Levites might, for they assisted the priests at the altar. The midrash quotes Num. 18:23, which states that the Levites bear their own iniquity. Again we learn that Scripture answers questions correctly, even those raised by logic. This section need not follow from the previous discussion. Its relationship to the section preceding it is its discussion of the iniquity of the priests.

Next, the midrash deals with the apparent repetition in the Scripture's stating *and also your brothers, the tribe of Levi.* The first phrase excludes women, and the second excludes the Israelites. Again, we learn that nothing in the Bible is superfluous or repetitious.

Aqiba now employs a *gezarah shavah* to explain the meaning of *with you* in Num. 18:2. He concludes that this refers to the songs the Levites sung as part of the sacrificial service. This issue will be discussed elsewhere, but it is not part of Numbers. We have here an attempt to show that all of the essential parts of the sacrificial service could be found in this passage from Numbers.

Next we find a rather long discussion of the meaning of *to accompany you and serve you* in Num. 18:2. The basic question is whether the Levites perform part of the priestly ritual or their own duties. The midrash follows a pattern we have seen many times. It offers an interpretation of the verse, brings a logical alternative, and quotes a verse from the Bible to establish that its initial interpretation was correct. Here we learn that the Levites do not serve the priests; they serve YHWH by performing their own tasks.

The midrash next takes up the rest of Num. 18:2. The form of this discussion is similar to the one which precedes it: The midrash offers an interpretation, brings a logical alternative which is refuted by citing Scripture, here Num. 18:4, and finally accepts its original interpretation of the verse.

Because Num. 18:3 was quoted above in the discussion of whom the Levites serve, we are told here that Num. 18:3 is the basis of the interpretation given it in the previous discussion.

The midrash next explains that Num. 18:3 teaches us that the Levites shall not draw near to the ark or to the portion of the Tent containing the ark, and it quotes Num. 4:20 to support this position. Nathan states, however, that Num. 4:20 (or Num. 18:3?) is the only text in the Torah which hints at the Levites' singing as part of the sacrificial ritual. He claims that only the Book of Ezra contains an explicit reference to this levitical task. Hananyah responds that Nathan was incorrect; for Ex. 19:19 refers to the levitical songs. Because Hananyah ignores Num. 18:3 and responds only to Nathan's comment, I assume that these two remarks were joined together before being included in this section.

The midrash now offers an alternate interpretation of Num. 18:3. It discusses the issue of the "warnings" and the "punishments," a subject we have encountered elsewhere. We are told that the opening of Num. 18:3 provides the warning to the Levites not to engage in the priestly activities, and the end of the verse refers to the punishment. We are further told that the end of the verse provides the punishment for the priest who engages in levitical tasks. In addition, this same phrase, *neither they nor you,* teaches us that one may not engage in an activity associated with his normal service but not usually performed by him or by his family. Although the questions are presented in logical order, they are all answered by the same verse, and especially by the phrase *gm . . . gm.* I noted in my comments that *gm* is an inclusive particle, and that fact is clearly illustrated here. The midrash next offers a narrative which illustrates its point.

Rabbi offers a long comment which demonstrates that one can learn that the Levites should not engage in the priestly tasks, that priests may not engage in activities usually assigned to the Levites, and that one may not engage in an "associated" activity from verses other than Num. 18:3. He concludes by stating that Num. 18:3 refers to Korah's rebellion against Aaron. Thus, Rabbi offers us a different interpretation of Num. 18:3, and, as usual, our text does not select one alternative over the other.

Because Num. 18:4 was cited in the discussion of the priests' serving within the sanctuary while the Levites served without, we are now told, in sequence, that it was the basis for that interpretation.

The next section of the midrash asks why we need Num. 18:4 because we already have Num. 3:38, which appears to say the same thing. We are told that one verse supplies the warning, while the other gives us the punishment.

Num. 18:5 is taken as a warning to the courts that they should direct the priests to act according to the rabbinic ordinances. This is clearly a rabbinic attempt to claim control of the priesthood. Only if the priests follow the rabbinic courts will the former prevent divine punishment from coming into the world.

Next we find a rather long, and obvious, discussion of the word *again,* in Num. 18:5. As I stated in my comments, this discussion is here because the word *again* could be viewed as superfluous in the verse. Because nothing in the Bible is superfluous, the midrash had to deal with this word, even though it interpreted it in an obvious way.

The midrash takes the end of Num. 18:6 literally; however, this is the second time and the second way in which it has established that the Levites serve YHWH directly and are not under the control of the priests. Obviously, this was an important issue to the author(s) of our midrash.

Eleazar states that Num. 18:7 teaches that the priests should *guard* their *priesthood concerning all the things* done by the priests, a rather literal interpretation of the verse. Unfortunately, he does not tell us exactly to what he refers.

The midrash next states that Num. 18:7 speaks of the place behind the curtain where the priestly genealogies were examined. As I noted in my comments, however, the Mishnah claims that this was done in a different place, in the Chamber of Hewn Stones.

On the basis of the next phrase in Num. 18:7, the midrash establishes that each of the tasks connected with the sacrificial ritual were assigned to various individuals or families. This was assumed above, where we were told that the priests and Levites could perform only those tasks which were assigned to them as individuals or as members of specific families. This was clearly an important issue to the author(s) of our midrash. It was probably something well known to everyone. Perhaps it received so much attention in this text because the Temple lay in ruins and the priests were no longer in power. Because it is logical to assume that the priests knew which family was responsible for what, it was important for the rabbis to demonstrate that they accepted the idea that certain duties were assigned to specific families and that they knew which duties were the responsibility of which families. In brief, this discussion was an important aspect of the rabbis' asserting their control over the priesthood.

The midrash next establishes the principle that the priests are to eat the holy things given to them now, after the Temple has been destroyed, in the same way in which they ate them in the Temple precincts while the Temple stood. This means that the priests should wash before they eat the holy things. The midrash assumes that the priests received some of the priestly dues even though the Temple was no longer standing.

The midrash next brings a narrative in which Tarfon's actions illustrate the above point: Tarfon missed a session in the schoolhouse because he was "performing the Temple ritual." Gamliel, the Patriarch, was surprised by Tarfon's comment until Tarfon explained that the members of the priestly families eat their priestly gifts now just as they did when the Temple stood. There may be a latent polemic here, for it is significant that the Patriarch, Gamliel, is surprised by Tarfon's claim that the priestly ritual is performed even without a Temple. Perhaps this reflects some area of tension between the Patriarchs and the priests, in this case a priest who was also a member of the rabbinic hierarchy.

Rabbi, the Patriarch, now suggests that in fact the priests do not perform the priestly ritual now as they did when the Temple was standing, for before they washed both their feet and their hands, because they approached the holy altar and used both their hands and their feet in the sacrificial ritual, but now they wash only their hands. Rabbi concludes that the priests now wash their hands not in order to replicate the sacrificial ritual but because they are told to do so in the Torah. Thus the priests now wash their hands because of the rabbinic interpretation of the Bible and not because they are actually performing the sacrificial ritual.

The midrash now takes up Num. 18:7. The anonymous midrash states that the verse teaches that a nonpriest who approaches the altar to perform the sacrificial service is subject to death. The midrash next raises the possibility that the nonpriest is subject to the death penalty even if he approaches the altar without performing the sacrificial service. The midrash then offers an *a fortiori* argument which supports its original interpretation. Therefore, instead of citing Scripture to refute a logical argument, this section of the midrash cites Num. 18:7 to support the *a fortiori* argument.

The midrash now suggests that Num. 18:7 refers only to an unclean nonpriest who approaches the altar in order to perform the sacrificial ritual. The midrash then raises the logical possibility that the verse teaches only about the impure nonpriest who approaches the altar. In this case, the midrash cites Num. 18:7 in order to refute the logical possibility that a pure nonpriest may approach the altar, while an impure nonpriest may not. This paragraph follows the normal pattern we have encountered frequently in this volume, while the previous paragraph does not follow the normal pattern.

Ishmael and Yohanan explain the type of death referred to in Num. 18:7. Each employs a *gezarah shavah,* but each reaches a different conclusion. Ishmael's conclusion is derived from the Bible, Deut. 13:6, while Yohanan's is not. The midrash next discusses the issues of "warning" and "punishment."

At Num. 18:8 the midrash again asks to whom God spoke. At this point it concludes that God spoke to Moses, even though the Bible explicitly states that He spoke with Aaron.

Ishmael states that the word *behold* in Num. 18:8 teaches that God acted with joy. His students respond that if *behold* signifies joy, we must conclude that God acted with joy when He destroyed those of the generation of the flood. Although this troubles Ishmael's students, it does not bother the master. The section ends by citing several verses which support Ishmael's contention that God is happy when the wicked are punished. The elongated conclusion to this section may be the result of one or several editorial expansions. In an independent unit, Nathan also interprets *behold* as a reference to joy, and he cites Ex. 4:14, in which Aaron's joy at greeting Moses appears in a verse which opens with the word *behold*. Both rabbis agree that *behold* signifies joy; however, the two interpretations are independent and unrelated.

The midrash next explains that Num. 18:8 was needed to make it clear to all that God had given certain gifts to the priests and that no one had the right to complain about these gifts. Specifically, the midrash again refers to Korah's complaining about Aaron. The issue of Korah's rebellion was raised above, almost out of nowhere, and here again it appears unrelated to what has occurred before.

The next section, an exegesis of Num. 17:5, interrupts the flow of the midrash. It was included here because it is taken as a reference to Korah's punishment; therefore, it is related to the paragraph which precedes it. It is an expansion of the previous comment; it is not an exegesis of the biblical text under consideration.

The midrash next offers two interpretations of the word *mšḥ* in Num. 18:8. In my comments I noted that Isaac's interpretation is awkward.

Finishing with Num. 18:8, the midrash establishes that the gifts were given to Aaron and his sons because they deserved them and that God's giving them to the Aaronides was an everlasting act. Like the discussion of Korah which appeared earlier in the exegesis of Num. 18:8, this section also underscores the fact that the priests have been given certain gifts which they deserve and about which no one has a right to complain. The everlasting nature of these gifts and the fact that the priests deserved to receive them was clearly an important issue for the author(s) of our text.

The midrash now explains the nature of the gifts mentioned in Num. 18:9. As I demonstrated in my comments, most of these gifts are mentioned elsewhere in the Bible. This exegesis is an attempt by its author(s) to demonstrate that all of the priestly gifts explicitly mentioned elsewhere in the Bible are alluded to in Num. 18:9. There may be a message here to those who wanted to expand or to limit the number of priestly gifts on the basis of what is explicitly mentioned in Num. 18:9. The point of this midrash may be that the priests are due everything which the rabbis have claimed they deserve, nothing more and nothing less.

Exegeting Num. 18:9, the midrash again claims that the priests deserve the gifts they are given.

The midrash now explains, on the basis of Num. 18:10, that the Most Holy Things were given the priests while the Temple stood. It implies that the Most Holy Things are no longer given to the priests since the Temple has been destroyed. Judah offers a second interpretation of Num. 18:10. He claims that the verse means that the priests were allowed to eat the Most Holy Things in the innermost parts of the Temple if they were prevented from eating them in the Temple courts. On the basis of Num. 18:10, the midrash also teaches that only the priestly males could eat the Most Holy Things and that nonedible items could be classified as Most Holy Things.

Num. 18:11 begins the midrash's discussion of the Lesser Holy Things. Again, the items mentioned in the midrash are found elsewhere in the Bible as interpreted by the rabbis. Again, the point seems to be that the priestly gifts have been determined by the rabbis and that the priests deserve these gifts, nothing more and nothing less. In this case, we are told that a ritually clean member of the priest's household may eat the Lesser Holy Things. The implication of the interpretation of Num. 18:12 is that the Lesser Holy Things were given to the priests even though the Temple had been destroyed. Again, we discover in the exegesis of Num. 18:12 that the priests should receive only those offerings allowed them by the rabbinic interpretation of the Bible.

In discussing the first fruits mentioned in Num. 18:13, the midrash follows its familiar form of offering an interpretation, presenting a faulty logical argument, and citing Scripture as a refutation of the logical argument. Here we learn, as we have so many times before, that logic uninformed by Scripture can lead one to incorrect conclusions. The midrash then takes Num. 18:13 literally and concludes that the first fruits were given to the priests.

Next follows a rather long section which is cast in a familiar pattern: The midrash explains that Num. 18:13 teaches that an Israelite woman engaged to a priest is considered part of his household so that she is allowed to eat the Heave-offering. It next raises the possibility that only a woman married to a priest is considered part of his household. The midrash states that Num. 18:11 refers to a woman married to a priest; therefore, Num. 18:13 must refer to the woman engaged to a priest.

The midrash next raises the possibility that the sojourner and the hired hand should be included in the priest's household just like the Israelite woman to whom he is engaged. The midrash cites Ex. 12:45 and suggests that its prohibition applies only to the sojourner and hired hand who are not under the priest's power and not part of his household. The midrash then suggests that Num. 18:13 applies to the sojourner and to the hired hand. However, Lev. 22:10 states that a sojourner and a hired hand cannot eat the holy things; therefore, Num. 18:13 cannot discuss the sojourner and the hired hand. It must, therefore, refer to the Israelite woman who is engaged to a priest. Although it is somewhat longer than other discussions we have encountered, this section of the midrash follows the pattern we have seen many times before.

The midrash next brings a narrative in which Judah and Yoḥanan both seem to agree that one can establish by means of an *a fortiori* argument that an Israelite woman engaged to a priest may eat the Heave-offering. Yoḥanan, however, must follow the ruling of sages, which is that an Israelite woman does not become a part of the priest's household until she has married him under the bridal canopy.

For the most part, this selection from Sifre Numbers has features similar to those we encountered in Sifra and Mekhilta. All three offer us a virtual word-by-word, verse-by-verse, exegesis of the Bible. They all assume that every word in the Bible is important, that nothing in the Bible is merely repetitious, that nothing in the Bible is superfluous. Like Sifra, our text often makes the point that logic unaided by Scripture is faulty. Logical conclusions can be demonstrated to be incorrect merely by citing Scripture. Like Mekhilta, our present text often makes the point that the whole Bible is interrelated and that each verse must be seen in light of every other verse.

Although this midrash looks the same as the other collections, it does seem to include some important polemical points. Like our selections from Mekhilta and Sifra, the present text discusses the issue of to whom God spoke, Moses or Aaron. In the present selection, we find two different answers: Ishmael says He spoke to Aaron, while the anonymous midrash states that He spoke to Moses. Our present selection also makes it clear that the priests are supposed to receive certain gifts, that these gifts were given to them by God because the priests deserved to receive them, that others should not complain about the fact that the priests receive these gifts, and that the priests should receive *only* those gifts which have been established by the rabbinic interpretation of the Bible. In addition, we are told that the priests should perform their sacrificial ritual according to the rules set down by the rabbinic courts. It is interesting to note that this section follows the claim that God revealed this portion of Numbers to Moses, that is, the rabbis, and not to Aaron, that is, the priests. We are told that both the priesthood and the rabbinic courts supervised the priestly ritual; however, we are not told over what each court had jurisdiction. In addition, there seems to be evidence of a disagreement between the Patriarch and the priests concerning the viability of a Temple ritual after the Temple had been destroyed.

Again, we have no way of discovering to whom this midrash was addressed. However, it was clearly composed by the rabbis, and its major theme is that the priests have certain rights and duties which are regulated by and administered by the rabbis, who have derived their specifics from the Bible itself.

NOTES

1. D. Hoffmann, *Zur Einleitung in die halachischen Midraschim* (Berlin, 1886–87), 52.
2. Z. Frankel, *The Paths of the Mishnah* [Hebrew] (Leipzig, 1859), 309. Hoffmann, 52–56, 66–72. Ch. Albeck, *Untersuchungen über die halakhischen Midraschim* (Berlin, 1927), 1–44, 45–86, 121–139. M. D. Herr, S. V. "Sifrei," *Encyclopaedia Judaica* XIV, 1519–1521.
3. Albeck, 91. Herr, 1519.
4. Herr, 1519–1520. J. N. Epstein, *Prolegomena ad Litteras Tannaiticas*, ed. E. Z. Melamed (Jerusalem, 1958), 605–608.
5. The translation is based on H. S. Horovitz, *Siphre d'be Rab* (Jerusalem, 1966), 131–137.
6. See Chap. 2, note 21.
7. R. DeVaux, *Ancient Israel* (New York, 1965), II, 415–417.
8. See *Toledot Adam* on *w'ynw ywd' lšm, my hqtyrw* and Rabbenu Hillel on *w'yn ywd' lmy zrqw*.
9. See Chap. 2, note 21.
10. See *Toledot Adam* on *hky grsnn 'th wbynk 'tk*.
11. On the levitical singers, see D. L. Petersen, *Late Israelite Prophecy: Studies in the Deutero-Prophetic Literature in Chronicles* (Missoula, 1977), *passim.*
12. At this point the Hebrew text is rather confused; I have made the best out of it that I could.
13. *Toledot Adam* on *r ntn 'wmr.*
14. Rashi's comment, loc. cit., on Babylonian Talmud *Arakhin* 11b.
15. See Chap. 3, note 25.
16. See Babylonian Talmud *Arakhin* 11b. On Joshua, see W. S. Green, *The Traditions of Joshua ben Hananiah* (Leiden, 1981).
17. *Toledot Adam* on *šb' qrḥ w'r'r.*
18. On the history of the Sanhedrin, see the rather uncritical studies of H. Mantel, *Studies in the History of the Sanhedrin* (Cambridge, 1961).
19. *Toledot Adam* on *mkyn 'l yhy 'l' bk.*
20. Toledot Adam on *mn mtnh bpyys.*
21. Horovitz, 133, note to line 13.
22. On Rabbi Ṭarfon, see J. Gereboff, *Rabbi Tarfon: The Tradition, the Man, and Early Rabbinic Judaism* (Missoula, 1979).

23. Compare Babylonian Talmud, *Pesaḥim* 72b–73a.

24. G. Porton, *The Traditions of Rabbi Ishmael [Ishmael]*, (Leiden, 1976–82), III, 105–106.

25. See Chap. 2, note 21, and the opening of this selection.

26. *Toledot Adam* on *wydbr yhwh*.

27. Rabbenu Hillel on *tlmwd lwmr*.

28. *Ishmael*, II, 172–173.

29. See Chap. 2, note 17.

30. There are scores of books and articles on the parable; however, most of them center on the Jewish parable only as an introduction to the parables of Jesus. W. O. E. Oesterley, *The Gospel Parables in the Light of Their Jewish Background* (New York, 1936). C. H. Dodd, *The Parables of the Kingdom* (London, 1950). J. Jeremias, *The Parables of Jesus* (New York, 1963).

31. *Toledot Adam* on *h' lmdnw šhyh qrḥ*.

32. F. Brown, S. R. Driver, and C. A. Briggs, *A Hebrew and English Lexicon of the Old Testament* (London, 1962), *mšḥ*, 602–603.

33. Wilna Gaon, loc. cit.

34. *Toledot Adam* on *wkl qrbmn*.

35. *Toledot Adam* on *zw mnḥt ḥwṭ'*.

36. Rabbenu Hillel on *lkl mnḥtm*.

37. Rabbenu Hillel on *lkl ḥṭ'tm*.

38. *Toledot Adam* on *w'šm nzyr*.

39. *Toledot Adam* on *wḥṭ't h'wp*.

40. *Toledot Adam* on *'šr yšybw zh gzl hgr*.

41. *Toledot Adam* on *zh lwg šmn šl mṣwr'*.

42. Neusner, *Judaism: The Evidence of Mishnah* (Chicago 1981) 53–55, 79–87, 126–132, 172–182, 287–300.

43. A. Peck, *The Priestly Gift in Mishnah: A Study of Tractate Terumot* (Chico, 1981), 2.

44. *Toledot Adam* on *lymd 'l hbkwrym*.

45. Palestinian Talmud, *Ketubot* 5:4.

5️⃣ Sifre Deuteronomy

Even though scholars agree the Sifre Numbers and Sifre Deuteronomy do not stem from one school and that they should not be printed together in one volume as is commonly done,[1] there is no clear indication of the provenance or the date of origin of the Midrash to Deuteronomy.[2] As in the case of Sifre Numbers, Sifre Deuteronomy does not offer us an exegesis of the entire biblical book; it contains comments to 1:1–30, 3:21–4:1, 6:4–9, 11:10–26, 15, 31:14, 32:1 ff.[3] Also similar to Sifre Numbers, scholars claim that sections of Sifre Deuteronomy derive from sources different from those of which the main body of the text was composed.[4]

The following passage from the midrash is an exegesis of Deut. 6:4–9, the portions of the liturgy known as the *Shema* and the *ve-'ahavtah*.

> *Hear, O Israel, YHWH is our God, YHWH is one. And you shall love YHWH, your God, with all your heart, with all your soul, and with all your might. And these words which I command you this day shall be upon your heart. You shall teach them intensely to your children, and you shall speak of them when you sit in your house, when you walk on the road, when you lie down, and when you rise up. You shall bind them for a sign on your hand, and they shall be a symbol (ṭṭpt) between your eyes. You shall write them on the doorposts of your house and on your gates.*

This section from Sifre Deuteronomy is a detailed exegesis of virtually every phrase of Deut. 6:4–9; in fact, we have more than one interpretation

119

of most phrases. However, the explanations move considerably beyond the text. The midrash opens by identifying the Israel of Deut. 6:4 with Jacob and discussing his concern for his sons' deserving God's love. After dealing with Reuben's sin and his repentance. we are told that Deut. 6:4 was the response of Jacob's sons to their father's admonition on his deathbed that they should remain faithful to YHWH, their God. Similarly, the long digression about chastisements which is juxtaposed with Deut. 6:5 has little to do with the biblical context or subject matter. In addition, the midrash contains several artificial and awkward discussions of the *tefilin*. These sections seem to establish points which must have been well known to everyone. One problem was the fact that the biblical injunction concerning where the *tefilin* should be worn was not taken literally by the rabbis. In short, this passage is not a simple or straightforward exegesis of Deuteronomy. It moves far afield from the biblical text. While the issue of reason versus revelation appears in this text, we discover that reason may prevail, especially where rabbinic custom was not in line with the literal meaning of Scripture. In brief, this midrash is much different from those we have reviewed to this point. Like Genesis Rabbah and Leviticus Rabbah, the theological points the author(s) wanted to make are more important than the actual biblical text.

Hear,[5] *O Israel, YHWH is our God, YHWH is one* (Deut. 6:4). Why was this said: [It was said] because it is said [in Ex. 25:2]: *Speak to the Children of Israel.* "Speak to the children of Abraham" [or] "speak to the children of Isaac" is not written here; rather, *speak to the Children of Israel* [is written here, and it indicates that] our father Jacob was worthy [enough so] that the [holy] words[s] should be spoken to his children. [He was worthy of this honor] because our father Jacob was anxious all his days, and he [would] say: "Woe is me, perhaps an unworthy [offspring] will come forth from me in the same way that one came forth from [each of] my forefathers. Ishmael came forth from Abraham, [and] Esau came forth from Isaac. Therefore, I [pray that] an unworthy [offspring] will not come forth from me in the same way that one came forth from [each of] my forefathers."

And thus it says: *And Jacob vowed a vow saying* (Gen. 28:20). One might think that our father Jacob [was] saying, "*If He gives me bread to eat and clothes to wear then YHWH shall be my God* (Gen. 28:20–22); [but] if not, He will not be my God." [However,] Scripture says, *And I return in peace to my father's house, and YHWH will be my God* (Gen. 28:21) [which means that Jacob said YHWH will be his God] no matter what happens. [If this is so,] why does Scripture say, *Then YHWH shall be my God?* [This was said to indicate that] His name would rest on me [Jacob] so that an unworthy [offspring] would not come forth from me, from the first [of my children] until the last [of them].

But thus it says: *When Israel dwelt in that land, Reuben went and lay with Bilhah, his father's concubine, and Israel heard* (Gen. 35:22). When Jacob heard about [it], he was shaken. He said: "Woe is me, perhaps an unworthy one has occurred among my sons." [He remained in this state] until he received good news from the Holy One that Reuben had repented, for it is said, *And the sons of Jacob were twelve* (Gen. 35:22). But was it not well known that they were twelve? [This verse is not meant to tell us the number of Jacob's sons;] rather, [it indicates] that [Jacob] received good news from the Holy One, blessed be He, that Reuben had repented. This is in order to teach you that Reuben used to fast all his days, for it is said: *And they sat down to eat bread* (Gen. 37:25). And do you really think that the brothers would sit and eat bread and their oldest brother was not with them? Rather, [this verse was said] to teach you that [Reuben] fasted all his days until Moses came and accepted [Reuben's] repentance, for it is said: *Let Reuben live and not die* (Deut. 33:6).

And thus you find when Jacob our father was [about to be] removed from the world he called to his sons and admonished each of them individually, for it is said, *And Jacob called to his sons, "Reuben, you are my firstborn; Simon and Levi are brothers; Judah, your brothers shall praise you"* (Gen. 49:1–8). After he admonished each one individually, he returned and called to all of them as one, [and] he said to them: "Perhaps it is in your heart[s to] break away from [the One] who spoke and the world came into being." They said to him: "*Hear* [us] *O Israel*, our father, just as it is not in your heart to break away from [God], so also it is not in our heart[s] to break away from the One who spoke and the world came into being; rather, *YHWH is our God, YHWH is one.*" Therefore, it says, *And Israel bowed himself on the head of the bed* (Gen. 47:31). And did he really bow himself on the head of the bed? Rather, [this indicates] that he gave thanks and praised [God] because an unworthy [offspring] had not come forth from him.

And there are those who say, "*And Israel bowed himself on the head of the bed* [indicates] that Reuben repented."

Another matter: [Why is it said that Israel bowed himself on the head of the bed? He did this,] for [when his sons recited the *Shema',*] he said: "Blessed is the name of His glorious kingdom for ever and ever." The Holy One, blessed be He, said to him, "Jacob, behold, you used to express [your] desire all your days that your sons would rise early [and begin their days by reciting the *Shema'*] and [would] bring on the evening by reciting the *Shema',* [and see, they are doing just that]."

[Hear, O Israel]. From here they said: "One who recites the *Shema'* but not [loud enough so that] his ears hear [his words], has not fulfilled [his] obligation [to recite the *Shema'*]."

YHWH is our God. Why was this said? Was it not already said, *YHWH is one?* Why does Scripture say, *Our God?* [This was said to indicate that] His name rests upon us in a special degree. Similarly, *Three times during the year all your males shall appear before the Lord, YHWH, the God of Israel* (Ex. 34:23). Why do I need [this repetition]? Isn't it already said: *Before the Lord, YHWH?* Why does Scripture say, *the God of Israel?* [It said this to indicate that] His name rested upon Israel in a special degree. Similarly: *Thus said YHWH Seba'ot, the God of Israel* (Jer. 32:14). Why do I need this [repetition]? Isn't it already said: *I am YHWH, the God of all flesh; is anything too difficult for Me?* [It said this to indicate that] His name rested on Israel in a special degree. Similarly: You say, *"Hear, O My people, and I will speak, O Israel, and I will testify against you, I am Elohim, your God* (Ps. 50:7)." [This teaches you that] My name rested upon you in a special degree.

Another matter: *YHWH is our* God [means He is God] over us. *YHWH is one* [means He is God] over all who come into the world. *YHWH is our God* [means] in this world; *YHWH is one* [means He will be our God also] in the world-to-come. And thus it says: *And YHWH will be king over all the earth. On that day YHWH shall be one, and His name shall be one* (Zech. 14:9).

And you shall love YHWH your God (Deut. 6:5). [This teaches us that one should] perform [the commandments] out of love. [This verse] distinguishes between those who perform [the commandments] out of love and those who perform [them] out of fear. One who performs [the commandments] out of love, his reward is doubled and redoubled. Because it says, *You shall fear YHWH, your God, and serve Him* (Deut. 10:20) you may [compare this to] a man [among you] who fears his compatriot, and thus [though] he needs him, he avoids him and goes his way. But you [should] perform [the commandments] out of love, for you cannot have love where there is fear, or fear where there is love, except in the attributes of the Omnipresent One, alone.

Another matter: *And you shall love YHWH your God.* You should cause Mankind to love Him [through your actions], like Abraham your father in the instance where it is said, *And the souls which he made in Haran* (Gen. 12:5). But [contrary to what is stated in Gen. 12:5] is it not so that if all who came into the world would unite for [the purpose of] creating one mosquito and placing a soul in it, they could not [do so! This verse does not mean that Abraham literally created souls;] rather, [the verse] teaches [you] that Abraham, our father, used to convert [the people] and bring them under the wing of the Holy Presence.

With all your heart (Deut. 6:5). With your two inclinations: With the inclination to do good and with the inclination to do evil.

Another matter: *With all your heart* [means] with all of the heart in you so that your heart will not divide [itself] against the Omnipresent One.

With all your soul (Deut. 6:5), even if He takes your soul [and you die]; and thus it says: *But for Your sake we are slain all day long and accounted as sheep for the slaughter* (Ps. 44:23). Rabbi Simeon the son of Menasya says: "And is this really so? How is it possible for a man to be slain all day? Rather, [this verse indicates that] the Holy One, blessed be He, accounts it to the righteous as if they were slain all day long."

Simeon the son of Azzai says: *With all your soul* [means] love him until the agony of death."

Rabbi Eliezer says: "If it says, *with all your soul,* why is it [also] said, *with all your might* (Deut. 6:5)? And if it says, *with all your might,* why is it [also] said, *with all your soul?* [It is necessary for Scripture to employ both phrases because] there [may] be a man for whom his body is more precious to him than his wealth; therefore, *with all your soul* is said. And [there may be] a man for whom his wealth is more precious to him than his body; therefore, it is said, *with all your might."*

Rabbi Aqiba says: "If [Scripture had said only] *with all your soul,* one [could have reasoned to] *with all your might* [by means of] an *a fortiori* [argument; therefore,] why does Scripture say, *with all your might?* [This was said to teach you that you should love God] for whatever measure He metes out to you, whether it is a good measure or a bad measure. And thus David says: '*A cup of salvation I shall lift up, and I shall call upon the name of YHWH* (Ps. 116:13). *I suffered distress and anguish, then I called on the name of YHWH*' (Ps. 116:3–4). And thus Job says: '*YHWH gives and YHWH takes away, may the name of YHWH be blessed*' (Job. 1:21). [If Job said this] when [he was experiencing a] good measure from God], how much the more [would he say this] at [a time when] an evil measure [befell him]. What did his wife say to him? '*Do you still hold fast to your integrity? Bless God, and die*' (Job. 2:9). And what did he say to her? '*You speak as one of the foolish women speak. Shall we receive good at the hands of God but not receive evil?*' (Job. 2:10)."

The men of the generation of the flood were repulsed by good, and when evil came upon them they accepted it against their will. But is this not the basis of an *a fortiori* [argument]? If one who is repulsed by good is pleased by evil, [how much the more] should we who are pleased by good be pleased by evil. And it is he who said to her: "*You speak as one of the foolish women would speak.*"

Moreover, a man should be happier with chastisements than with good [fortune], for if a man [experiences only] good [fortune] all his days, his iniquities are not pardoned [during his lifetime]. Then, through what means are his iniquities pardoned? [They are pardoned] when [he experiences] chastisements.

Rabbi Eliezer the son of Jacob says: "Behold, it says, *For YHWH chastises (ywkyh) him whom He loves, as a father the son in whom he is pleased* (Prov. 3:12). What happens to the son who is pleasing to [his] father? You must say [that he experiences] acts of chastisements [at his father's hands]."

Rabbi Meir says: "Behold, it says, *Know in your heart that as a man disciplines (yysr) his son, YHWH, your God, chastises you (mysryk)* (Deut. 8:5). [YHWH says:] 'You and your heart know the deeds you have done and the chastisements I have brought upon you, for I did not bring [them] upon you [in an amount] equal to your deeds which you have done.' "

Rabbi Yosi the son of Rabbi Judah says: "Precious are chastisements, for the name of the Omnipresent One rests upon him to whom chastisements come, for it is said, *YHWH, your God, chastises you* (Deut. 8:5)."

Rabbi Nathan the son of Joseph says: "Just as a covenant was made for the Land [of Israel], so [also] a convenant is made by means of chastisements, for it is said: *YHWH, your God, chastises you*

(Deut. 8:5), and it says, *For YHWH, your God, will bring you into a good land* (Deut. 8:7)."

Rabbi Simeon the son of Yoḥai says: "Precious are chastisements, for three valuable gifts were given to Israel [as a result of them], which the [other] nations of the world desired; however, they were given [to Israel alone,] only as a result of the chastisements [which God brought upon her]; and these are they: [The] Torah, the Land of Israel, and the world-to-come. From where [do we learn that the Torah] was given to Israel as a result of chastisements? Scripture says:] *That men may know wisdom and instruction (mwsr)* (Prov. 1:2); and it says: *Happy is the man whom You chastise, O, YHWH, and whom You teach out of Your Torah* (Ps. 94:12). From where [do we learn that] the Land of Israel [was given to Israel as a result of chastisements? Scripture says:] *YHWH, your God, chastises you, for YHWH, your God, will bring you into a good land* (Deut. 8:5–7). From where [do we learn that] the world-to-come [was given to Israel as a result of chastisements? Scripture says:] *For the commandment is a lamp, and YHWH is a light, and the chastisements are the path of life* (Prov. 6:23). Which is the path that brings man to the world-to-come? You must say that these are chastisements."

Rabbi Nehemiah says: "Precious are chastisements, for just as [offering] sacrifices makes one pleasing [to God], so also [experiencing] chastisements makes one pleasing [to God]. Concerning sacrifices it says, *And it shall be accepted from him to make atonement for him* (Lev. 1:4). Concerning chastisements it says, *And they shall be payments for their iniquity* (Lev. 26:43). Moreover, chastisements make one more acceptable [to God] than sacrifices [do], for sacrifices [come from a man's] property, but chastisements [come upon a man's] body; and thus it says, *Skin for skin, and all that a man has he will give for his life* (Job. 2:4)."

And one time Rabbi Eliezer was sick, and Rabbi Ṭarfon, Rabbi Joshua, Rabbi Eleazar the son of Azariah, and Rabbi Aqiba entered to visit him. Rabbi Ṭarfon said to him: "Rabbi, you are more precious to Israel than the orb of the sun, for the orb of the sun lights up [only] this world, but you bring light to this world and to the world-to-come." Rabbi Joshua said to him: "Rabbi, you are more precious to Israel than the gift of rain, for rain gives life [only] in this world, but you give [life] in this world and in the world-to-come." Rabbi Eleazar the son of Azariah said to him: "Rabbi, you are more precious to Israel than [a person's] father or mother, for [a person's] father and mother bring [him/her] into this world, but you bring [him/her] into this world and into the world-to-come." Rabbi Aqiba said to him: "Rabbi, chastisements are precious." Rabbi Eliezer said to his students: "Support me." Rabbi Eliezer sat up [and] said to him: "Aqiba, speak [to me." Aqiba] said to him: "Behold it says, *Manasseh was twelve years old when he began to reign, and he reigned in Israel for fifty-five years* (II Chron. 33:1); and it says, *Also these are the proverbs of Solomon which the men of Hezekiah, king of Judah, copied* (Prov. 25:1). And do you really believe that Hezekiah taught [the] Torah to all of Israel, but to Manasseh, his son, he did not teach [the] Torah? Rather, [we learn] that all of [the] learning which Hezekiah taught him and all of the labor which he lavished on him did not profit him, for only [his suffering] chastisements [from God succeeded in helping him], for it is said: *And YHWH spoke to Manasseh and to his people, but they gave no heed. Therefore, YHWH brought upon them the chiefs of the army of the king of Assyria, who took Manasseh with hooks and bound him with fetters of bronze and brought him to Babylon. And when he was in distress, he entreated the favor of YHWH, his God, and greatly humbled himself before the God of his fathers. He prayed to Him, and God accepted his entreaty and returned him to Jerusalem unto his kingdom* (II Chron. 33:10–13). Behold, [from this we learn that] chastisements are precious."

Rabbi Meir says: "Behold it says: *And you shall love YHWH, your God, with all your heart.* Love Him *with all your heart*, as Abraham your father [did] as [in the following] instance, for it is said, *But you Israel, my servant, Jacob, whom I have chosen, the offspring of Abraham, the one who loves Me* (Isa. 41:8). And *with all your soul*, like Isaac who bound himself to the altar as in the instance where it is said, *And Abraham sent forth his hand and took up the knife* (Gen. 22:10). *With all your might (m'dk):* Be thankful *(mdh)* to Him, as was Jacob, your father, for it is said: *I am not worthy of the least of all the steadfast love and all the faithfulness which You have shown Your servant, for with my staff alone I have crossed the Jordan, and now I have become two companies* (Gen. 32:11)."

And these words, which I command you this day, shall be upon your heart (Deut. 6:6). Rabbi Meir says: "Why was this said? [It was said] because it says [in Deut. 6:5], *And you shall love YHWH, your God, with all your heart.* But [from this verse] I do not know how [one should express his or her] love [for] the Omnipresent One; [therefore], Scripture says, *And these words which I command you this day shall be upon your heart* [which means] put these words in your heart so that you may acknowledge Him who spoke and the world came into being and cleave to His paths."

Which I command you this day so that they will not [appear] in your eyes like an outmoded ordinance, for a man respects only a new ordinance, for [when it is new] everyone runs to read it.

Upon your heart. From here Rabbi Yoshiah used to say: "A man needs to control his inclination [to do evil], for thus you always find that righteous ones control their inclination [to do evil]. Concerning Abraham it says, *I have sworn to YHWH, God Most High, Maker of heaven and of earth, that I would not take a thread or a sandal-thong or anything that is yours* (Gen. 14:22–23). Concerning Boaz it is said, *As YHWH lives, I will perform the part of the next of kin for you. Lie down until the morning* (Ruth 3:13). Concerning David it is said, *And David said: 'As YHWH lives, YHWH will smite him; or his days shall come to die, or he shall go into battle and perish'* (I Sam. 26:10). Concerning Elisha it is said, *As YHWH lives, whom I serve, I will receive none* (II Kgs. 5:16). And just as the righteous ones [must] control their inclination [to do evil], so that they would not do [evil], so also the wicked ones [must] control their inclination [to do good] so that they would do [evil], for it is said, *As YHWH lives, I will run after him, and get something from him* (II Kgs. 5:20)."

And you shall teach them intensely to your children (Deut. 6:7) so that they might be ever ready in your mouth, for when a man asks you something, you should not hesitate about it; rather, you should tell it to him immediately. And thus it says, *Say to Wisdom, "you are my sister," and call insight your friend* (Prov. 7:4); and it says, *Bind them on your fingers, write them on the tablet of your heart* (Prov. 7:3); and it says, *Your arrows are sharp* (Ps. 45:6). What is the reward for this? [The reward is that] *the peoples fall under you, in the heart of the king's enemies* (Ps. 45:6). And it says, *Like arrows in the hand of the warrior are the sons of one's youth* (Ps. 127:4). And what is said about them? [It says,] *Happy is the man who has his quiver full of them. He shall not be put to shame when he speaks with his enemies in the gate* (Ps. 127:5).

Another matter: *And you shall teach them intensely to your children.* These [words] must be memorized. But [one need] not [memorize] *every firstborn is holy to Me* (Ex. 13:2) [or] *and when*

YHWH brings you (Ex. 13:11). But it [could be] argued by analogy: If *and YHWH said* (Num. 15:37), [a passage] which is not bound [in the *tefilin*], is memorized, how much the more [should we conclude that] *holy to Me* (Ex. 13:2) [and] *and when YHWH brings you* (Ex. 13:11), which are bound [in the *tefilin*], should be memorized; [however,] Scripture says, *And you shall teach them intensely,* [which means] these [words should be] memorized, but *holy to Me* [and] *and when YHWH brings you* [need] not be memorized. Yet I [might] say [that] if *and YHWH said,* which is preceded by other commandments, should be memorized, the Ten Commandments, which are not preceded by other commendments, how much the more should they be memorized. You say that it is an *a fortiori* argument: If *every firstborn is holy to Me* [and] *and when YHWH brings you,* which are bound [in the *tefilin*], are not memorized, the Ten Commandments, which are not bound [in the *tefilin*], how much the more should they not be memorized. And, *and YHWH said* supports the analogy with the Ten Commandments, for even though they are not bound [in the *tefilin*], they are to be memorized. [However,] Scripture says, *And you shall teach them intensely to your children* [which means] these [should be] memorized and the Ten Commandments [should] not be memorized.

To your children. These are your students. And thus you find that in every place students are called children, for it is said: *And the children of the prophets who were in Beth El came out to Elisha* (II Kgs. 3:2). Were these really the prophets' children? Rather, from here [we learn] that students are called children. And thus it says: *And the children of the prophets who were in Jericho met Elisha* (II Kgs. 2:5). Were these really the children of the prophets? Were they not [their] students? Rather, from here [we learn] that students are called children.

And thus you find concerning Hezekiah the king of Judah that he taught the whole Torah to Israel and [that] he called them children, for it is said: *My children, do not be negligent* (II Chron. 29:11).

And just as students are called children, so also the teacher is called the father, for it is said: *And Elisha saw and he cried out, "My father, my father, the chariot of Israel and its horsemen." And he saw him no more* (II Kgs. 2:12). And it says: *Now when Elisha became ill with the illness from which he was to die, Joash, the king of Israel, went down to him and wept before him crying, "My father, my father. The chariot of Israel and its horsemen"* (II Kgs. 13:14).

And you shall speak of them (Deut 6:7). Make them the main subject [of your conversations,] and do not make them [only] a secondary subject, for you [should] engage in everyday actions only through them. You should not mix other matters with them like so-and-so. Perhaps you [might] say that I have learned the wisdom of Israel, [and now] I shall go and learn the wisdom [of the rest of] the nations of the world; [however,] Scripture says: *To walk with them* (Lev. 18:4) and not to depart from their midst. And thus it says: *Let them be for you alone, and not for the strangers with you* (Prov. 5:17). And thus it says: *When you walk it will lead you; and when you lie down, it will watch over you; and when you wake up it will talk with you* (Prov. 6:22). *When you walk it will lead you* [means] in this world. *When you lie down, it will watch over you* [refers to] the hour of your death. *And when you wake up* [refers to] the days of the Messiah. *It will talk with you* [means] in the world-to-come.

And when you lie down (Deut. 6:7). One might think that even if one lies down in the middle of the day [he *must* meditate on these words and recite the *Shemaʿ*; however,] Scripture says, *When you sit in your house and when you walk on the road* (Deut. 6:7) [which means] the Torah speaks of ordinary actions [done at their normal times].

One time Rabbi Ishmael was reclining and expounding, and Rabbi Eleazar the son of Azariah was standing. [When] the time for reciting the *Shemaʿ* arrived, Rabbi Ishmael stood, and Rabbi Eleazar the son of Azariah reclined. Rabbi Ishmael said to him: "What is this [you are doing], Eleazar?" He said to [Ishmael]: "Ishmael, my brother, they say to one, 'Why is your beard grown?' He said to them, 'May it be against the destroyers.' " [Ishmael] said to him: "You reclined according to the words of the House of Shammai, but I stood according to the words of the House of Hillel." Another matter: [They acted thus] so that the matter would not be fixed as a requirement, for the House of Shammai say: "In the evening every man should recline and recite [the *Shemaʿ*], but in the morning, [every man should] stand [and recite the *Shemaʿ*]."

And you shall bind them (Deut. 6:8). These are bound [in the *tefilin*], but *and YHWH said* is not bound [in the *tefilin*]. For it could be argued by analogy. If [with regard to] *holy to Me* and *when*

YHWH brings you, which are not memorized, but behold they are bound [in the *tefilin*, with regard to] *and YHWH said*, which is memorized, is it not logical that it should be bound [in the *tefilin*? However,] Scripture says: *And you shall bind them*, [which means] these are bound [in the *tefilin*] and *and YHWH said* is not bound [in the *tefilin*]. Still, I [might] say, if *holy to Me* and *when YHWH shall bring you*, which are preceded by other commandments, behold they are bound [in the *tefilin*], the Ten Commandments, which are not preceded by other commandments, how much the more should they be bound [in the *tefilin*]! You [might] say it is an *a fortiori* argument: If *and YHWH said*, which is memorized, is not bound [in the *tefilin*], the Ten Commandments, which are not memorized, is it not logical that they should be bound [in the *tefilin*]? Behold, *holy to Me* and *when YHWH shall bring you* will prove the matter, for they are not memorized but, lo, they are bound [in the *tefilin*]. And they prove the case for the Ten Commandments, for even though they are not memorized, they should be bound [in the *tefilin*. To prove that this reasoning is incorrect.] Scripture says: *And you shall bind* [which means] these are bound, but the Ten Commandments are not bound [in the *tefilin*].

And you shall bind them for a sign on your hand (Deut. 6:8). [There should be] one roll with four inscriptions, for it is an argument by analogy: Because [the] Torah said [to] put [the] *tefilin* on your hand and [to] place the *tefilin* on your head, [I might think that] just as on the head there are four [rolls with] inscriptions, so also on the hand there should be four [rolls with] inscriptions; [however,] Scripture says, *And you shall bind them for a sign on your hand* [which means there should be] one roll with four inscriptions. Or, [perhaps, you can reason as follows:] Just as on the hand there is one roll, so also [the *tefilin*] of the head [should contain] one roll [with four inscriptions; however,] Scripture says: *And they shall be ṭṭpt* (Deut. 6:8), *ṭṭpt* (Ex. 13:16) *ṭwṭpt* (Deut. 11:18); [therefore,] four inscriptions are mentioned. Or, [perhaps] one should make four receptacles for four inscriptions; [however,] Scripture says: *As a memorial between your eyes* (Ex. 13:9) [which means that there should be] one receptacle [which contains] four inscriptions.

On your hand [means] the thick part of the upper arm. You say [it refers to] the thick part of the upper arm or *on your hand* in its literal sense. One can make an argument by analogy: Because Scripture said [to] put [the] *tefilin* on your head [and to] put [the] *tefilin* on your hand, [you might conclude that] just as [with regard to your head you put it on] the thick part of [your] upper head, so also *on your hand* [means you should put it] on the thick part of your upper arm, [and this line of reasoning is correct].

Rabbi Eliezer says: "*On your hand* [means] on the thick part of your upper arm. You say [it means] on the thick part of your upper arm or [it means] *on your hand* in its literal sense; [however,] Scripture says: *And it shall be a sign for you on your hand* (Ex. 13:9). *It shall be a sign for you*, but it shall not be a sign for others."

Rabbi Isaac says: "[You should put the *tefilin* on] the thick part of your upper arm. You say [it means] on the thick part of your upper arm or [it means] *on your hand* in its literal sense; [however,] Scripture says: *And these words . . . shall be upon your heart* (Deut. 6:8) [which means] opposite your heart. And which [place] is this [that is opposite your heart? It is] the thick part of your upper arm."

On your hand. This [refers to your] left hand. You say this is [your] left hand or, perhaps, it [refers to] only [your] right hand? Even though there is no clear proof for the matter, there is a hint [supporting] this position, [for it is said:] *My hand laid the foundations of the earth, and My right hand spread out the heavens* (Isa. 48:13); and it says, *She put her hand to the tent peg and her right hand to the workman's mallet; she struck Sisera a blow, she crushed his head, she shattered and pierced his temple* (Jdgs. 5:26). Behold, in every place [where] *your hand* is said, [it refers to] only the left hand.

Rabbi Nathan says: "*And you shall bind them* (Deut. 6:8), *And you shall write them* (Deut. 6:9). Just as writing [is done] with the right hand, so also [the] binding [should be done] with the right hand."

Rabbi Yosi the net-maker says: "We find that also the right hand is called [merely] "hand," for it is said: *When Joseph saw that his father laid his right hand upon the head of Ephraim, it displeased him; so he took his father's hand, to remove it from Ephraim's head to Manasseh's head* (Gen. 48:13). If this is so, why does Scripture say *on your hand*? [It said this] to include the one [who merely] has a stump [for his left arm] so that he might place [the *tefilin*] on [his] right arm."

And you shall bind them for a sign on your hand, and they shall be a symbol between your eyes (Deut. 6:8) [teaches us that] each time [one places the *tefilin*] of the hand on the hand [he should] place [also the *tefilin*] of the head on the head. From here they used to say: "When one puts on [his] *tefilin*, he places [the *tefilin*] of the hand first, and after that he places [the *tefilin*] of the head. When he removes [them], he removes [the *tefilin*] of the head first, and after that [he removes the *tefilin*] of the hand."

Between your eyes (Deut. 6:8) [means] on the thick part of [your] upper head. You say [it means] the thick part of [your] upper head or perhaps [it means] between your eyes in its literal sense? You can employ an argument by analogy: Because [the] Torah said [to] put [the] *tefilin* on the hand and [to] put [the] *tefilin* on the head [you can conclude that] just as "on the hand" [means] on the thick part of the upper arm, so also "on the head" [means] on the thick part of the upper arm.

Rabbi Judah says: "Because [the] Torah said [to] put [the] *tefilin* on the hand [and to] put [the] *tefilin* on the head [you can conclude that] just as "on the hand" [means] on a place which can be considered unclean by a single [symptom] of skin disease, so also "on the head" [means] on a place which can be considered unclean by a single [symptom] of skin disease."

And you shall write them (Deut. 6:9) [means with a] correct writing. From here they said: "[If] he wrote *ayyins* for *alephs*, *alephs* for ayyins, kafs for *bets*, *bets* for *kafs*, *gimmels* for *ṣaddiks*, *ṣaddiks* for *gimmels*, *reshes* for *daleds*, *daleds*, for *reshes*, *ḥets* for *heys*, *heys* for *ḥets*, *yods* for *vavs*, *vavs* for *yods*, *nuns* for *zyyins*, *zyyins* for *nuns*, *peys* for *ṭeṭs*, *ṭeṭs* for *peys*, straight letters for bent letters, bent letters for straight letters, *samechs* for *mems*, *mems* for *samechs*, opened letters for closed letters, closed letters for opened letters, [or if] he wrote an opened section for a closed section [or] a closed [section] for an opened [section, or if] he did not write with ink, or [if] he wrote a poetic passage similar [to the prose passage he was supposed to write], or [if] he wrote the Divine Name in gold, behold, these [scrolls] must be hidden away [and not used]."

And you shall write them. I might think [that one should write them] on stones. Behold, you can made an analogy: *Write* is said here, and *write* is said elsewhere [in Deut. 27:8: *And you shall write upon the stones all the words of this law very plainly*]. Just as *write* which is said elsewhere [means] on stones, so also *write* which is said here [means] on stones. Or [perhaps] you should turn to this path: *Write* is said here, and *write* is said elsewhere [in Num. 5:23:

Then the priest shall write these curses on a scroll]. Just as *write* which is said elsewhere [means] on a scroll with ink, so also *write* which is said here [means] on a scroll with ink. You make an analogy with this expression, but I will make an analogy with an expression which is different: *Write* is said here, and *write* is said elsewhere. Just as *write* which is said elsewhere [means] on stones, so also *write* which is said here [means) on stones. You say, "It is different!" I learn a thing from [a similar] thing, and I draw an analogy from a thing to a [similar] thing. I learn [about] a thing which is practiced throughout the generations, from a thing which is practiced throughout the generations. I do not learn [about] a thing which is practiced throughout the generations from a thing which [was done] only at [one] time: *Write* is said here, and *write* is said elsewhere. Just as *write* which is said elsewhere [means] on a scroll with ink, so also *write* which is said here [means] on a scroll with ink. Even though there is no proof for this position, there is a hint [which supports] this position, [for it is said,] *Baruch said to them, "He dictated all these words to me, while I wrote them with ink on a scroll"* (Jer. 36:18).

On the doorposts (Deut. 6:9). I might think that there [must be] two doorposts; [however], Scripture says a second time, *doorposts* (Deut. 11:20). "An inclusive term follows an inclusive term [and] serves only to limit"—the words of Rabbi Ishmael. Rabbi Isaac says: "There is no need [for Ishmael's argument]. Behold it says: *And they shall take from the blood and place it on the two doorposts and on the lintel* (Ex. 12:7). This is a prototype. Every place where *doorposts* is said, behold, it includes [instances in which there is] one [doorpost], unless Scripture specifies for you [that there should be] two doorposts."

Your house [means] on the right when [you] enter. You say [it means] on the right when [you] enter, or [perhaps it means] on the right when [you] leave? [However,] Scripture says: *On the doorposts of your house* [which indicates] on your coming [into the house; therefore, you place it] on the right [side] when [you] enter.

And on your gates. I might think [that this means] on the gates of houses, chicken-coops, a cattle shed, straw-shed, a cattle barn, a storehouse, and storehouses of wood, wine, grain, and oil are included; [however,] Scripture says: *Your house.* Just as *your house* is the house in which one dwells, so also *your gates* [refers to the gate of] the house in which [you] dwell. I might think that even the gates of the basilica, the *damasia*, and bathhouses [are included] in this category; [however,] Scripture says, *Your house.* Just as *your house* is a place of honor and the house of [your] dwelling, so also *your gates* [refers to] a place of honor and the house of [your] dwelling. I might think that even the gates of the Temple [are included] in this category; [however,] Scripture says, *Your house.* Just as your house is a profane place, so also *your gates* [refers to] a profane place. From here they said: "The chambers [of the Temple] which open upon sanctified [space] are [themselves] holy; [but the ones] which open upon profane areas are [themselves] profane."

Precious is Israel, for Scripture surrounds them with commandments, *tefilin* on their heads, *tefilin* on their arms, *mezuzot* on [the] openings [of] their [dwellings], fringes on their garments. And David said about them: "*Seven times a day I praise You for Your righteous ordinances* (Ps. 119:164)." He entered to wash, and he saw himself naked. He said: "Woe is me, for I am naked of commandments." He reflected upon [his] circumcision, and he began to compile a praise for it, for it is said: *To the choirmaster, about the eighth, a Psalm of David* (Ps. 12:1). [This can be] compared to a king of flesh and blood who said to his wife: "Wrap yourself in all your jewelry so that you will be pleasing to me." Thus, the Holy One, blessed be He, said to Israel: "My child, be frequently engaged in the commandments so that you will be pleasing to Me; and thus it says, *My love, you are beautiful as Tirsah (ktrṣh)* (Cant. 6:4) [which means] you are beautiful when you are pleasing *(rṣwyh)* to Me."

COMMENTS

Why was this said. The opening section plays with the word *Israel* in Deut. 6:4. The initial midrash takes "Israel" as a reference to Jacob, who was named Israel after his struggle with the angel at Peniel, Gen. 32:22–32. The midrash notes that in Ex. 25:2 Moses is commanded to speak to Israel's, that is, Jacob's, children, and not to the children of Abraham or Isaac, the two other Patriarchs. The midrash suggests that Jacob's children were selected because they were worthy of God's communicating with them. This was the case because Jacob had not produced an unworthy child, such as Ishmael[6] or Esau. Jacob, realizing that he had not yet produced a child unworthy of God's love and protection, constantly worried about the possibility that he might, in fact, produce such an offspring who would be unworthy of having a special relationship with God.

And Jacob vowed a vow saying. The midrash now raises the possibility that Jacob himself was unworthy of having a special relationship with God, for he seems to have said that only if YHWH gave him food and clothes would he accept Him as his God. The midrash offers a different reading for Gen. 28:20–22: And Jacob vowed a vow saying: "If God will be with me and guard me on this road upon which I am walking and give me bread to eat and clothes to wear, so that I will return in peace to my father's house, [I will know that] YHWH [has chosen] to be my God [and that He will not allow me to produce any unworthy children]."[7]

But thus it says. The midrash now brings up the issue of Jacob's first son, Reuben, who had intercourse with his father's concubine. Upon hearing this, Jacob concludes that in fact he has had a son unworthy of God's special concern. In light of the above section, Jacob could have taken this as a sign that YHWH had not chosen to be his God. Jacob remained unsure of the situation until he learned that Reuben had repented and had been forgiven for his misdeed.

And the sons of Jacob were twelve. The midrash asks why Gen. 35:22 states the obvious, that Jacob had twelve sons. It concludes that it was possible for someone to assume that in fact Jacob no longer had twelve sons, for Reuben's sin had made him unworthy to be included among Jacob's offspring. Therefore, by specifically mentioning that Jacob had twelve sons, the Bible indicates that Reuben's sin had been forgiven and that he was worthy enough to be included among Jacob's children.

And they sat down to eat. The midrash suggests that Reuben's sin was forgiven because he fasted as he sought repentance. The midrash asks why the Bible specified that *they* sat down to eat bread. It concludes that this was to teach us that *they* sat down to eat while Reuben fasted.

Let Reuben live and not die. The midrash suggests that Reuben's repentance was accepted, for Moses stated *let Reuben live,* for his sin has been forgiven and his repentance has been accepted, *and not die* as a sinner deserving of death and not deserving of life in the world-to-come. The reference to Reuben's living and not dying is taken by the rabbis as a reference to his no longer deserving death for the sin which he had committed.

After he admonished each one individually. Gen. 49:1 ff. demonstrates that Jacob admonished each of his sons individually, for each is mentioned in the chapter. The midrash states that after Jacob finished speaking to each of his sons individually, he addressed them as a group and warned them not to break away from God. His sons responded by reciting Deut. 6:4, a response to their father in which they assured him that they accepted the fact that YHWH was their God and the only God.

Therefore, it says. The midrash's problem centers on Jacob's prostrating himself at the head of his bed, for the word "prostrate," *hšthwh*, normally, signifies an act of worship.[8] Why did Jacob bow, and to whom did he bow? The midrash answers that Jacob prostrated himself before God and thanked Him for seeing to it that all of his children were worthy of God's love, for they had told Jacob that they accepted the fact that YHWH was their God and that He was the one and only God. The midrash takes up Gen. 47:31 because it discusses the things which Jacob did when he was about to die, the same period of time to which the previous discussion about his admonishing his sons refers.

And there are those who say. These anonymous authorities believed that when Jacob prostrated himself before God at the head of his bed, he did so to thank God for accepting Reuben's repentance.

Another matter. When Jacob prostrated himself upon hearing his sons reciting the *Shema'*, he recited the traditional response: "Blessed be the name of His glorious kingdom for ever and ever." J. Heinemann argues that this line was part of the Temple service and that it was recited at several different times during that service. Because this line was not taken from Bible, as was the *Shema'* and the three paragraphs which follow it in the liturgy, and in fact interrupts the flow of Deut. 6:4–9, it is said under one's breath. The exact time of the introduction of this line after the recitation of Deut. 6:4 and the reason for its inclusion in the worship service is the subject of scholarly disagreement.[9]

From here they said. This anonymous opinion attributed to "they" is the same as Rabbi Yosi's comment in Mishnah *Berakhot* 2:3. The opinion is based on the fact that *Hear, O Israel* can mean that one should recite the line loudly enough so that one's ears hear that *YHWH is our God, YHWH is one*. An anonymous opinion in the above Mishnah disagrees and states that one fulfills the obligation to recite the *Shema'* even if one did not recite it loudly enough for one's ears to hear the words. Yosi's opinion is the one which is eventually accepted.

YHWH is our God. The midrash focuses on what appears to be a needless repetition: Why does the Bible need to state that *YHWH is our God*, for it also stated that *YHWH is one*, which the midrash takes to mean the one and only God? The midrash points to the word *our* in the first part of the verse and concludes that this first part signifies that God has a special relationship with Israel.

Similarly. The midrash brings four examples in which we find a seemingly superfluous reference to that fact that YHWH or ELHYM is the God of Israel. These specific references are not superfluous, and they indicate that YHWH has a special relationship with Israel. We here learn that the Bible does not needlessly repeat itself.

Another matter. Here we find two interpretations of Deut. 6:4. In the first, the midrash focuses on the word *our* in *YHWH is our God;* it states that this means that YHWH is the God over Israel. Next, the midrash interprets the word *one* in *YHWH is one* to mean "only"; therefore, this part of the verse means that YHWH is the God over all those who dwell on the earth. In the second interpretation, the midrash probably began with the end of the verse, for Zech. 14:9, which speaks of the end of time, mentions that *on that day YHWH will be one;* therefore, the reference to YHWH's being one in Deut. 6:4 must refer to the end of time or to the world-to-come. If this is the case, we must conclude that the mention of YHWH's being our God must refer to the present time.[10]

And you shall love. The midrash states that to love God means to perform His commandments out of a feeling of love, and not out of a feeling of fear.[11]

Because it says. Deut. 10:20 states that one should fear YHWH. If we had only Deut. 10:20, we might conclude that just as we usually avoid one whom we fear and approach him or her only when we need something from that person, so also we should avoid God out of fear and approach Him only when we need something from Him. Therefore, Deut. 6:5 was included in the Bible to teach us to love Him so that we learn not to treat Him as we treat a being whom we fear. The midrash ends by making an interesting point: One should not fear God, for it is impossible for a human being to fear and to love the same object. We are supposed to love God, and we can do this only if we do not fear Him. For God, however, things are different. Because there are no distinctions in God, He alone could possess the feelings of fear and love for the same object, for all of His feelings, if in fact God could have feelings, would be the same.[12]

Another matter. He created us, because He alone has the power to create living beings. Although Gen. 12:5 states that Abraham *made* souls in Haran, we should not take this verse literally, for if all of the people on earth joined together and used all of their creative powers and ingenuity, they could not grant life to something as small and as insignificant as a mosquito. Therefore, Gen. 12:5 means that Abraham converted people to a belief in YHWH, and this is accounted to him as if he had given them life.[13]

With all your heart. The rabbis had a realistic view of people, for they realized that each one of us possesses an inclination to do good as well as an inclination to do evil. In addition, the rabbis taught that we need both of these inclinations if the world is to exist. Here, the midrash tells us that we must love God with both of our inclinations; that is, we must love Him with all of our feelings and emotions.[14]

Another matter. With all your heart means that you should unite all of your feelings, thoughts, and emotions so that all of you will love God, and you will not struggle within yourself over your love for Him.

With all your soul. The midrash states that you should love God even at the time of your death, perhaps even if you die because of your allegiance to God. This may be an oblique reference to the martyrdom suffered at the hands of the Romans or others. The reference to Ps. 44:23 seems to support this interpretation.

Rabbi Simeon the son of Menasya says. Suffering for the sake of Judaism or one's belief in God is a good thing; therefore, even though one cannot be slain "all day long," as Ps. 44:23 states, God considers those who have died for the sanctification of His name as if they had suffered every day. [Rabbi Simeon plays on *kl hywm* (all day) as *kl ywm* (every day).] Because the more you suffer the better off you are, this is a form of God's recognizing the value of one who has suffered for His sake.

Simeon the son of Azzai says. Simeon's statement does not appear to refer to martyrdom or to any special death; rather, it simply means that you should love God your whole life, even while you are at death's door. We should never give up our faith in or love of God. For both Simeons, the key word in the verse is "soul," which can also mean "life" or "living one."[15]

Rabbi Eliezer says. Eliezer explains the difference between "soul," *npš*, and "might," *m'd*. "Soul," *npš*, refers to one's life, while "might," *m'd*, refers to one's wealth or property. Thus, we must love God with everything which we have, our whole body and all of our possessions. Both terms were needed so that each of us would be warned to love God with whatever we consider to be most important to us as individuals.

Rabbi Aqiba says. Aqiba notes that if Scripture had said only *with all your soul*, we could have used logic to reach the conclusion that we should love God also with all our material wealth. Therefore, why was this injunction specifically stated? Aqiba's interpretation is a pun; he connects *m'd*, "might," with *mdh*, "measure," and *mdd*, "to mete out." Therefore, *with all your might, m'dk,* means "with every measure, *mdh,* that God metes out, *mwdd,* to you."[16]

And thus David said. In Ps. 116:13, David, the reputed author of the Psalms, states that he called upon YHWH when he was saved from those who threatened him, and in 116:3–4, he called upon YHWH while he was suffering. Thus, David expressed his faith in YHWH when things were good and when things were bad.

And thus Job says. In Job 1:21, things still are going well for Job; yet here he recognizes that YHWH can give benefits to people and that He can take away those benefits if He wishes. However, even at this time, Job states that one should bless God in either case. If while things were going well for him, Job realized that God should be blessed even if He removed the benefits He hàd once granted, is it not logical to assume that when things were bad Job would bless God and have faith that He would again be good to him?

What did his wife say. Job's wife's statement serves as an introduction to Job's claim that we cannot expect to receive only good things from God. How can we expect not to receive some bad things, if we have been rewarded by God? Again, this statement underlies Job's conviction that we should praise God no matter what happens to us.

The men of the generation of the flood. The point which must be established throughout this section is that we should praise God even for the evil which befalls us. We saw that both David and Job praised God no matter what happened to them. We now turn to a logical argument. We know that those who lived at the time of Noah reveled in evil and hated good, Gen. 6:5–13. Is it not logical, therefore, that those of us who are pleased by good should also accept evil? The logic seems to be that if there are those who are pleased when evil occurs, even though they have no good to balance out the evil, how much the more should we who have good things befall us accept the evil which comes upon us. The argument is, of course, weak, for the men of the generation of the flood enjoyed *doing* evil things; we do not know how they felt when evil things occurred *to* them.

Moreover, a man should be happier with chastisements. The midrash now enters into a rather long discourse on the value of suffering. It is one way in which the rabbis addressed the problem of good and evil. Why do the good—the rabbis, the Jews, or whoever—suffer while the wicked—the enemies of the Jews—seem to prosper? The next few sections attempt to explain why this is the case.[17]

For if a man experiences only good. The first answer to the question of why the good suffer is that suffering in this life is a way to balance out one's iniquities. We suffer in this life because we have sinned; that is, we deserve to suffer, and our suffering *now* means that we shall not have to experience punishment for our sins after we die. Note that suffering is deserved and that it is brought about by God. Clearly, evil happens for a reason, and it is all under the control of the one and only God.

Rabbi Eliezer the son of Jacob says. Eliezer also stresses the fact that suffering comes from God. In fact, our suffering is a sign that God loves us and is concerned for our well-being. God chastises us when we err, just as a father punishes his children when they commit a wrong. Thus, our suffering is a form of education, for when we suffer we know that we have done something wrong and that we must reexamine our past actions so that we shall not again act improperly.

Rabbi Meir says. Meir also draws the parallel between the loving father, who punishes his son, and God, who punishes his beloved children, Israel. Meir makes the additional point that no matter how severe the punishment appears, it really was not as severe as it could have been, for God does not punish us in a way equal to the enormity of our sins. Thus, while Meir teaches that God punishes Israel for her sins, he also underscores God's mercy, for He was less harsh than he could have been.

Rabbi Yosi the son of Rabbi Judah says. Yosi argues that suffering is a sign of God's love. Thus, the righteous suffer because God cares about their actions and is concerned about them.

Rabbi Nathan the son of Joseph says. Nathan argues that God made a covenant with Israel, promising her that if she followed His commandments, He would bring her into a good land, the Land of Israel. This promise is preceded by the statement that as a father disciplines his children, so YHWH will chastise Israel if she acts incorrectly. Nathan views God's promise of the Land as equal to His promise that He will treat Israel as His children. Nathan also may imply that the promise of the Land was given because God warned that He would punish Israel if she deserved it.

Rabbi Simeon the son of Yoḥai says. Simeon argues that Israel received the Torah, the Land of Israel, and the promise of the world-to-come only because she also received chastisements from God. It is possible, given the flow of the text, that in this context we are supposed to read Simeon's statement as follows: Because I punish Israel, as a father punishes his beloved children, I will reward Israel, as a father rewards his beloved children. Furthermore, only Israel will receive these gifts, because I consider Israel alone to be My beloved children.[18]

From where do we learn that the Torah. The citation of Prov. 1:2 is based on a pun and a symbolic interpretation of the word "wisdom." The rabbis believed that the word "wisdom" in Proverbs referred to the Torah. In addition, the word for "instruction," *mwsr,* can be connected to the word "chastisement," *ysr.*[19]

The chastisements are the path of life. The word "life" is taken to mean "eternal life," and as we have seen above, when people suffer for their sins in this world they will not be punished after they have died; therefore, they will be worthy to live in the world-to-come. Thus, chastisements in this life assure that our sins are forgiven and that we are worthy to receive the reward of living in the world-to-come.

Rabbi Nehemiah says. Both sacrifices and chastisements are equal and make one pleasing to God, because both bring forgiveness of one's sins. Moreover, chastisements are better than sacrifices, for the former affect a person's body, while the latter come from his or her possessions. This would have been an important concept after the Temple had been destroyed, for with the cessation of the sacrificial cult, the Jews had to discover new ways to achieve forgiveness for their sins.[20]

And one time Rabbi Eliezer was sick. The same assumption underlies the comments of Tarfon, Joshua, and Eleazar: By teaching Torah to his students, a rabbi allows them to live properly in this world and to be worthy of the reward of living in the world-to-come.[21] The rabbis believed that the Torah contained the secrets of the universe and the proper guide to a person's actions. The Torah had two components: the Written Torah, which was available to all and was contained in the Torah scroll of Genesis, Exodus, Leviticus, Numbers, and Deuteronomy, and the Oral Torah, which had been transmitted in an unbroken chain from God to Moses and from Moses to the rabbis. Thus, the rabbis alone possessed the whole of revelation. Because revelation was given by the same God who created the world, it contained the proper duties of human beings. By learning the Torah, one could learn one's proper role in the complexity of creation. and therefore would know what God expected of humans. Because only those who knew the whole Torah, its written and its oral components, could act as they were supposed to act, only they would be worthy of the reward of living in the world-to-come. In brief, a rabbi taught a guide for life in this world and a promise of life in the world-to-come when he taught his Torah to his students and to the population in general. For this reason, a rabbi was indeed a precious thing.[22]

Behold it says. Aqiba argues that chastisements are precious; therefore, Eliezer should be glad he is ill. Aqiba establishes his point by referring to Hezekiah and Manasseh.[23] Prov. 25:1 refers to Hezekiah's having the proverbs of Solomon, and by implication, the rest of the books of the Bible, copied. We are to assume from this that he taught what was in these books to his subjects. In fact, we must assume that Hezekiah knew and taught the Torah because II Kgs. 18:3–6 tells us that *he did right in the eyes of YHWH, trusted in YHWH, the God of Israel, and held fast to YHWH; he did not depart from following him, but kept the commandments which YHWH commanded Moses.* If Hezekiah taught the Torah to Israel, surely he taught it to his own son, Manasseh. If this is the case, why did Manasseh do evil? And if Manasseh did evil, as II Chron. 33:10–11 states, why did he rule in Israel for fifty-five years? Aqiba answers that although Manasseh's father had taught him the Law of God, Manasseh ignored his father's teachings and did not follow God's commandments. In fact, he accepted God's teachings only after he had suffered at the hands of the Assyrians. We learn, however, that after he had suffered at their hands, he humbled himself before YHWH and accepted His teachings. Because of this, YHWH restored him to his throne. From this we learn that chastisements are important; in fact, they are more important than merely being taught Torah.[24]

Rabbi Meir says. Meir suggests that the three elements in Deut. 6:5, *heart, soul,* and *might,* refer to the three Patriarchs, Abraham, Isaac, and Jacob. Isa. 41:8 employs the word *w'hby,* which could mean "My beloved"; however, it could also be read as "he loves Me." Neh. 9:7–8 stated: *You are YHWH, the God who chose Abram . . . and You found his heart faithful before You.* The Wilna Gaon (18th cent.) suggests that this is how Meir made the connection between Abraham's love for God and the word "heart."[25]

With all your soul. Soul is again used in the sense of "life." Meir suggests that Isaac so loved God that he voluntarily bound himself on the altar as a willing sacrifice to God. The story of Abraham's binding of Isaac, Gen. 22, was much discussed by the rabbis. Their comments moved the story well beyond what is contained in Genesis. Although the tradition that Isaac willingly bound himself on the altar is not in the biblical account, it was widespread among the Palestinian Jews of the first centuries of the common era.[26]

With all your might. Might means "wealth," as it did above. Jacob states that he is unworthy to have received all of the wealth which he had acquired from Laban. He states that his wealth is a sign of God's *steadfast love and faithfulness.*

Rabbi Meir says. Although Deut. 6:5 states that we should love God with all our heart, it does not tell us how to accomplish this act; therefore, the Bible had to include Deut. 6:6, which tells us that by taking these words into our heart, we express our love for God. By taking these words to heart, we acknowledge and accept God's existence.

Which I command you this day. The midrash focuses on the word *this.* We are to consider God's words as if they were continually revealed to us and as if they were always relevant. The midrash makes the interesting point that if we do not accept God's revelation as always contemporaneous, we shall probably consider it outdated and possibly ignore it.

From here Rabbi Yoshiah used to say. Yoshiah's comment opens with a pun, for the word "inclination," *yṣr,* could also mean "create," *yṣr.* Thus, Yoshiah's opening statement *ṣryk 'dm lhšby' 't yṣrw* could mean either "a man needs to control his inclination" or "a man needs to adjure his Creator [so that he may subdue his inclination to do evil]." I favor the latter interpretation because each of the examples from the Bible opens with one's taking an oath in the name of God. The conjunction of "heart" with "inclinations" was made above. Whatever is the correct translation of Yoshiah's comment, the verses he cites suggest that one must work at doing good. We must constantly be on our guard to avoid evil, as Abraham did when he refused to take anything except what he absolutely needed for his men from the king of Sodom, whom he had defeated (Gen. 14:10), as Boaz did when he lived up to his obligation as Ruth's kinsman, as David did when he refused to kill Saul, the king appointed by God, when the former snuck into the king's camp, and as Elisha did when he refused to be paid for healing Naaman. Just as the righteous person must constantly be on guard so as not to do evil, and must constantly strive to overcome the inclination to do evil, so also a wicked person must overcome the inclination to do good, as Elisha's servant, Gehazi, did when he ignored Elisha's wishes and ran after Naaman to accept payment from him for Elisha's healing him.

And you shall teach them intensely. The midrash states that one should teach his children God's word so that they can respond immediately to any question they are asked. In effect, God's words must become so ingrained in our minds that they flow automatically from our lips. God's words must become as an intimate friend; again, we must assume that the rabbis read *wisdom* in Prov. 7:4 as "Torah."[27]

Your arrows are sharp. The words of Torah are equated with arrows which protect us from our enemies. Just as arrows protect us from evil, so the words of Torah protect the Jews. Furthermore, Ps. 127:4 equates the arrows with one's children. Therefore, we learn that just as we must prepare our arrows so that they might protect us, so also we must educate our sons in the words of Torah so that they might grow to bring credit to us and to themselves. Just as one who has a quiver full of arrows will not be put to shame, so also one who has properly educated his children in God's law will not be put to shame.[28]

Another matter. At this point, the midrash begins a discussion of the *tefilin*, the ritual boxes which are bound on a person's forehead and on his arm. Here, all of the midrash's arguments lead to conclusions which appear to have been well known. Thus, the midrash attempted to find biblical support for rabbinic practices which were well known and perhaps even widespread. The biblical basis for the use of the *tefilin* is Deut. 6:8, *and you shall bind them for a sign on your hand, and they shall be ṭṭpt between your eyes.* The box on the arms contains Ex. 13:1–10, Ex. 13:11–16, Deut. 6:4–9, and Deut. 11:13–21 written on one scroll and placed in one compartment. The box on the forehead contains each of these passages written on a separate scroll and placed in its own compartment in one box. In addition to the passages which are contained in the *tefilin*, our midrash also discusses the sections which comprise the portion of the liturgy entitled the *Shemaʿ*. In the *Shemaʿ* portion of the service, the worshiper recites Deut. 6:4–9, Deut. 11:13–21, and Num. 15:37–41. Deut. 6:4–9 and Deut. 11:13–21 compose part of the *Shemaʿ* in the liturgy and appear in the *tefilin*.

These should be memorized. The midrash states that to *teach intensely* means to memorize; therefore, Deut. 6:4–9 should be memorized. However, one need not memorize the passages which appear only in the *tefilin*, Ex. 13:1–10 and Ex. 13:11–16.

But it could be argued by analogy. The midrash warns us, for the first time in this selection, that reason unaided by Scripture can lead to incorrect conclusions: If Num. 15:37–41, which is not placed in the *tefilin*, is memorized, should we not conclude that the rest of the passages which appear only in the *tefilin* should be memorized? Therefore, we need Deut. 6:7 to teach us that only the passages of the *Shema'* are memorized, and not the passages which appear only in the *tefilin*.

Yet I might say. This passage is less than clear, and I am not sure of its meaning. The traditional commentators to our text are not much help. Rabbenu Hillel (12th cent.) draws the obvious conclusion that between the giving of the Ten Commandments and Num. 15:37 God revealed "other laws" to Moses.[29] It is possible that this refers to more or less important commandments. Perhaps nothing "precedes," that is, is more important than, the Ten Commandments.[30] In any case, the midrash suggests that logic leads one to conclude that the Ten Commandments should be memorized.

You say that it is an a fortiori argument. The midrash offers an argument which suggests that, contrary to the above conclusion, the Ten Commandments should not be memorized. Just as *when YHWH brings you*, which is included in the *tefilin*, is not memorized, so also the Ten Commandments, which are not included in the *tefilin*, should not be memorized. The argument is as follows: If sections which are in the *tefilin* are not memorized, should we not conclude that any biblical section not in the *tefilin* also should not be memorized?

"And YHWH said" supports your analogy. The midrash now claims that the proper argument by analogy should be made between Num. 15:37 ff. and the Ten Commandments: Because the former is memorized even though, like the latter, it does not appear in the *tefilin*, we should conclude that the Ten Commandments also should be memorized. Because our reason could lead us to the conclusion that the Ten Commandments should be memorized, we need Deut. 6:7 to teach us that this is not the case.

To your children. The equating of rabbis with parents and students with children was popular in talmudic times. Above, we saw that rabbis are more precious than parents, for the former bring people into this world, in a proper sense, and also into the world-to-come, while the latter merely bring their children into this world. The biblical passages cited are clear. We saw above that the rabbis believed that Hezekiah taught Torah to the people of Israel. Furthermore, Elijah was Elisha's teacher, and Elisha was Joash's advisor/guide and also, the rabbis assumed, his teacher.[31]

And you shall speak of them. The midrash states that we should make God's words the main object of our concern; they should direct all of our actions. In short, we should cause our acts to conform to the will of God.[32]

Like so-and-so. David Hoffmann suggested that this refers to Elisha the son of Abbuyah, who, according to tradition, rejected his rabbinic training in favor of Greek philosophical wisdom. Although Elisha is usually called 'aḥer, "the other one," and not "so-and-so," the reference to Lev. 18:4 and the midrash's interpretation of this passage lends credibility to Hoffmann's suggestion.[33]

And thus it says. Prov. 5:17 is taken to mean that the words of Torah shall be the only thing for Jews to study. Furthermore, the study of Torah should not be combined with the wisdom of the non-Jews among whom the Jews lived.

And thus it says. Prov. 6:22 is brought here because it contains three of the four activities mentioned in Deut. 6:7, walking, lying, and rising. In fact, Prov. 6:20 ff. could be seen as an allusion to our text, for it opens by stating: *My son, keep your father's commandment, and forsake not your mother's teaching. Bind them upon your heart always; tie them about your neck. When you walk, it will lead you . . .* Above, we saw that the rabbis are equated with one's parents; therefore, the rabbis could have read this biblical text as follows: My student, keep the commandments of YHWH which the rabbis teach you. The rest of the text could be seen as an obvious reference to Deut. 6:5–9. The three acts mentioned in Proverbs probably led to the interpretation that these refer to life while you are walking on this earth, life when you lie down to die, and life when you rise up again at the time of the Messiah. "Talking" could refer to the discussions which will take place in the world-to-come, for some of the rabbis believed that in the world-to-come the Jews' main activity would be the study and discussion of Torah.[34]

When you lie down: Tannaitic tradition ruled that one was required to recite the *Shema'* twice during the day: In the morning and in the evening. The basis for this ruling was Deut. 6:7. Our passage argued that lying down and rising up refer to the times when one normally lies down to sleep and when one normally gets up in the morning. These terms do not refer to every lying down or rising up. Normal actions are meant because Deut. 6:7 refers to normal activities when it mentions walking on the road and sitting in the house.

One time Rabbi Ishmael: Mishnah *Berakhot* 1:3 contains the following dispute: The House of Shammai say: "In the evening, one should recline and recite [the *Shema'*], but in the morning one should stand up [and recite it], for it is said, *And when you lie down and when you rise up* (Deut. 6:7)." But the House of Hillel say: "Everyone recites [the *Shema'*] in his own way." This Mishnah forms the basis of the story which appears here. There are several versions of this story, and it is interesting to compare them, for they are not all the same.[35]

And you shall bind them: This section of our text is similar to the one discussed above; however, instead of learning which portions are memorized, this passage determines which biblical portions belong in the *tefilin*. The arguments are much the same as those which appeared above, and they assume that the portions which we were told above should be memorized were in fact memorized. Both in this passage and in the similar section above, one has the impression that the author(s) knew which portions were memorized and which were not, which appeared in the *tefilin* and which did not. Both sections appear to be attempts to ground well-known and probably widely accepted practices in the Bible.[36]

And you shall bind: The midrash now derives from the biblical text how many scrolls, boxes, and compartments there are for each of the *tefilin*. I assume that this was well known by the author(s) of our midrash, for clearly the first argument presupposes that the box on the forehead contains four rolls, while the second argument assumes that the box on the hand contains one roll.

For it is an argument by analogy: This argument assumes that the box on the head contains four rolls, each with one inscription. Because we could reason that the box on the hand should contain the same thing as the box on the forehead, we need Deut. 6:8 to teach us that this is not the case. I assume that this conclusion is based on the phrase *for a sign.* Because *sign* is singular, there should be one scroll.

Or perhaps you can reason: The midrash now assumes that the box on the hand contains one scroll; therefore, one should conclude that the box on the forehead should also contain one scroll. For this reason, we need Deut. 6:8, Ex. 13:16, and Deut. 11:18 to teach us that this is not the case. The conclusion that we need four compartments in the box on the forehead is based on the spelling of *twtpt*. In two places, Deut. 6:8 and Ex. 13:16, the word is spelled *ttpt*; however, in Deut. 11:18, the word is spelled *twtpt*. The extra *w* in the latter verse signifies two, not one, compartments, while the other forms of the word each signify one compartment. Therefore, we must conclude that the box on the forehead, the *totapot,* contains four compartments. It is obvious that this argument is forced. It would have been a little better had one of the spellings been *ttpwt*, for the *wt* ending is the feminine plural ending, and one could have argued more reasonably that this spelling signifies "two," while the other spelling signifies "one." Again, the nature of this argument suggests that the conclusion was well known before the argument was advanced.[37]

Or perhaps one should make: The midrash now accepts the above argument and raises the possibility that there should be four boxes on the forehead, instead of just one. This logical conclusion is rejected because Deut. 13:9 mentions that it should be *a memorial,* in the singular; therefore, there should be one box with four compartments, each containing one roll.

On your hand: The problem with the *tefilin* is that rabbinic tradition decided that the *tefilin* of the hand should be worn on the upper arm and that the *tefilin* between the eyes should be worn on the forehead. The midrash now attempts to prove that *on your hand* means the upper arm and that *between your eyes* means the forehead. We have an attempt to ground in Scripture a well-known practice which deviates from the exact wording of the biblical text.

One can make an argument by analogy: This is one of the few instances in which we accept a logical argument. The reason for this is probably the fact that we do not follow the literal meaning of the verse. In fact, the *tefilin* of the hand is not worn on the hand.

Rabbi Eliezer says: The *tefilin* of the hand is worn on the upper arm with the box on the inner part of the arm. Eliezer states that this is so because *a sign for you*, Ex. 13:9, means that it should be seen by you and not by others.

Rabbi Isaac says: Isaac says that the *tefilin* of the hand is worn on the inside of the upper arm because Deut. 6:8 says that *these words . . . shall be upon your heart.* He takes this to mean that they should be opposite your heart; that is, the *tefilin* should be placed on the inside of the upper arm opposite the heart.

On your hand: The midrash now proves that the *tefilin* is to be worn on the left arm. In both Isa. 48:13 and Jdgs. 5:26 the word *hand* is used, and the phrase *right hand* also appears. Therefore, it is logical to conclude that when the word *hand* appears in the Bible without any specification as to which hand it refers, it refers to the left hand.

Rabbi Nathan says: Deut. 6:8 states that *you shall bind them [these words],* and Deut. 6:9 states that *you shall write them [these words].* Therefore, the two acts are analogous. Just as one writes with the right hand, so also one should bind with the right hand. This latter act is possible only if one binds the *tefilin* on the upper part of the left arm.

Rabbi Yosi the net-maker says: Yosi's comment would have been placed better after the anonymous comment which preceded Nathan's remarks. Yosi notes that in Gen. 48:13 the word *hand* clearly refers to the right hand, not to the left hand, as the anonymous comment had claimed. However, Yosi knew that one normally placed the *tefilin* on the left arm; therefore, he concluded that the reference in Gen. 48:13 was needed so that a person who did not have a left arm could be allowed to fulfill the commandment by placing the *tefilin* on his right arm.

And you shall bind them: Because Deut. 6:8 mentions the *tefilin* of the hand and the head, the midrash concludes that if one places the *tefilin* on the hand, he must also place the *tefilin* on the head; that is, both must be worn at the same time. Furthermore, "they" ruled that one must put the *tefilin* on in the same order that they are mentioned in the biblical text; that is, one places the *tefilin* on the hand before one places the *tefilin* on the head. When the *tefilin* are removed, they are removed in the opposite order from the way they were put on.

Between your eyes: This discussion *assumes* that *hand* refers to the thick part of the upper arm. Remember, above the midrash *assumed* that the *tefilin* of the head was placed on the thick part of the upper head and not between the eyes in the literal sense.

Rabbi Judah says: The key to Judah's statement seems to be the phrase by "a single [sympton.]" If there is a place which has both hair and skin, one needs two signs of the skin disease in order to determine whether or not the area is unclean, for both the hair and the skin must change color; see Lev. 13:30. Therefore, the *tefilin* must be placed on a location where there is skin but no hair. This applies to the forehead and to the inner side of the upper arm.

From here they said: "They" warn us that the scrolls must be written correctly. The *ayyins* and the *alephs* are both silent; therefore, they could easily be written for each other. The sets of letters from "the *kafs* for *bets*" to "the *tets* for *peys*" are written similarly, as you can see from the transliteration chart in the front of this volume; therefore, one is warned to write the letters carefully. The "straight letters" are the final forms of the *kaf, nun, pey,* and *saddik;* one is warned to use the final form only at the end of words. *Samechs* and final *mems* are similar in shape; therefore, again one is warned to write them with care. The "open letters for closed . . . " seems to refer to the medial and the final *mem.* According to tradition, some chapters or sections of the Bible are considered opened, while others are considered closed; however, there seems to be little agreement among the medieval authorities concerning the definition of these terms. According to present practice, both opened and closed sections end in the middle of a line. In the case of a closed section, the next section begins on the same line on which the previous section ended. The opened section is marked by the next-line beginning on the line following the one on which the previous section ended. The reference to the poetic passages probably refers to the fact that in the two poems in the Torah, Ex. 15:1–18 and Deut. 32:1–43, the lines of the biblical text are not continuous across the parchment but contain breaks in them. There are open spaces at approximately the same place on each line of the scroll. The spaces in a prose passage occur at irregular intervals across the parchment.[38] The passage tells us that the scrolls must be written with ink and that the Divine Name must not be written with special gold ink. If any of these defects appear, the scroll must be hidden away. It cannot be destroyed because it contains the name of God. These rules apply to the writing of all holy scrolls.

And you shall write them: The midrash now employs several *gezarot shavot* in order to determine if, in fact, the words are to be written on a scroll or on the stonework of the doorpost's themselves. A *gezarah shavah* is an exegetical device which juxtaposes two biblical verses which contain the same word or phrase. In this case, what applies to one passage also applies to the other. The midrash suggests that one should write on the doorposts, because the word *write* occurs in Deut. 6:9 and in Deut. 27:8. Because in the latter context one writes on stone, we could argue that one should also write on stone in the former context. The midrash then responds that one could use a *gezarah shavah,* juxtaposing Deut. 6:9 with Num. 5:23, to prove that one should write on scrolls.[39]

You say it is different: The midrash now objects to the first *gezarah shavah.* It notes that the stones mentioned in Deut. 27:8 are not comparable to what is discussed in Deut. 6:9, for the former were to be erected only once, while the latter refers to an act which is supposed to be done over and over, forever. Therefore, one must reject the former *gezarah shavah* and rely on the latter one. The midrash seems dissatisfied with this conclusion, probably because the practice of the priest's writing on the scrolls concerning the suspected wife was not practiced after the Temple was destroyed; therefore, one could claim that the writing on the doorposts, which was done even after the Temple was destroyed, was not really comparable with the writing of the scrolls for the suspected wife, which probably was suspended shortly after the Temple was destroyed.[40] The midrash then states that although there is no clear proof that one should write the words mentioned in Deut. 6:9 on a scroll, there is a hint that this is the case from the fact that Baruch wrote *these words,* a phrase which also occurs in the context of Deut. 6:9, on a scroll, with ink.

On the doorposts: The midrash now asks whether, if there are not two doorposts, one still needs to place *these words* on a single doorpost. Logic suggests that one needs two doorposts because the word *mzwzt* seems to be plural, for *wt,* even spelled without the *w,* is a feminine plural ending.

The words of Rabbi Ishmael: The midrash attributes to Ishmael the exegetical principle that if a plural form follows a plural form, it is only to limit the application of the rule. I have no idea exactly how this principle works; although it is attributed to Ishmael in several places.[41] From this context, we are to conclude that Ishmael would have argued that this pattern limits the application of the rule to a single doorpost.

Rabbi Isaac says: Isaac rejects Ishmael's exegetical principle, and the former argues by means of a prototype. In a prototype, one verse (or two verses) is taken as the example of what should be done. In this case, Ex. 12:7 specifically refers to *two doorposts;* therefore, when two doorposts are meant, the Bible will specifically state that *two* are required. Isaac's argument is based on the fact that the Bible does not employ words needlessly: If "two" were implied in the word *mzwzt,* the word *two* would not have been needed in Ex. 12:7; therefore, we must conclude that the word *mzwzt* by itself does not imply the number two.

Your house: According to Rabbenu Hillel (12th cent.), *bytyk* was read as *b'tk,* "your coming"; therefore, the text refers to the side of the doorposts as you come into the house.[42] In the Babylonian Talmud, *Menaḥot* 34a, II Kgs. 12:10 is quoted to establish that we are talking about the right side of the door as one enters: *And Jehoiada the priest took a chest, and bored a hole in its side, and set it beside the altar, on the right side as one comes into YHWH's house.* Also, in the Babylonian Talmud, Rabbah explains that because men normally place their right foot forward first when entering a house, the *mezuzah* should be placed on the right side when entering a house. Yet neither Rabbah's statement nor II Kgs. 12:10 appears in our midrash; therefore, we have no idea why the author(s) of this text decided that the *mezuzah* must be placed on the right side. Again, it appears that our text has attempted to find biblical justification for a well-established practice.

On your gates: The midrash now establishes that a *mezuzah* is placed only on the gates surrounding your house and not on all the gates which may be on your land. The midrash employs an argument by analogy: Just as *your house* refers to your dwelling, so also *your gates* must refer to the gates around your dwellings. Just as *your house* refers to your dwelling, which is a respectable place, so also *your gates* refers to a place in which you dwell, which is also a respectable place. For the Jews, neither a bathhouse nor a church would be a respectable place.[43]

Precious is Israel: This section of Sifre Deuteronomy ends with a short "homily." The people of Israel's special relationship with God is evidenced by the fact that they and their belongings are surrounded with commandments; that is, everywhere they turn, the people of Israel encounter things which remind them of their God and with which they testify to His existence.

For it is said: Ps. 12:1 refers to circumcision because it is *about the eighth,* which is taken as a reference to the eighth day, the day on which a Jewish male is circumcised.[44]

Thus, the Holy One, blessed be He: We have a pun. The word *trṣh* is connected with the word "pleasing," *rṣwyh.* The root of both is *rṣh.*

CONCLUSIONS

As I noted in the introduction, we have before us an exegesis of the biblical section which composes the *Shema'* in the liturgy. The midrash opens with a surprising discussion, for it takes *Israel* in Deut. 6:4 as a reference to Jacob. The theme of the opening paragraph is that Jacob and his sons, and by implication all upright Jews, all Children of Israel, were worthy of having a special relationship with God. This is evidenced by the fact that Jacob was concerned that his sons would be worthy of God's love, and that his sons assured him that they did believe that YHWH was the one and only God. This point is made by their recitation of Deut. 6:4. Therefore, every time a Jew, one of the Children of Israel, recites the *Shema'*, he or she demonstrates that an unworthy offspring has not arisen among Jacob's, Israel's, children.

The midrash opens by stating that *Hear O Israel* refers to Jacob. We are told that Jacob was honored to be addressed in this fashion because he daily worried that an unworthy offspring would appear among his children.

The next paragraph deals with Gen. 28:20 and states that Jacob would know that YHWH would be his God if in fact no unworthy children appeared among his offspring. In this paragraph the midrash establishes Jacob's integrity even though some had read the verse in a way which was derogatory to Jacob.

The midrash brings forth the case of Reuben's having had intercourse with his father's concubine as a possible challenge to the assumption that all of Jacob's sons were worthy of God's special love. We are told that Reuben did sin; however, he repented, and his repentance was accepted. From this we may conclude that all of Jacob's sons were worthy of God's special love.

After an aside, which discusses Reuben, the midrash returns to a treatment of Deut. 6:4. We learn that upon his death, Jacob admonished his sons to love God. His sons responded by reciting Deut. 6:4, thus assuring their father that they accepted YHWH as their God, for He is the one and only God. This section ends by quoting Gen. 47:31. It is included here because it appears in the context of Jacob's dying. The verse becomes the subject of the next two paragraphs.

We are presented with three interpretations of Gen. 47:31. The verse signifies that (1) Jacob gave thanks to God that all of his sons were worthy of God's love, (2) Jacob gave thanks that Reuben had repented, (3) Jacob recited the liturgical response to Deut. 6:4.

151

The midrash now offers a point of halakhah; the word *hear* in Deut. 6:4 tells us that we should recite the *Shema'* loudly enough so that our ears hear our words. This legal point intrudes into a nonlegal discussion of the biblical text.

We next find two interpretations of the phrase *YHWH is our God.* The first focuses on the seemingly repetitious nature of Deut. 6:4, for if YHWH is one, is it not logical that He is also our God? The midrash answers that the repetition teaches us that God loves Israel in a special degree. The point is further illustrated by four other biblical passages. The second and third interpretations also deal with the repetition in Deut. 6:4: We learn that YHWH is our God and the God of all people, and we discover that He is God in this world and in the world-to-come.

The midrash now brings us two explanations of the word *love* in Deut. 6:5. The first explanation tells us that one must worship God out of love, and not from fear, and the midrash makes the interesting point that there are no distinctions in God. The second interpretation tells us to love God as Abraham did; however, the point of the section is that Abraham loved God by converting people to a belief in Him.

Next, we are presented with two explanations of the phrase *with all your heart* in Deut. 6:5. The first tells us that we should love God with all our "inclinations," while the second tells us that *all* means that we should not divide our heart against God. These two interpretations seem to be two ways of saying the same thing.

The phrase *with all your soul* serves as an introduction to a long aside about the importance of chastisements. This is a rabbinic attempt to deal with the problem of evil. First, we are told to love God even while we are dying. The paragraph also makes the point that suffering martyrdom for the sake of YHWH is a good thing. The more we suffer for the sake of a belief in God, the better it is. Simeon makes a similar point: We should love God until we die. Eliezer offers an aside: Deut. 6:5 refers to both *soul* and *might* so that we might learn to love God with whatever is more precious to us, our life or our wealth.

Aqiba changes the direction of the discussion. Aqiba argues that Deut. 6:5 teaches us that we must love God no matter what happens to us. To illustrate his point, he refers to David and to Job, and either Aqiba or the anonymous midrash offers the example of the men of the generation of the flood.

At this point, the midrash moves into a rather long discussion of the value of chastisements. The lesson is that the righteous—rabbis, Jews, or whoever—suffer as a sign of God's special care for them. We learn that God causes suffering, and that suffering is not necessarily bad. Chastisements bring pardon for iniquities, provide evidence that God treats the sufferer as a father treats his children, are not as bad as they could have been, and prove that the name of God rests on the sufferer.

Nathan now states that a covenant, that is, a promise by God to Israel, was made through chastisements. Simeon's comment, although independent of Nathan's, expands on the latter's discussion. Simeon argues that the Torah, the Land of Israel, and the world-to-come were all given through chastisements. Next, Nehemiah argues that chastisements make one pleasing to God, just as the sacrifices did while the Temple stood. In fact, Nehemiah argues, chastisements make one more pleasing to God than did the sacrifices.

Next follows a story about a time when Eliezer was sick. Tarfon, Joshua, Eleazar, and Aqiba visited the ailing sage. The first three focus on the importance of a rabbi and his value to his students in particular, and to Israel in general. Aqiba, however, discusses the chastisements. While the others had claimed that rabbis are precious, Aqiba argues that chastisements are precious. The flow of the story suggests that Eliezer accepted Aqiba's analysis of the situation. Aqiba proves that one deserves chastisements and that they improve a person's character from the example of Hezekiah and Manasseh. The example implies that a rabbi may fail to influence his student in a positive way; therefore, God may have to send chastisements upon the student in order to shape his character. One could draw the analogy further from the rabbis' students in particular to the Jews in general.

Meir offers an interpretation of the whole of Deut. 6:5 and equates each of the bodily elements in the verse with one of the Patriarchs. Meir's comment returns us to the biblical text. His interpretation of Deut. 6:6 demonstrates that Deut. 6:5 and 6:6 must be interpreted in light of each other. By reading these two verses together, we learn that one loves God (Deut 6:5) by taking His words to heart (Deut. 6:6).

The anonymous midrash now makes an interesting point: The phrase *this day* in Deut. 6:6 indicates that the Bible must be made relevant to each new generation and each new situation. Because people follow only new ordinances, we must be sure that the Bible is never viewed as old or outdated.

Yoshiah takes the phrase *upon your heart* in Deut. 6:6 as an admonition that one must work hard to do good. As I noted in my comments, we seem to have a pun. The lesson is that we must seek God's help to overcome our inclination to do evil. However, even people who are evil by nature must strive extra hard not to do good.

Next we find two interpretations of the phrase *teach them intensely to your children.* The first argues that we always should be ready with words of Torah so that we might easily respond to questions which are posed to us. One who possesses the words of Torah is compared to one who has a quiver full of arrows, for both the arrows and the words of Torah offer protection.

The second interpretation of the phrase from Deut. 6:7 discusses the biblical sections which appear in the *tefilin* and those which form the liturgical section of the *Shemaʿ*. The question is, which of these phrases are to be memorized and which are not? The argument seems artificial and circular. It appears that we have an attempt to ground in the Bible a well-known practice. This is the process I identified above as finding a proof-text. This passage does share with the previous one the assumption that to teach intensely means to memorize.

The next three paragraphs equate children in Deut. 6:7 with students, and rabbis with parents. This latter equation was found earlier, in the story about Eliezer's illness, where we were told that rabbis are more important to us than our parents. The identification of children with students and parents with teachers is supported by references to several biblical passages.

From *you shall speak of them* in Deut. 6:7, we learn that the words of Torah should be our main topic of conversation and that we should use them to guide our normal activity. In addition, we are told that we should not mix revelation with the wisdom of other nations. This paragraph ends with an aside which teaches us that the words of Torah will be relevant at all times: In this life, in the life in the world-to-come, and in the days of the Messiah.

The midrash now makes another halakhic, legal, point: We are supposed to recite the *Shemaʿ* when we normally lie down and when we normally rise up.

The story of Ishmael and Eleazar, which follows, appears in several places. The account is based on a disagreement between the House of Hillel and the House of Shammai, two early groups of sages, which appears in Mishnah. In fact, the story makes no sense without that disagreement. It is included here because Deut. 6:7 underlies the disagreement in Mishnah and explains why the actions of the rabbis are important. The story seems to be an attempt to ensure that people will follow the rulings of the Hillelites and not the Shammaites. It discusses the posture one takes when reciting the *Shemaʿ*, a logical next step after the midrash has determined when this section of Deuteronomy should be recited.

The midrash now moves to several discussions of halakhah, law; however, in each case the arguments are circular and artificial. Throughout, it appears as if the midrash is attempting to ground accepted practices in the biblical text, another example of finding proof-texts. Constantly, one part of the argument assumes something *which will not be assumed elsewhere*. The clause *and you shall bind them* serves as the introduction to a discussion of which biblical sections are bound in the *tefilin*. This paragraph assumes points made earlier about which sections are memorized and which are not. The earlier section, on the other hand, assumed that certain sections were bound in the *tefilin* while others were not. Each section assumes what the other section attempts to demonstrate.

The next section attempts to establish the number of scrolls and sections each box of the *tefilin* contains. As I noted in my comments, the conclusion is based on an artificial interpretation of the spellings of *ṭwṭpt*.

The next section *assumes* that the *tefilin* of the head is not placed between the eyes but is placed on the thick part of the upper head. Below, the midrash will attempt to prove that this is the case, while *assuming* that the *tefilin* of the hand is placed on the thick part of the upper arm, the point established here. The final ruling is based on a logical argument, because we do not, in fact, follow the literal meaning of the biblical text.

There follow two additional proofs for the rule that one places the *tefilin* of the hand on the thick part of the upper arm. Eliezer bases his proof on Ex. 13:9, which states that *it shall be a sign for you*. Eliezer suggests that this means that the box should be placed where only *you* can see it. Isaac states that the phrase *on your heart* in Deut. 6:8 means that the box should be opposite your heart.

After establishing that the *tefilin* of the hand goes on the thick part of the upper arm, the midrash demonstrates on which arm the box should go. It argues that the word *hand*, without any modification, refers to the left hand. Nathan argues that the "binding" in Deut. 6:8 should be interpreted in conjunction with the "writing" in Deut. 6:9. Just as the "writing" is done with the right hand, so also the "binding" should be done with the right hand. Yosi argues that *hand* without any modification could refer to the right hand. He accepts the principle that the *tefilin* should be placed on the left arm; however, one who does not have a left arm may place the *tefilin* on the right arm. In my comments, I suggested that Yosi's comment would have fit better after the anonymous statement preceding Nathan's remarks.

The next paragraph notes that the *tefilin* of the hand and the *tefilin* of the head are mentioned in the same verse; therefore, they both must be worn. One cannot wear only one of them. The midrash also claims that one should put them on in the order in which they appear in the biblical text. However, they are to be removed in reverse order.

The midrash now proves, by means of a logical argument, that one places the *tefilin* of the head on the thick part of the upper head. This argument *assumes* that one places the *tefilin* of the hand on the thick part of the upper arm. It is a logical argument because we do not follow the literal meaning of the biblical text.

Judah also demonstrates that one should place the *tefilin* of the hand on the thick part of the upper arm, and the *tefilin* between the eyes on the thick part of the upper head; however, he bases his proof on the laws of purity. For a reason which is not made explicit in his comment, Judah argues that one should place the *tefilin* on a spot which can be declared unclean by the appearance of one of the symptoms of a skin disease. This means that one should place the *tefilin* on a spot where there is skin without any hair.

We next find two interpretations of the clause *and you shall write them*.

The first tells us that one must be careful when preparing the scrolls. The text refers to letters which may be confused with one another either because they sound the same or because they are written in a similar manner. In addition, the midrash warns us about the proper use of the final and medial forms of certain letters. We are also told that the biblical portions should be written on the parchment to be included in the *tefilin* and *mezuzot* in the exact same way in which they appear on the Torah scroll.

The second interpretation of this phrase raises the possibility that one should write the passages on the stonework of the doorway instead of on a scroll. The midrash offers two *gezerot shavot*, analyzes the appropriateness of each analogy, and ends by arguing that even the analogy which the text favors may not be good enough to establish the point the midrash wishes to make.

The midrash next discusses the word *doorposts* in Deut. 6:9 and asks if there must be two doorposts before one is required to affix a *mezuzah*. Ishmael offers an obscure exegetical principle to prove that this is not the case, and Isaac employs a prototype to prove that one needs to attach a *mezuzah* even if there is only one doorpost.

After establishing that one needs to affix a *mezuzah* even if there is only one doorpost, the midrash proves that one places the *mezuzah* on the right side of the door as one enters, and that one should place them only on the doors and gates to houses in which people dwell. We are told, in addition, that *mezuzot* need not be placed on those doors of the Temple and its environs which open onto holy space.

The midrash ends with a short homily which states that Israel's special relationship to God is evidenced by the fact that she is surrounded by commandments. In fact, it is her observance of these commandments which makes her pleasing to God. The end of this section of Sifre Deuteronomy complements the opening of the section, for both the beginning and the end stress the special relationship which exists between YHWH and Israel.

Although an exegesis of Deut. 6:4–9, the midrash moves far beyond the biblical text. From its opening interpretation of the word *Israel* until its closing homily, the midrash seems less concerned with the text of Deuteronomy than with making specific theological points. The midrash's foremost concern is the special relationship which exists between Israel and YHWH, for our selection opens and closes with this point. This relationship is evidenced by the commandments which the Jews observe and by the suffering which they have experienced. In a rather lengthy discussion of chastisements, our text makes the point that God causes Israel to suffer and that this suffering is positive. Although our text does deal with some legal matters, the discussion of the *tefilin* and the *mezuzot* seems forced, circular, and artificial. Throughout, it appears that our author(s) have attempted to supply biblical proof-texts for well-known practices.

This selection has features in common with the other selections we have read to this point. Frequently, they all contain several interpretations of a given verse. They all assume that nothing in the Bible is superfluous and that given verses should be interpreted in light of other verses. They all move beyond the biblical text; however, our selection from Sifre Deuteronomy seems to move farther away from the text it interprets than our other midrashic passages. Again, every word and element of the biblical text is interpreted; details of the Bible are the source for many and varied comments.

It is impossible to determine the audience of this midrash. The messages which it contains would have been important to all Jews. However, the emphasis on the special relationship between YHWH and Israel, which is marked by God's surrounding Israel with commandments and Israel's following the commandments, and the attempt to demonstrate that the rabbinic practices should be followed with regard to the *tefilin* and *mezu-zot*, even when these practices do not conform to the exact wording of the biblical text, suggest that this may be a propagandistic text in support of the rabbinic movement. This suggestion is also supported by the glowing description of the rabbis vis-à-vis one's natural parents. Whether this was directed toward the rabbis or the nonrabbinic Jewish population is unclear. There is no doubt, however, that this text was composed by men deeply embedded in the rabbinic tradition and learned in its laws and methods of biblical interpretation.

NOTES

1. D. Hoffmann, *Zur Einleitung in die halachischen Midraschim* (Berlin, 1886–87), 52.

2. M. D. Herr, s.v. "Sifrei," *Encyclopedia Judaica* XIV, 1519–1521.

3. Ibid., 1519–1520.

4. J. N. Epstein, *Prolegomena ad Litteras Tannaiticas*, ed. E. Z. Melamed (Jerusalem: 1958), 703–724.

5. This translation is based on L. Finkelstein, *Siphre ad Deuteronomium* (New York, 1959), 49–68.

6. The rabbinic tradition did not picture Ishmael in a positive light because of the Bible's focus on Isaac, the son of Abraham *and* Sarah. L. Ginzberg, *The Legends of the Jews* (Philadelphia, 1913), I, 237–240.

7. See Babylonian Talmud *Pesaḥim* 56a.

8. F. Brown, S. R. Driver, and C. A. Briggs, *A Hebrew and English Lexicon of the Old Testament* (Oxford, 1962), šḥh, 1005–1006.

9. J. Heinemann, *Prayer in the Talmud,* translated by R. Sarason (Berlin, 1977), 127.

10. The issue of the Messiah and what will occur at the "end of time" is a complex and contradictory matter in rabbinic Judaism. E. E. Urbach, *The Sages—Their Concepts and Beliefs,* translated by I. Abrahams (Jerusalem, 1975), 492–649. G. Scholem, *The Messianic Idea in Judaism* (New York, 1972), 1–36. L. Landman, *Messianism in the Talmudic Era* (New York, 1979). S. H. Levey, *The Messiah: An Aramaic Interpretation* (Cincinnati, 1974).

11. Urbach, 400–419.

12. On the oneness of God and His attributes, see Urbach, 19–65. G. F. Moore, *Judaism in the First Centuries of the Christian Era: The Age of the Tannaim* (Cambridge, 1966), I, 357–444. A. Marmorstein, "The Unity of God in Rabbinic Literature," *Hebrew Union College Annual,* I, 467–499.

13. Ginzberg, I, 195–217.

14. Urbach, 471–483. S. Schechter, *Aspects of Rabbinic Theology: Major Concepts of the Talmud* (New York, 1961), 242–292.

15. M. Jastrow, *A Dictionary of the Targumin, the Talmud Babli and Yerushalmi, and the Midrashic Literature* (New York, 1971), 926.

16. Eliezer's and Aqiba's statements appear on Babylonian Talmud *Berakhot* 61b. See also Babylonian Talmud *Berakhot* 54a and Mishnah *Berakhot* 9:5.

17. On the issue of "chastisements," see Urbach, 444–448, and Moore, II, 248–256.

18. See Babylonian Talmud *Berakhot* 5a.

19. On the identification of Torah with Wisdom, see M. Hengel, *Judaism and Hellenism: Studies in Their Encounter in Palestine during the Early Hellenistic Period*, translated by J. Bowden (Philadelphia, 1974), 188–195.

20. See, for example, J. Neusner, *A Life of Rabban Yohanan ben Zakkai* (Leiden, 1970), 188–195.

21. Ibid., 57–117.

22. Urbach, 286–399. J. Neusner, *A History of the Jews in Babylonia* (Leiden, 1965–70), III, 94–194. Babylonian Talmud *Sanhedrin* 101a.

23. On Hezekiah and Manasseh, see Ginzberg, IV, 266–281.

24. Compare *Mekhilta deRabbi Ishmael, BaHodesh* 10.

25. Wilna Gaon, loc. cit.

26. On the legends concerning the "binding of Isaac," see S. Siegal, *The Last Trial* (Philadelphia, 1967).

27. See Babylonian Talmud, *Qiddushin* 30a.

28. Ibid.

29. Rabbenu Hillel on *mṣwt 'ḥrt*.

30. This interpretation was suggested by Professor Alan Avery-Peck.

31. See Babylonian Talmud *Sanhedrin* 19a.

32. On Babylonian Talmud *Yoma* 19a this is attributed to Aḥa.

33. Quoted by Finkelstein, 61–62, comment on line 16. For an excellent *novel* about Elisha the son of Abbuyah, see M. Steinberg, *As a Driven Leaf* (New York, 1939).

34. J. Neusner, *There We Sat Down* (Nashville: 1972), 72–97.

35. G. Porton, *The Traditions of Rabbi Ishmael* (Leiden, 1976–1982), I, 15–22.

36. See Babylonian Talmud *Menahot* 34b.

37. Ibid. Compare the dispute between Ishmael and Aqiba, Porton, III, 123–124. See also *Mekhilta deRabbi Ishmael, Pisha* 17.

38. See Babylonian Talmud *Shabbat* 103b. For a good discussion of the issues discussed here and a diagram of the poetic and prose passages, see H. Freedman, *Shabbat*, in *The Babylonian Talmud*, ed. I. Epstein (London, 1938), 497, notes 2–8, and 498, notes 1–3.

39. See Babylonian Talmud *Menahot* 34a.

40. On the issue of the Red Heifer and the *Soṭah* after the destruction of the Temple, see the rather uncritical article by V. Eppstein, "When and How the Sadducees Were Excommunicated," *Journal of Biblical Literature*, LXXXV, 2 (June 1966).

41. Porton, IV, 203, no. 30; 177, no. 32; 181, no. 17; 182–183, no. 34.

42. Rabbenu Hillel on *bytk*.

43. See Babylonian Talmud *Yoma* 11a.

44. For a passage similar to the one attributed to Meir, see Tosefta *Berakhot* 6:25.

⑥ Genesis Rabbah

Genesis Rabbah is our premier example of an expositional aggadic (nonlegal) midrash. The collection includes a commentary on virtually the whole Book of Genesis; only genealogical passages and those which furnish no material for exposition, such as the reenactment account of Abraham's servants in Gen. 24:35–48, are omitted.[1] The text is divided into *parashot* (sections) and is characterized by proems *(petihot)*, either one or many, at the opening of most sections. The proem serves as an introduction to the *parashah*. Most of the proems open with a verse from the Writings and move to the first verse or verses of the *parashah* they introduce.[2] Genesis Rabbah contains a wide variety of material. Some of its passages are highly philosophical, and much of it is designed to counter the popular philosophical theories of the period of its composition.[3] Often, the commentary contains references to contemporary events and persons, and J. Theodore, the editor of the Hebrew critical edition of the text, suggested that "it is characteristic [of Genesis Rabbah] to view the personages and conditions of the Bible by light of contemporary history."[4]

The organization of the text is rather loose, and this allows the editor(s) to include rather long digressions which may relate either to the verse upon which the text is commenting or to an exegetical comment included as an interpretation of the verse or word.[5] The text contains many repetitions, and as often as not, a passage is not changed to fit its new context when it is repeated.[6] Although most scholars seem to agree that Genesis Rabbah was edited sometime in the fifth century of the common era, neither its exact date of appearance nor the name(s) of its editor(s) are known to us.[7]

Our selection expounds Genesis 1:26–28.

And God said: "Let us make Adam in our image, according to our likeness. And they shall have dominion over the fish of the sea and the birds of the heavens, and the beasts, and all the earth and all the creeping things that creep on the earth." And God created Adam in His image; in the image of God He created him; male and female He created them. And God blessed them, and God said to them; "Be fruitful and multiply, and fill the earth and subdue her, and have dominion over the fish of the sea, and the birds of the heavens, and all the wild beasts that creep on the earth."

The passage opens with two proems. The first centers on the Primordial Adam, and we learn that he was not at all like us. The second tells us that we should not inquire about the things God was doing before He created the world, for these matters are too mysterious for us to understand. The midrash deals with the obvious problem of Gen. 1:26: With whom did God take counsel when He said, "Let us make Adam"? Several answers appear; however, they all stress that there is only one God, that He is supreme, and that He can do whatever He wishes to do. Even when God took counsel with the angels, He ignored them or withheld information from them. There are two major themes in this section: (1) the nature of the Primordial Adam, and (2) the Oneness of God. Because the rabbis considered Gen. 1:28 to speak of the Primordial Adam, Adam's nature is much different from what we would expect, and the discussion of his nature is probably not what we thought we would find. Unlike Sifra, Mekhilta, and Sifre Numbers, Genesis Rabbah does not deal with the issue of revelation versus reason. Like Sifre Deuteronomy, this selection from Genesis Rabbah is more interested in theology than in the plain meaning of the biblical text.

And[8] God said: "Let us make Adam . . ." (Gen. 1:26). Rabbi Yohanan opened [his discourse with] *You hemmed me in behind and before ('ḥwr wqdm ṣrtny)* (Ps. 139:5). Said Rabbi Yohanan: "If man is worthy, he [may] partake of two worlds [this world and the world-to-come], for it is said, *You hemmed me in behind and before.* [But] if [he] is not [worthy], he shall be brought to account, for it is said: *And You laid Your palm upon me* (Ps. 139:5)." Said Rabbi Jeremiah the son of Leazar: "When the Holy One, blessed be He, created the Primordial Adam, He created him [as] an androgynous being, for it is said, *Male and female He created them [and He blessed them and He called their name Adam]* (Gen. 5:2)." Said Rabbi Samuel the son of Nahman: "When the Holy One, blessed be He, created the Primordial Adam, He created him double-faced [in one body], and He divided him and made [for] him a back here and a back there." They objected to this: "But, behold, is it [not] written: *And He took one of his ribs (mṣl'tyw)* (Gen. 2:21)?" He [Samuel] said to them: "[This means that God made Eve] from his side, [for the root ṣl' could mean 'side' as well as 'rib',] just as you say [it does in Ex. 26:20, *And from the second] side (ṣl') of the Tabernacle.*" Rabbi Tanḥuma in the name of Rabbi Banayah [and] Rabbi Berekhyah in the name of Rabbi Eleazar [said]: "He created him [as] an unformed mass *(gwlm)* and he stretched from one end of the universe to the other; thus it is written, *Your eyes beheld my unformed substance (gwlmy)* (Ps. 139:16)." Rabbi Joshua the son of Rabbi Nehemiah [and] Rabbi Judah the son of Simon in the name of Rabbi Leazar [said]: "He created him [so that] he filled the whole universe. From where [do we learn that he stretched] from the east to the west? [We learn it from Ps. 139:5,] for it is said, *You formed me from west to east ('ḥwr wqdm ṣrtny).* From where [do we learn that he stretched] from the north to the south? [We learn it from Deut. 4:32,] for it is said, *[Since the day that God created Adam upon the earth,] from one end of the heavens until the other end of the heavens.* And from where [do we learn that Adam filled] even the voids of the universe? Scripture says: And You placed Your palm on me (Ps. 139:5), thus you say *Withdraw Your hand from me* (Job 13:21)." Said Rabbi Leazar: "*Behind ('ḥwr)* [refers to his being] the last of the deeds of the last day [of creation] *('ḥrwn)* and *before (qdm)* [refers to his being] first of the deeds of the last day [of creation]." This agrees with the opinion of Rabbi Leazar, for said Rabbi Leazar: "*[And God said:] 'Let the earth bring forth living creatures'* (Gen. 1:24). This [refers to] the soul of the Primordial Adam." Rabbi Simeon the son of Laqish said: "*Behind ('ḥwr]* [refers to his being last of] the deeds of the last day [of creation], and before *(qdm)* [refers to his being created among the] deeds of the first day [of creation]." This agrees with the opinion of Rabbi Simeon the son of Laqish, for said Rabbi Simeon the son of Laqish: "*And the spirit (rwḥ) of God hovered [over the face of the waters]* (Gen. 1:2). This (refers) to the soul of the Primordial Adam; thus you say, '*And the spirit of YHWH shall rest upon him* (Isa. 11:2).' " Said Rav Naḥman: "[Adam] was last ('ḥwr) of the deeds [of creation], but [he was] the first qdm [to receive the] punishments." Said Rabbi Samuel the son of Tanḥum: "Also [Adam's] praise [of God] only [came] last *(b'ḥrwnh),* for thus it is written: *Praise YHWH. Praise YHWH from the heavens.* The passage continues until *He has made a dcree and it shall not be transgressed.* After than [it says], *Praise YHWH from the earth.* And after that [it says], *Kings of the earth [and all peoples, princes and all rulers of the earth! Young men and maidens together, old men and children! Let them praise the name of YHWH]* (Ps. 148:1–11)."

Said Rabbi Simlai: "Just as [Adam's] praise [of God] came only after [the praise given Him by the] domesticated animals, the wild beasts, and the birds, thus [Adam's] creation was only after [the creation of the] domesticated animals, the wild beasts, and the birds. At first [we read], *And God said: 'Let the waters swarm'* (Gen. 1:20), and after all of them [were created] it is said, *'Let us make Adam'* (Gen. 1:26)."

Rabbi Ḥama the son of Ḥanina opened [his discourse with] *Do you not know this from of old, since Adam was placed on earth* (Job. 20:4). Said Rabbi Ḥama the son of Ḥanina: "[It is] comparable to a country which was supplied by ass-drivers, and they would ask one another what the market price was in the country that day. The sixth [ass-driver to arrive in the country] would ask the fifth [ass-driver who was just leaving the country]. The fifth [to arrive in the country] asked the fourth. The fourth asked the third. The third asked the second. The second asked the first. But the first [ass-driver], of whom would he ask? Would he not ask the people of the country, for they were engaged in the public affairs of the country? Thus, the things [which God created] each day would ask one another: 'What has the Holy One, blessed be He, created among you today?' Those [created on the] sixth [day] asked those [created on the] fifth [day]. Those of the fifth asked those of the fourth. Those of the fourth asked those of the third. Those of the third asked those of the second. Those of the second asked those of the first. But those of the first [day of creation], of whom would they ask? Would they not ask the Torah, for she preceded the creation of the universe [by two thousand years]; thus it is written: *[YHWH created me at the beginning of His work]* then *I was beside Him, like a master workman, and I was daily His delight* (Prov. 8:22–30)? And one of the days of the Holy One, blessed be He, [is equivalent to] one thousand [of our] years, for it is said: *For a thousand years in Your sight are but as yesterday* (Ps. 90:4). Behold, this is [the meaning of] *Do you not know this from of old.* The Torah knows what was before the creation of the world, but you may only investigate [those things which occurred] *since Adam was placed on earth.*" Rabbi Leazar in the name of Ben Sira [said]: "Do not investigate [things] which are too great for you, [and] do not examine [things] which are too mighty for you, [and] do not [attempt to] to know [things] which are too marvelous for you, [and do not ask about things which are hidden from you]. You may study [things] which are permitted you; [but] do not busy [yourself] with hidden matters."

And God said: "Let us make Adam" (Gen. 1:26). With whom did He take counsel? Rabbi Joshua the son of Levi said: "He took counsel with the works of heaven and earth. It is comparable to a king who had two advisors and would not do anything without their knowledge." Rabbi Samuel the son of Naḥman said: "He took counsel with the works of each day. It is comparable to a king who had an associate and would not do anything without his knowledge." Rabbi Ami said: "He took counsel in His heart. It is comparable to a king who had a palace built by an artisan. [The king] saw it, and it did not please him. With whom would be be angry? Surely with the artisan! Thus [we read in Gen. 6:6: *And YHWH was sorry that He had made Adam on the earth,] and it grieved Him in His heart.*" Said Rabbi Yassai: "It is comparable to a king who did business through an agent, and he suffered a loss. With whom would he be angry? Surely with the agent! Thus we read [in Gen. 6:6], *And it grieved him in His heart.*"

Said Rabbi Berekhyah: "When the Holy One, blessed be He, came to create the Primordial Adam, He saw that [both] righteous ones and evil ones would come forth from him. He said [to Himself]: 'If I create him, evil ones will come forth from him. [If] I do not create him, how will righteous ones come forth from him?' What did the Holy One, blessed be He, do? He removed the ways of the wicked ones from before His face, and He joined His attribute of mercy to Himself; then He created [Adam]. Thus it is written, *For YHWH knows the way of the righteous, but the way of the wicked will perish* (Ps. 1:6). What [is the meaning of] *the way of the wicked] will perish?* It will perish from before His face. He joined the attribute of mercy [to Himself], and He created [Adam]." Rabbi Ḥanina did not say thus; rather, [he said]: "When [the Holy One, blessed be He,] came to create the Primordial Adam, He took counsel with the ministering angels. He said to them: *'Let us make Adam.'* They said to him: 'What will be his character?' He said to them: 'Righteous ones will come forth from him'; thus it is written, *For YHWH knows the ways of the righteous* [which means] He made known the ways of the righteous to the ministering angels. *But the way of the wicked will perish* [means] it was hidden from them. [God] revealed to them that righteous ones would come forth from him, but He did not reveal to them that wicked ones would come forth from him, for if He had revealed to them that wicked ones would come forth from him, the attribute of justice would not have let [Him] create [Adam]."

Said Rabbi Simeon: "When the Holy One, blessed be He, came to create the Primordial Adam, the angels of service formed groups and associations. Some of them said, 'Let him be created,' and some of them said, 'Let him not be created.' Thus it is written, *Love and Truth fought together, Righteousness and Peace combated each other* (Ps. 85:11). Love said: 'Let him be created, for he will do acts of loving-kindness.' Truth said: 'Let him not be created, for [he will be] full of lies.' Righteousness said: 'Let him be created, for he will perform righteous deeds.' Peace said: 'Let him not be created, for [he will be] full of strife.' What did the Holy One, blessed be He, do? He took Truth and cast her to the earth. The ministering angels said before the Holy One, blessed be He, 'Master of the universe, why did You despise Your seal? Bring Truth up from the earth.' Thus it is written, *Truth shall spring forth from the earth* (Ps. 85:12)."

All our rabbis say the following in the name of Rabbi Ḥanina, [while] Rabbi Phineḥas [and] Rabbi Ḥilkiah say [it] in the name of Rabbi Simeon: "*Very (m'd)* [refers to] Adam, *'dm;* thus it is written, *And God saw all that He had created, and behold, it was very good* (Gen. 1:31) [which means] 'and behold, Adam was good'."

Rabbi Hunah the Great of Sepphoris said: "While the ministering angels were contending with one another and were busy arguing one with the other, the Holy One, blessed be He, created [Adam. He] said to them: 'What can you accomplish [by your arguing]? Adam has already been created.' "

Rabbi Hunah in the name of Rabbi Aibu [said]: With forethought He created him. [This is proven by the fact that only] after He had created the requirements for his food did He create him. The ministering angels said before the Holy One, blessed be He: 'Master of the universe, *What is man that You are mindful of him, the son of Adam that You care for him* (Ps. 8:5)? This troublesome one, for what was he created?' He said to them: 'If [one were to follow your reasoning he could ask], *All sheep and oxen* (Ps. 8:8), why were they created? *Birds of the heavens and fish of the sea* (Ps. 8:9), why were they created? [If there were] a tower full of good things but no guests, what benefit [would the tower be] to its owner who filled it?' They said before Him: 'Master of the universe, *YHWH, our Lord, how majestic is Your name in all the earth!* (Ps. 8:10). Do what pleases you.' "

Rabbi Joshua of Siknin in the name of Rabbi Levi [said]: "He took counsel with the souls of the righteous. Thus it is written: *These were the potters and inhabitants of Netaim and Gedarah; they dwelt there with the king for his work* (I Chron. 4:23). *These were the potters (hywṣrym)* [refers to Adam's creation] because [it is said,] *YHWH, God, formed (wyyṣr) Adam* (Gen. 2:7). *And inhabitants of Netaim (ntʿym)* [refers to the placing of Adam into the garden] because [it is said], *and YHWH, God, planted (wytʿ)* [*a garden in Eden]* (Gen. 2:8). *And Gedarah (wgdrh)* [refers to His creating dry land] because [it is said], *I placed the sand as the bound for the sea [a perpetual barrier it cannot be passed]* (Jer. 5:22). *They dwelt there with the king for his work* [which means] with the King of Kings, the Holy One, blessed be He. The souls of the righteous sat, and with them He took counsel, and then He created the world."

Rabbi Samuel the son of Naḥman in the name of Rabbi Yonatan [said]: "When Moses wrote the Torah, he would write the deeds of each day [separately]. When he came to the verse, *And God said, 'Let us make Adam,'* he said: 'Master of the universe, why do You give an opening for the heretics [to speak]?' He said to him: 'Write! He who wishes to err, let him err.' The Holy One, blessed be He, said to him: 'Moses, the man whom I am creating, will I not bring forth from him important ones and [seemingly] unimportant ones? Now, if an important one comes to seek permission [for an action] from one less important than himself, he [would] say to [himself], "Why [must] I seek permission from the unimportant ones?" But they [would] say to him: "Learn from your Creator, for He created the upper regions and the lower regions [by Himself], but when He came to create Adam he took counsel with the ministering angels." ' "

Said Rabbi La: "There is no [actual] taking counsel here; rather, [it is comparable] to a king who was walking [near] the door of [his] palace, and he saw a boulder that had been cast away. He said to himself: 'What shall we do with it?' Some of them said: '[Make] public baths [with it].' Others said: '[Make] private baths [with it].' The king said: 'I shall make it into a statue [of myself]. Who will stop me?' "

The heretics asked Rabbi Simlai: "How many gods created the world?" He said to them: "I and you shall ask the first days; thus it is written, *For ask now of the first days* (Deut. 4:32). 'Gods created'

(br`w) is not written there; but *God created (br`)* [is written there]."
They returned and asked him: "What [is the meaning of] that which
is written [in Gen. 1:1], *When God (`lhym) began to create?*" He
said to them: " 'When gods began to create' *(br`w)* is not written there,
but *God created (br`) the heavens and the earth* [is written there]."
Said Rabbi Simlai: "Every place where you find an opportunity for
the heretics [to ask a question], you find its answer at its side." They
returned and asked him: "What [is the meaning of] that which is
written [in Gen. 1:26], *And God said: 'Let us make Adam'?*" He said
to them: "Read what follows it. 'And gods created *(wybr`w)* Adam' is
not [written there], but *And God created (br`)* [is written there in
Gen. 1:27]." When [the heretics] went out, his students said to him:
"Them you pushed over with a reed; what will you answer us?" He
said to them: "In the past, [at the time of the first creation,] Adam
was created from the earth, and Eve was created from Adam. From
that time forward, *In our image and in our likeness* [shall our
children be created, which means] a man [cannot be created] without a woman, and a woman [cannot be created] without a man, and
neither of them [can be created] without the Divine Presence."

Said Rabbi Hoshiya: "When the Holy One, blessed be He, created
the Primordial Adam, the ministering angels erred with regard to
him, and they sought to say 'holy' before [Adam, thinking that he
was divine]. To what may this thing be compared? [It may be
compared] to a king and a governor who were placed in a chariot,
and the people of the province sought to say 'Sovereign' before the
king; however, they did not know which one he was. What did the
king do? He pushed out [the governor] and cast him [outside] the
chariot. Then [the people of the province] knew [which one] was the
king. Thus, when the Holy One, blessed be He, created the Primordial Adam, [and] the angels erred, what did the Holy One, blessed be
He, do? He caused sleep to fall upon [Adam], then all knew that he
was a mere mortal. Thus it is written, *Turn away from Adam* (Isa. 2:22)."

Male and female (nqbh) He created them (Gen. 1:27). This is one
of things which they [changed when they] wrote [it] for King Ptolemy
[in the Septuagint. They wrote,] "A man and his apertures *(nqw-
byw)*, He created them."

Rabbi Joshua the son of Rabbi Nehemiah in the name of Rabbi
Ḥanana the son of Isaac, and the rabbis in the name of Rabbi Leazar
[said]: "He created in [Adam] four attributes [from the higher beings
and four] from the lower creatures. From the higher beings [God

took the following attributes and gave them to Adam:] He stands like the ministering angels, he speaks like the ministering angels, he comprehends like the ministering angels, and he sees like the ministering angels." But do not animals [also] see? ["Yes, they see,] but this [Adam can see] sideways [without turning his head, and animals cannot do that. God took the following] four [characteristics] from the lower beings [and gave them to Adam]: He eats and drinks like the animals, he procreates like the animals, he defecates like the animals, and he dies like the animals."

Rabbi Tifdai in the name of Rabbi Aḥa [said: "The Holy One, blessed be He, said to Himself,] 'The higher beings were created in [My] image and likeness, and they do not procreate. But the lower beings procreate, for they were not created in [My] image and likeness.' The Holy One, blessed be He, said, 'Behold, I will create [Adam] in the image and likeness of the upper beings, [but he will have the trait] of procreation from the lower beings.' "

Rabbi Tifdai in the name of Rabbi Aḥa [said: "The Holy One, blessed be He, said to Himself], 'If I [were] to create him [with characteristics solely] from the upper beings, he would live and not die. But if [I were to create Adam with characteristics solely] from the lower beings, he would die and not live [forever]; therefore, I shall create him [with characteristics] from the upper beings and from the lower beings. If he sins he shall die; but if he does not sin, he shall live [forever].' "

And they shall have dominion (wrdw) over the fish of the sea (Gen. 1:28). Said Rabbi Ḥanina: "If he is worthy, then *they shall have dominion (wrdw),* and if he is not worthy let him descend *(yrdw).*"

Said Rabbi Jacob of Kefar Ḥanan: "He that is *in our image and our likeness, shall have dominion;* but he who is not *in our image and our likeness,* let him descend."

And God blessed them (Gen. 1:28). There we learn that a virgin is married on the fourth day [Wednesday], but a widow [is married] on the fifth day [Thursday]. Why [were these days designated as wedding days? They were so designated because the word] "blessing" is written with regard to them. But "blessing" is written only with regard to the fifth day [Thursday] (Gen. 1:22) and the sixth day [Friday] (Gen. 1:28). Bar Qapara said: "The fourth day is the eve of the fifth, and the fifth is the eve of the sixth."

Rabbi Leazar in the name of Rabbi Yosi the son of Zimra [said]:

"*[Be fruitful and multiply and fill the earth] and subdue her* (Gen. 1:28). *Subdue her (wkbšh)* is written. [This means that] the man [alone] is commanded concerning [the commandment] to *be fruitful and multiply,* but not the woman." Rabbi Yoḥanan the son of Beroqa says: "It is the same with regard to the man and the woman; about both of them it says [in Gen. 1:28] *And God blessed them;* [therefore, both are commanded to *be fruitful and multiply]. And subdue her* is written. [This means] that a man controls his wife so that she will not go out to the marketplace [alone], for every woman who goes out to the marketplace [alone] will eventually be led to sin. From where do we [learn this? We learn it] from Dinah, for it is written, *And Dinah went out* (Gen. 34:1)." Rabbi Isaac in the name of Rabbi Ḥaninah [said]: "The law is according to Rabbi Yoḥanan the son of Beroqa."

Said Rabbi Abbahu: "The Holy One, blessed be He, took a cup of [wine for] a blessing and blessed them."

Said Rabbi Judah the son of Rabbi Simeon: "[The angels] Michael and Gabriel were the Primordial Adam's groomsmen."

Said Rabbi Simlai: "We find that the Holy One, blessed be He, blesses the grooms, adorns the brides, visits the sick, buries the dead, and recites the blessing of the mourners. [We learn that He] blessed the grooms [from Gen. 1:28], for it is written, *And God blessed them.* [We learn that He] adorns the brides [from Gen. 2:22], for it is written: *And God formed the rib.* [We learn that He] visits the sick [from Gen. 18:1], for it is written: *And YHWH appeared to him.* [We learn that He] buries the dead [from Deut. 34:6], for it is written: *And He buried him in the valley.*"

Rabbi Samuel the son of Naḥman said: "He even appears to the mourners, for it is written: *And YHWH appeared to Jacob again when he came from Padan Aram and He blessed him* (Gen. 35:9). What blessing did He recite over him? [It was] the blessing of the mourners."

COMMENTS

Rabbi Yoḥanan opened. This is the first of two proems with which our section of Genesis Rabbah opens. The appearance of the proems, *petiḥot*, at the opening of sections is a characteristic of Genesis Rabbah. The proem begins with a verse which usually appears to be unrelated to the text upon which the midrash is commenting. Often, the opening verse is chosen from the Writings, or Hagiographa, the last of the three divisions of the Hebrew Bible. The proem then moves from its opening passage down several paths until it arrives at the opening verse, or sometimes the second verse, of the section with which the midrash is concerned. While there are many reasons for the structure of the proem, one clear purpose is to demonstrate the unity of the Bible. By starting with the Prophets or the Writings in a commentary on Genesis, the author(s) demonstrated that the three sections of the Bible are interrelated and that each serves to elucidate the others.[9]

Said Rabbi Yoḥanan. Yoḥanan interprets Ps. 139:5 as follows: A person who lives a proper life will be hemmed in by two worlds: this world, which is *before* him/her now, and the world-to-come, which will occur as the "last", '*ḥr*, days, a pun with "behind," '*ḥwr*, However, if people act improperly, the palm of God will rest upon them when they are brought before God to account for their misdeeds.[10]

Said Rabbi Jeremiah the son of Leazar. I assume that the basis of Jeremiah's comment is the end of Gen. 5:2, *And He called their name Adam,* for the name Adam is singular and was given to both sexes. Jeremiah argues that this teaches us that Adam possessed both male and female characteristics.

Said Rabbi Samuel the son of Naḥman. Samuel suggests that God created Adam with two distinct bodies, one male and one female. Originally, these bodies were joined together. However, when God created Adam and Eve, He divided the two bodies and made them into two distinct beings. It is unclear to me exactly how these two bodies were connected. The discussion about "backs" suggests that they were originally connected back to back; i.e., on one side Adam was male, but when he was turned around, he was female. However, Samuel's response to the objection "they" raised suggests that the two were joined at the side so that they stood next to each other.

They objected to this. Because Gen. 2:21 states that Eve was made from

Adam's rib, how can Samuel claim that Adam and Eve were originally two parts of a single body? Samuel responds that the word ṣl' can mean "rib" or "side"; therefore, Gen. 2:21 means that God separated Eve from Adam's side.

Rabbi Tanḥuma in the name of Rabbi Banayah. Tanḥuma suggests that at first Adam was an unformed mass with neither male nor female attributes. According to Tanḥuma, Gen. 5:2 should probably be read as follows: "Potentially male and female He created them, and called their name in this unformed state Adam." Ps. 139:16 supplies clear support for the position that Adam was originally created as an unformed mass.

Rabbi Joshua the son of Rabbi Nehemiah. Joshua suggests that originally Adam filled the whole universe; he occupied all space. This seems to be the same as Tanḥuma's claim that Adam stretched from one end of the universe to the other. The difference between the two opinions may be that Tanḥuma believed that the Primordial Adam was an undifferentiated mass, while Joshua thought that Adam was originally of cosmic proportions.

From east to west. Ps. 139:5 proves that the Primordial Adam stretched from east to west: ṣrtny, "hemmed in," is taken as a form of the root yṣr, "to create"; qdm, "before," can also mean "east."[11] If qdm means "east," then 'ḥwr must mean "west."

From the north to the south. Deut. 4:32 is read as follows: "From the day that God created Adam upon the earth, when he stretched from one end of the heavens until the other end of the heavens." Although "from one end of the heavens until the other end of the heavens" could mean from north to south or from east to west, it means the former because the latter directions have been derived from Ps. 139:5. Therefore, Joshua's interpretation of Deut. 4:32 depends on his explanation of Ps. 139:5.

And from where do we learn that Adam filled. The end of Ps. 139:5 proves that Adam filled the entire space of the universe. It is possible that the text means that Adam reached from the earth to God's abode in the heavens, for God was able to place His hand upon Adam's head. It is also possible, however, that this means that God, wherever He was, was able to place His palm on Adam because he, like God, was everywhere at once. Some have suggested that *your palm*, kpkh, should be read as kypt hšmym, "dome of heaven." This interpretation is based on the "extra" h at the end of kpkh. In this case, Ps. 139:5 should be read as follows: "The dome of heaven rested on Adam; therefore, he filled all the space between the earth and the dome of heaven."[12]

Said Rabbi Leazar. Leazar states that Adam's body was the last thing created on the last day of creation, for Gen. 1:24, which also records the events of the sixth day of creation, states that the earth brought forth *living creatures*, animals, creeping things, and the beasts of the earth, at the beginning of the last day. Adam was not created until Gen. 1:26, after these other beings were already on the earth. However, Leazar claims that *before* also applies to Adam's creation on the last day of creation.

This agrees with the opinion of Rabbi Leazar. Above, Leazar stated that the terms *before* and *behind* mean that Adam was the first and the last to be created on the sixth day of creation. We saw that Gen. 1:24–26 clearly placed the creation of Adam at the end of the things created on the last day. Here, Leazar interprets Gen. 1:24 as referring to the creation of Adam's soul at the beginning of the process of creation on the sixth day. Therefore, Adam's soul was created as the first thing on the last day of creation, and Adam's body was the last thing created on that day. I assume that the phrase *living creatures* is taken by Leazar as referring to Adam's soul, which gave him life.

Rabbi Simeon the son of Laqish said. Simeon argues that *behind* refers to Adam's creation on the last day of creation; that is, as we learn from Gen. 1:24–26, Adam's body was created last among the things created on the sixth day. However, his soul was created on the first day of creation, and we learn this from the word *before* in Ps. 139:5. Simeon takes *qdm*, "before," in the sense of "first."

This agrees with the opinion of Rabbi Simeon the son of Laqish. Simeon argues that the word *spirit, rwḥ,* in Gen. 1:2 refers to the soul of Adam, the spirit of God which He placed into him, Gen. 2:7. Isa. 11:2 proves that the *rwḥ 'lhym* in Gen. 1:2 refers to the spirit of God which He placed in Adam, because it clearly states that the *rwḥ yhwh* was upon man.

Said Rav Naḥman. Naḥman agrees that Adam was the last thing created on the sixth day of creation; however, he implies that both his soul and his body were created at this time, for *before* does not refer to the creation of Adam's soul. According to Naḥman, *before* indicates that Adam was the first to be punished. However, it is unclear exactly to what Naḥman refers. Rashi (11th cent.) suggests that Naḥman referred to the time of Noah: *So YHWH said: "I will blot out Adam whom I have created from the face of the ground, from Adam to the beast, creeping thing, and bird of the air"* (Gen. 6:7).[13] Others suggest that this means that Adam was the first to receive a commandment for which he would be punished if he violated it, and they refer to Gen. 2:17: *But of the tree of the knowledge of good and evil you shall not eat, for on the day that you eat of it you shall die.*[14]

Said Rabbi Samuel the son of Tanḥum. Samnuel argues that *behind* in Ps. 139:5 means that Adam was the last to praise God. Ps. 149 lists those that should praise God in the following order: angels, host, sun, moon, stars of light, heavens of heaven, the waters which are above the heavens, *taninim,* depths, fire, hail, snow, frost, winds of storms, mountains, hills, fruit trees, cedars, wild beasts, domesticated animals, creeping things, birds, kings, princes, judges, young men, maidens, old, young.

Said Rabbi Simlai. Simlai draws a causative connection between Ps. 148

and Gen. 1:24–26. Just as Adam was the last thing that praised God, so he was the last thing created on the sixth day of creation. It seems to me that Simlai wants to argue that Adam's being created last on the day is a result of his being the last to praise God. With Simlai's comment, we come to the end of the first proem. Notice that our proem began with Ps. 139:5 and that a good deal of the proem discussed that psalm and its connection to the creation of Adam. It should be noted that Ps. 139 is an appropriate psalm to be discussed at this point, for in it the psalmist praises YHWH, who has "examined" and "known" him and who created his "inner parts." Although Ps. 139:5 seems to be the major text interpreted in the proem, Simlai's comment brings us to Gen. 1:26; therefore, the proem serves as an introduction to this section of Gen. 1:26–28.[15]

Rabbi Ḥama the son of Ḥanina opened. This proem is defective, for although its theme is that one may study only the things which were created during the week of creation and onward, a theme appropriate to our section, it does not end by quoting the opening verse of our section.

Said Rabbi Ḥama the son of Ḥanina. Ḥama seems to read Job 20:4 as follows: "Learn things from those who have been there for a long time." Ḥama draws an analogy between the things created during the first week of creation and the ass-drivers who supply a city. Just as the latter learned about the market situation from those who had been in the market before them, so each item of creation learned about creation from the things which had experienced creation before it. Ḥama's point is that the creation of the Torah predated the creation of the world, and that the Torah contains all the information that one needs to know. Because the Torah begins with God's creating the universe, everything we need to know and all the questions which are proper for us to ask begin with that event.[16] Although Prov. 8 discusses Wisdom, it was common for the rabbis to identify Wisdom with Torah.[17] The point that the Torah preceded creation and that it is the blueprint of creation is made at the opening of Genesis Rabbah.

And one of the days of the Holy One, blessed be He. Ps. 90:4 states that 1,000 years are equal to one day *(ywm),* yesterday, in God's sight; therefore, "daily," *ywm ywm,* in Prov. 8:30, is equal to 2,000 years.

Behold, this is the meaning of. At this point, Ḥama seems to read Job 20:4 as follows: "You may not know this from of old, only the Torah knows that. You may know only those things which occurred since Adam was placed on earth."

Rabbi Leazar in the name of Ben Sira [said]. Joshua the son of Sira was a Palestinian Jew who flourished approximately in the first quarter of the second century before our era. He was a scribe who seems to have run a school for the men of the upper classes of Jewish society in Jerusalem. Probably by the year 175 B.C.E. the son of Sira had created his rather long "wisdom-book." The work, modeled on the biblical Book of Proverbs, was originally written in Hebrew; however, it has survived mainly in a Greek version derived from his grandson's translation, completed in Egypt in the last third of the second century before the common era.[18] Our passage seems to reflect 3:21–23 of the Hebrew version of Ben Sira.[19]

You may study things which are permitted you. Whatever the son of Sira meant in his original comment, we usually read this section as an admonition to avoid the study of gnosticism, mysticism, and other speculative forms of Judaism in the first century of our era. In order to study the texts produced by these Jews, one had to be well grounded in the standard rabbinic texts and to be confident in his acceptance of the truth of the Bible, as interpreted by the rabbis. Only after a person had matured could he study mysticism, and then only with a qualified teacher. Our text has two possible interpretations: (1) Avoid mystical speculation completely; (2) avoid mystical speculation until you are prepared to engage in it. I favor the first interpretation of this text.[20]

And God said: "Let us make Adam." The problem with this verse is that God said *let us make, n˘sh.* If there is only one God who created everything, with whom was He speaking at this point?

Rabbi Joshua the son of Levi said. In order to avoid any suggestion that Adam was created by any of the heavenly beings other than the One God, Joshua states that God took counsel with the works of heaven and earth, not with the angels. Joshua seems to suggest that *let us make* is the "royal we," for like a king who seeks the advice of his advisors before he alone acts, God talked matters over with the things He had created to this point before He alone created Adam. If we accept Joshua's analogy, he viewed the works of heaven as one entity and the works of earth as another, for the king had two advisors. We shall see below that some of the rabbis viewed people as a combination of the upper and lower beings, and this may be implied in Joshua's statement. It is unclear, however, exactly to what Joshua is referring, because he seems to consider these works as only two distinct items.[21]

Rabbi Samuel the son of Naḥman said. Samuel suggests that God took counsel with the works of each day, just like a king who has an associate without whose knowledge he would not act. Samuel seems to suggest that God took counsel with the works of each day individually and that He made the works of each day think that they were His only associate, for Samuel speaks of the king's associate. The only difference between Samuel's comment and that of Joshua is that each envisions in a unique way the manner in which God treated the things which He had created before Adam.

Rabbi Ami said. Ami suggests that God did not take counsel with anyone or anything else; He merely took counsel with Himself, for He was the creator. Ami compares this to a king who would be angered with an artisan if the latter created a work with which the former was not pleased. Therefore, God, who alone created Adam, would seek the advice of the one responsible for the latter's creation, for this is the one with whom He would have to deal if He were displeased with the finished product. We know that God alone created Adam, for just as a king who is displeased by a creation is angry with the artisan, so God in Gen. 6:6 was angry with Adam's creator, His heart.

Said Rabbi Yassi. Yassi's comment seems to be virtually the same as that attributed to Ami. While the latter speaks of an artisan with whom the king would be angry, the former speaks of an agent with whom the king would be angry if he suffered a loss through the agent's actions. Both rabbis quote Gen. 6:6; therefore, I assume that Yassi also believed that God took counsel in His heart.

Said Rabbi Berekhyah. Berekhyah raises the issue of human nature. Because people are both good and evil, how did God justify Adam's creation? Berekhyah suggests that although He realized that evil people would be descended from Adam, He still created him, for if He had not created Adam, righteous people would never have existed. According to Berekhyah, the *us* refers to God's joining His attribute of mercy with Himself when He created Adam.[22] There are a number of important themes running through Berekhyah's comment. First, Berekhyah raises the problem of evil and evil people.[23] Was there a separate creator for evil, or did the one, good God create both good and evil? Berekhyah affirms that there is only one creator and that He created both good and evil. Second, why did God create evil along with good? Berekhyah's answer is somewhat problematic, for he implies that good and evil complement each other. However, he also seems to imply that God could not have prevented the evil ones from coming into the world unless He refused to create Adam. This suggests that humans have free will and that God is powerless to control the actions of individuals. The evil ones were allowed to exist because they would be balanced off by the existence of the good ones. Berekhyah also suggests that God very much wanted the good ones to exist; He wanted this so much that He was willing to allow evil to exist as the price for the existence of good. Third, how could the good God create evil? Berekhyah suggests that only through His attribute of mercy could God suffer the existence of evil. He further suggests that this attribute of mercy is somehow distinct from God Himself, or at least, it does not come into play at all times unless God makes a conscious effort to allow it to act. Berekhyah finds support for his conclusion in Ps. 1:6, which he reads as follows: "When God set out to create Adam He took into account the ways of the righteous who would descend from Adam, and He ignored the ways of the wicked who would come from him."

Rabbi Ḥanina did not say thus. Ḥanina states that the *us* refers to the angels of service, for God took counsel with them when He set out to create Adam.[24] When the angels asked about Adam's character, God lied to them, or at least withheld part of the truth from them, for He told them only about the righteous ones who would come forth from Adam. It is an interesting theological point that God lied to the angels when He created Adam, for if He had not lied, the angels would not have allowed Him to create him. For Hanina, the attribute of justice seems to be an angel. The rabbis believed that God had two major attributes, the attribute of mercy and the attribute of justice. Both of these had to work together, for if the attribute of mercy predominated, there would be chaos in the world, because God would never demand right action. On the other hand, if the attribute of justice prevailed, the world would never have been created, for nothing is just and deserving of existence when measured against the perfection of God. At times, these attributes are viewed as part of God; at other times, they seem to be angels, or at least independent of God.

Said Rabbi Simeon. Simeon believes that the angels knew Adam's character; therefore, they debated God's plan to create him. Simeon bases his picture on Ps. 85:11, for what else could be meant by the clause *love and truth fought together* than that the angels Love and Truth argued? Simeon raises the interesting theological point that God had to reject the claims of Truth, that is, that people would be evil and full of lies, if He was to create Adam; therefore, God cast Truth out of the heavens. Simeon implies that if God had listened to Truth He could not have created Adam. This is even more curious because Truth, *emet,* is one of the names of God, or, in the words of the midrash, His seal.

All of our rabbis say the following. This is an intrusion into the text, for although it challenges the assumption that people are evil, it comes between two discussions of the angels' forming groups or contending with one another. In any case, this comment argues that Adam was good, and this is why he was created. The remark is based on the fact that "very," *m'd,* and "Adam," *'dm,* are spelled with the same Hebrew letters; therefore, they are the same thing. Thus, when God looked over His total creation He stated that Adam was good.

Rabbi Hunah the Great of Sepphoris said. Hunah returns to the above picture of the angels' arguing over the question of God's creating Adam. Hunah claims that while the angels were arguing with one another, God created Adam before they could prevent Him from doing so. Hunah suggests either that God ignored the angels or that He tricked them by creating Adam before they could prevent Him from creating him.

Rabbi Hunah in the name of Rabbi Aibu said. Hunah states that before God created Adam, He carefully prepared for him by first creating those things which he would need for food. When the angels asked Him why He created Adam, God responded that it would have been useless to have created the animals, birds, and fish had He not created Adam, for they were created only to serve as Adam's food. This raises the interesting theological point that God created the animals only to supply food for humans, and that if Adam had not been created, there would have been no reason for God to have created the animals. Hunah has God respond that just as it would be useless for one to store up food and delicacies unless there were guests to whom to serve them, so it would have been pointless for God to have created Adam's sources of food if He had not created Adam to eat them. The angels reply that God is so wonderful that He should do whatever He wishes to do.

Rabbi Joshua of Siknin in the name of Rabbi Levi said. Joshua argues that the word *us* refers to the souls of the righteous, and he brings I Chron. 4:23 to support his claim. There is a rabbinic tradition which states that God created all the souls of those who would appear on earth from the beginning through the end of time and that these souls remained with Him until it was time for them to enter their appropriate bodies. Perhaps our midrash alludes to this tradition.[25] I am not at all sure exactly what Joshua meant to say, and in the traditional commentaries I cannot find any clear indication of what this text means. However, it seems that I Chron. 4:23 is taken to mean that the righteous ones were with the King of Kings when He created Adam, when He planted the Garden of Eden and placed Adam there, and when He separated the waters and the dry land. The first two points are based on puns; *ywṣrym*, "potters," is connected with *yṣr*, "create," and *nṭʿym* is related to "plant," *nṭʿ*. The last point is not a pun, for the root *gdr* does not occur in Jer. 5:22. I assume that it merely refers to God's creation of the dry land because there He limited the extent of the water. I must say that I have come up with at least one other possible interpretation of the passage: The righteous ones were with the King of Kings when He created Adam, placed him in the garden, and limited his actions.

Rabbi Samuel the son of Naḥman. Samuel introduces another topic: The plural form of the verb, *let us make,* in Gen. 1:26 could lead the heretics to claim that more than one God created the world. He then asks why God dictated the text in this manner to Moses. When Moses arrived at Gen. 1:26, he asked God why He wanted the verse written in this way, for it would allow the heretics to press their claims that more than one God created the world or that God actually was a plurality. God responded that Moses should do what he was told to do, and that those who wanted to misread the verse were free to do so. Although we do not know exactly to whom the word "heretics," *mynym,* refers, it has been suggested that it often refers to Christians.[26]

Will I not bring forth from him. God explains to Moses why He wanted Moses to write the clause *let us make.* God says that the clause provides an example to men and women: Just as God discussed His actions with beings less than Himself, so also humans should take counsel with others, even those who appear to be less than themselves.

Said Rabbi La: La argues that *let us make* does not mean that God took counsel with anyone; rather, it is the "royal we." Just as a king, upon finding a clod, might say "what shall we do with it," even though he will, in the end, do anything he wants to do with it, so also God said, *"Let us make."*

The heretics asked Rabbi Simlai. We have here a rather long section in which Simlai answers the heretics concerning the number of gods who created the world. The answers all center on the same linguistic issue: the number of the verb. The problem arises from the fact that "God," 'lhym, has the ending, ym, of a plural masculine noun; therefore, it might appear to be a plural noun. The answer to this objection is that although the noun looks like a plural noun, we know that it is singular from the form of the verb with which it is used, for the verb is always in the singular. Thus we find 'lhym br', and not 'lhym br'w.[27]

When the heretics went out. This type of story, in which the heretics come to ask a rabbi a question, often ends with a discussion between the rabbi and his students. It is assumed that the rabbi has given the heretics a simple answer which would not have sufficed had the heretics been as sophisticated and as learned in the Torah as the rabbi's students; therefore, the rabbi must answer his students in a way appropriate for them. Simlai tells his students that *let us make* means that Adam and Eve were created directly by God; that is, they were created in a unique manner. *In our image and in our likeness* refers to the fact that the rest of the human race will be created by man, woman, and the Divine Presence. Those created after Adam and Eve were only an image and likeness of Adam and Eve, for they were not created in the same manner as the first couple. Therefore, this plural form refers not to a plurality in the Divinity but to the fact that creation now needs two humans and the Divine Presence.

Said Rabbi Hoshiya. It is likely that Hoshiya's coment is ralated to the phrases *in our image* and *in our likeness,* for the angels mistook Adam for the Divinity. This could have been the case only if Adam actually did reflect the image and likeness of God. In any case, in order to demonstrate to the angels that Adam was not divine, God caused Adam to sleep. Hoshiya compares this to a king who is traveling with his appointed governor. When the people cannot distinguish between the king and the governor, the former demonstrates his superior power. Thus, when the angels could not distinguish between God and Adam, the former demonstrated His superior powers.

Male and female He created them. This verse presents a problem because this clause is preceded by *in the image of God He created him.* In order to demonstrate that God is not a plurality, as *them* in our phrase implies, the verse is changed to read that God created a male with his apertures; that is, God created a single entity. Note also that this being is not bisexual; clearly it is a male. We are told that this change was made when the Hebrew Bible was translated from Hebrew to Greek for Ptolemy. Thus, the change was made so that a non-Jew would not misread the text. The Septuagint to the Torah seems to have been written during the first half of the third century before the common era. To my knowledge, we do not find this "change" in the versions we now possess.[28]

Rabbi Joshua the son of Rabbi Nehemiah. We have here a rather long discussion of the dual nature of humans, for they possess both divine characteristics and animal instincts. The rabbis had a realistic view of humans, and they realized that while God made people *a little lower than the angels* (Prov. 8:5), He also made them "a little higher than the animals." Joshua explains that people possess traits common to the higher beings, the angels, and characteristics common to the lower beings, the animals.[29]

Rabbi Tifdai in the name of Rabbi Aḥa. Tifdai here suggests that the trait which humans and the animals have in common is the act of procreation, and he implies that this is the only trait which they share, or at least the most constitutive trait of the animals which people have in common with them.

Rabbi Tifdai in the name of Rabbi Aḥa. Here Tifdai focuses on the fact that God and the angels are eternal. If God had created Adam solely with the traits of the higher beings, he would be eternal. On the other hand, if He had created him solely like the lower beings, he would die. Therefore, God created Adam with the characteristics of both types of beings: Although humans die, they have the possibility of eternal life, for if they do not sin, they achieve eternal life.[30]

Said Rabbi Ḥanina. Ḥanina's comment is similar to that of Tifdai: If a person is worthy, that is, obeys God's will, he or she will be the most important being on earth and will rule over others. However, if this person does not live a life according to the Torah, he or she will descend into the depths of Sheol and will not be the most important creature on earth. Ḥanina's comment is a pun which juxtaposes *rdh*, "to have dominion," and *yrd*, "to descend."

Said Rabbi Jacob of Kefar Ḥanan. Jacob employs the same pun as Ḥanina, and both sages say virtually the same thing. Jacob, however, brings together *in our image and in our likeness* from Gen. 1:27 and *shall have dominion* from Gen. 1:28.

And God blessed them. Our midrash attempts to find biblical support for the accepted practice that virgins were married on Wednesdays and widows were married on Thursdays.[31] The awkward exegesis before us suggests that the custom was widespread before this exegetical comment was constructed, for the text notes that the word "blessing" does not really occur with reference to Wednesday and Thursday. I assume that the midrash focuses on the word "blessing" because the "Seven Blessings" are a central feature of the marriage ceremony.[32]

Bar Qapara said. Bar Qapara attempts to bridge the gap between the actual days on which the word "blessing" appears and the fact that the weddings take place on Wednesday and Thursday. His attempt is awkward, for the word "blessing" appears with reference to Thursday and Friday; that is, it appears with reference to one of the days on which a wedding was to occur or to the two days after the weddings should have been performed. The traditional commentators suggest that the word "blessing" appears on the days after the weddings because the marriage was consummated on those days.[33] This is a possible interpretation of Bar Qapara's comment; however, it is less than satisfactory.

Rabbi Leazar in the name of Rabbi Yosi. Leazar's exegesis is based on the spelling of subdue her, *khšh,* for this appears to be a singular form of the verb, with a direct-object suffix, *kbš h;* therefore, we could read it as "he shall subdue her." Because this word follows the admonition to *be fruitful and multiply,* Leazar concludes that the verse means that the man is obligated to procreate; therefore, if he must, he may force his wife to have intercourse with him in order to fulfill his obligation to produce children.

Rabbi Yohanan the son of Beroqa says. Yohanan states that both men and women were commanded to procreate, for God blessed *them,* both of them. Therefore, what does the Bible mean when it says that *he shall subdue her?* This means that the husband shall have control over his wife's actions so that she does not place herself in danger, or does not flaunt her beauty. Specifically, he should not allow her to go out alone to the market, for we know from the case of Dinah, who was raped by Shechem, that a woman who goes out by herself places herself in danger.

Rabbi Isaac in the name of Rabbi Hanina. This is one of the few places in our collection where a legal ruling is specifically given. Isaac says that the law follows Yohanan; therefore, both men and women were commanded to procreate. I assume that this also means that a man does have the right to control his wife's public activities, such as her going out into the marketplace. Note, also, that according to this interpretation a man cannot force his wife to have intercourse with him so that *he* can fulfill *his* obligations, for the obligation rests on each one of them, and each one must act freely to fulfill it.

Said Rabbi Abbahu. Abbahu states that the word "blessing" indicates that God blessed the bride and groom, Adam and Eve, at their wedding.

Said Rabbi Judah the son of Rabbi Simeon. Judah expands on the theme of Adam and Eve's wedding and states that the archangels served as Adam's groomsmen.

Said Rabbi Simlai. Simlai states that God Himself presided at a wedding, adorned a bride, visited the sick, buried the dead, and accompanied a mourner. The implication is that if God Himself engaged in these acts, should we not also participate in these activities? Gen. 1:28 tells us that God presided at the wedding of Adam and Eve. Gen. 2:22 tells us that God fashioned Adam's rib, which is taken to mean that He made it pleasing to Adam so that Eve would be a suitable bride. At Gen. 18:1 we read that God visited Abraham. Because Gen. 17 tells us that Abraham was just circumcised, the rabbis assumed that Abraham was recovering from his operation when God visited him in Gen. 18:1. Deut. 34:6 tells us that God buried Moses. The importance of the wedding and the funeral are testified to on Babylonian Talmud *Ketubot* 17a: "Our rabbis taught: One interrupts the study of Torah for the sake of a funeral procession and the leading of a bride

[under the bridal-canopy]." Visiting the sick apparently was also an important obligation for Jews of late antiquity. Above we saw a story of the rabbis
who visited Rabbi Eliezer when he was ill.[34]

Rabbi Samuel the son of Naḥman said. Something is wrong with our
text, for Simlai mentioned at the opening of his comment that God "recites
the blessing of the mourner;"[35] however, he did not offer a verse to support
this as he did in the case of the other actions he attributed to God. This is
established by Samuel, who cites Gen. 35:9, which states that God appeared to Jacob and blessed him shortly after Deborah, Rebekah's nurse,
had died, Gen. 35:8. It is curious that this point was not made by Simlai
directly or that Simlai did not quote Samuel's opinion. I assume that
something has fallen out of Simlai's comment because of its similarity with
what Samuel said. On the other hand, the list attributed to Simlai might
have been altered in light of Samuel's remark; however, I think this latter
possibility less likely.

CONCLUSIONS

The section opens with a proem, which is typical of Genesis Rabbah. The carefully constructed *petiḥah* offers several interpretations of Ps. 139:5. Although we have a variety of interpretations of this verse from Pslams, they all attempt to explain the physical characteristics of the Primordial Adam. This Primordial Adam was much different from the Adam who was eventually exiled from the garden after he ate the fruit from the tree of the knowledge of good and evil. In fact, it was because he ate this fruit that Adam became like all other humans.[36]

The second proem does not fit the form, for it does not end with the opening of the section of Genesis to which this section of Genesis Rabbah is a commentary. It is related to Adam's creation because Job 20:4, which refers to the time *since Adam was placed upon earth*, forms the basis of the *petiḥah*. If we take the reference to Job 20:4 literally, we are told that we can inquire only into those events which occurred from the sixth day of creation and onward.

The midrash now addresses the issue of the plural verb *n'śh*. Joshua and Samuel suggest that God took counsel with the heaven and the earth or with the works of the days of creation, respectively. Both compare God's actions to those of a king who always discussed his actions with his favorite advisors. Ami and Yassi argue that God took counsel with Himself and that the plural verb reflects the "royal we." Berekhyah also argues that God took counsel with Himself. He focuses on the idea that God acted with the aid of His attributes by ignoring the evil ones who would come forth from Adam and joining His attribute of mercy with Himself so that He might create Adam despite the inevitable presence of evil ones on the earth.

Ḥanina suggests that God took counsel with the angels of service. Building on Berekhyah's concern with the evil ones who would appear among Adam's descendants, Ḥanina agrees that God withheld this fact from the angels so that His attribute of justice would not prevent Him from creating Adam. Thus, Ḥanina's comment serves as a transition to Simeon's discussion of the angels' forming groups to discuss God's plan of creating Adam.

Simeon suggests that when God told the angels that He planned to create Adam, the latter formed groups to discuss the plan. God ended the argument by thrusting Truth, one of the angels, out of heaven. At this point we find an intrusion in the midrash in which Adam is declared good, for

"Adam" and "very" have the same Hebrew letters. Hunah brings the discussion back to the angels' groups and contends that God created Adam while the angels were arguing with one another.

Hunah changes the direction of the discussion and argues that God created Adam only after He had created the sources of his food. This section fits here because Hunah pictures the angels as arguing with God and asking why He created Adam.

Joshua also discusses the plural *n'sh;* however, he suggests that God took counsel with the souls of the righteous. As I noted in my comments, Joshua's interpretation of I Chron. 4:23 is less than clear.

Although discussing the verb *n'sh,* Samuel moves the midrash in an entirely new direction. He asks why God allowed Moses to write this verse, for surely it would provide the occasion for the heretics to suggest that more than one God created Adam. God responds to Moses' objection by stating that the verse is meant to teach a lesson to humans. They should act as God acted, and they should seek advice even from those who appear to be lesser than themselves. La's comment provides an indirect answer to Samuel's problem by stating that God spoke in the "royal we."

The heretics' questions to Simlai would fit better directly following Samuel's comment, for Samuel was the first to raise the issue of the heretics. Simlai answers the heretics by drawing their attention to the number of the verbs which follow the word *'lhym* and those which appear when the Bible states that God created. Because the verb *br'* occurs only in the singular, we must conclude that only one God created Adam and the world. Simlai's students object to what their teacher told the heretics. He replies to them by quoting the end of Gen. 1:26, *in our image and in our likeness.* This serves as a transition to Hoshiya's remark that the angels mistook Adam for God. Although Hoshiya does not cite this part of the verse, it is assumed by his comment.

We have seen that this section of the midrash has several intrusions and several comments which appear out of place. However, the section has been fairly well constructed because there appear to be transitional comments which allow the text to change subjects and issues smoothly. However, we do have a variety of interpretations of the meaning of *n'sh,* and no choice is made among the several possible explanations of the verb. Also, we have seen that several sections of the midrash do not even deal directly with this verb but seem to be based on the issues raised in the rabbis' comments.

The anonymous midrash now suggests that Gen. 1:27 was translated for Ptolemy in a way which would prevent the Pharaoh from assuming that more than one God created Adam. Although this serves as an exegesis of Gen. 1:27, it indirectly discusses the issue of the number of gods who created Adam. Thus, its content follows logically from what has preceded it.

At this point the midrash ignores Genesis and moves in a completely new direction. Joshua suggests that God created man with attributes taken from the higher beings and the lower beings. While Joshua discusses the creation of Adam, the theme of Gen. 1:26, he ignores the biblical text. There is, however, an implicit connection with Gen. 1:26, for God should be included among the higher beings. There follow two comments by Tifdai in the name of Aḥa. Both comments follow from Joshua's suggestion that Adam contained traits of the higher and the lower beings. Tifdai suggests that Adam procreates like the lower beings but has the possibility of eternal life like the higher beings.

The text now moves to a discussion of Gen. 1:28. Ḥanina and Jacob say virtually the same thing. Their comments are based on a pun, for they juxtapose *wrdw* with *rdh* and *yrd.*

The midrash now discusses Gen. 1:28. It opens by suggesting that the word "blessing" in Gen. 1:28 refers to the blessings one receives at a wedding. As I noted in my comments, this section is awkward, and it appears to be a rabbinic attempt to ground a well-known practice in the biblical text.

Leazar ignores the issue of the blessings and focuses on the word *wkbšh.* He suggests that the admonition to *be fruitful and multiply* which precedes this word means that only the man must fulfill the commandment to procreate. Yoḥanan refers to the fact that God blessed both of them, Adam and Eve, and argues that the commandment to procreate, which he implies was a sign of God's blessings, is incumbent on both men and women. Isaac concludes the section by stating that the law follows Yoḥanan.

Abbahu returns to the issue of God's blessing and claims that it refers to the wedding of Adam and Eve. Judah also discusses the first wedding and suggests that Michael and Gabriel served as Adam's groomsmen.

Apparently basing himself on the connection between God's blessing Adam and Eve at their wedding, Simlai claims that God performed several acts. I noted in my comment that Simlai's comment is awkward because he does not cite a verse to support his claim that God recited the blessing of the mourners. This verse is supplied by Samuel.

This section of the midrash moves far beyond the biblical text, and, at points, it seems to be less carefully constructed than the middle section of our selection. However, the comments do flow smoothly from one another.

This selection is vastly different from the ones we have read so far. First, the midrash is less tied to the biblical text than the previous midrashim. In fact, it includes sections which seem to be based on the rabbinical interpretations of Genesis and not on the biblical text itself. Second, there is no attempt, outside of the first proem, to relate the various sections of the Bible or to claim that the verses in the Bible are needed to explain each other. Third, the Bible is not pictured as a necessary counter to logic; in fact, the issue of revelation versus human logic is never raised. This may be due to the fact that this is not a "legal midrash." The trait which this selection has in common with the other texts is the appearance of several alternative interpretations of a given word or verse.

The basic issue of the midrash is not logic versus revelation; rather, it focuses on the issues of how many gods created Adam and of Adam's nature. Both topics were widely discussed in Palestine during the rabbinic period, and our midrash offers the rabbinic interpretation: One God created Adam and the world, and Adam is *not* totally evil. At least, Adam is a combination of good and evil; at most, he is totally good. It is difficult to determine to whom these exegetical comments were addressed. These arguments, directed against those who claimed that more than one god created the world or that Adam was evil or created by an evil God, would have been useful to rabbis and nonrabbis alike. The interpretations are not obscure and do not depend on a sophisticated knowledge of the Bible or on methods of biblical interpretation. The proems most clearly testify to the ingenuity of the rabbis.

NOTES

1. J. Theodor, s.v. "Bereshit Rabbah," *Jewish Encyclopedia*, III, 62–65.

2. H. Albeck, *Einleitung und Register zum Bereschit Rabba* (Jerusalem: 1965), 11–19.

3. Theodor, 63.

4. Ibid.

5. Ibid., 64.

6. Albeck, 1 ff.

7. Theodor, 64. M. D. Herr, s.v. "Genesis Rabbah," *Encyclopaedia Judaica*, VII, 399.

8. The translation is based on J. Theodor and H. Albeck, *Midrasch Bereshit Rabba* (Jerusalem, 1965), I, 54–67.

9. W. Bacher, *Die Proomien der alten jüdischen Homilie* (Leipzig, 1913). J. Heinemann, "The Proem in the Aggadic Midrashim: A Form-Critical Study," *Scripta Hierosolymitana*, XXII (1971), 100–122. E. Stein, "Die homiletische Peroration im Midrasch," *Hebrew Union College Annual*, VIII–IX (1931–32), 335–371.

10. On sin and punishment, see E. E. Urbach, *The Sages—Their Concepts and Beliefs*, translated by I. Abrahams (Jerusalem, 1975), 420–444; S. Schechter, *Aspects of Rabbinic Theology: Major Concepts of the Talmud* (New York, 1961), 219–241; G. F. Moore, *Judaism in the First Centuries of the Christian Era: The Age of the Tannaim* (Cambridge, 1966), I, 445–552.

11. F. Brown, S. R. Driver, and C. A. Briggs, *A Hebrew and English Lexicon of the Old Testament* (Oxford, 1962), 869.

12. Comment of Zev Wolf on *wtšt ʿly kpk*.

13. Comment of Rashi on *ʾḥwr lkl mʿšh brʾšyt*.

14. Comment of Issacar Ber Ashkenazi on *wqdm lkl ʿwnśym*.

15. Compare this version with Leviticus Rabbah 14:1.

16. Compare with the proem to the opening of Genesis Rabbah 1:1 and J. Neusner, *There We Sat Down* (Nashville, 1972), 72–98.

17. On the identification of Torah with Wisdom, see M. Hengel, *Judaism and Hellenism: Studies in Their Encounter in Palestine during the Early Hellenistic Period*, translated by J. Bowden (Philadelphia, 1974), 153–175.

18. On Ben Sira, see Hengel, 131–153; V. Tcherikover, *Hellenistic Civilization and the Jews*, translated by S. Applebaum (Philadelphia, 1966), 142–151.

19. *The Book of Ben Sira* (Jerusalem: 1973), 3.

20. See G. Scholem, *Major Trends in Jewish Mysticism* (New York, 1973), 40–79.

21. On the rabbinic parable, see W. O. E. Oesterley, *The Gospel Parables in the Light of Their Jewish Background* (New York, 1936); C. H. Dodd, *The Parables of the Kingdom* (London, 1950); J. Jeremias, *The Parables of Jesus* (New York, 1963).

22. On God's attributes of mercy and justice, see Urbach, 448–461.

23. Ibid., 483–511.

24. On the angels of service, see ibid. 155–183.

25. Ibid., 483–511.

26. On the *mynym*, "heretics," see A. Segal, *Two Powers in Heaven: Early Rabbinic Reports about Christianity and Gnosticism* (Leiden, 1977).

27. Compare Palestinian Talmud *Berakhot* 9:12

28. On the Septuagint, see E. Bickerman, *From Ezra to the Last of the Maccabees* (New York, 1966), 72–92. E. Bickerman, "The Septuagint as a Translation," *Proceedings of the American Academy of Jewish Research*, XXVIII (1959), 1–39.

29. Compare Genesis Rabbah 14:3; Urbach, 214–254.

30. Urbach, 420–436.

31. Mishnah *Ketubot* 1:1.

32. See Babylonian Talmud *Ketubot* 8a for the seven blessings recited in Babylonia, and S. Lieberman, *Tosefta Kifshutah: Zeraim* (New York, 1955), I, 250, for the Palestinian custom.

33. Comment of Issacar Ber Ashkenazi on *'wr lḥmyšy*.

34. Supra, 125–126.

35. Not much is known about the "blessing of the mourner" in the rabbinic period; see L. Hoffman, *The Canonization of the Synagogue Service* (South Bend, Ind., 1979), 146–148.

36. See L. Ginzberg, *The Legends of the Jews* (Philadelphia, 1913), I, 49–90.

7 Leviticus Rabbah

Unlike the other collections which form the basis of our anthology, Leviticus Rabbah is not an expositional midrash; it is not a running commentary on the entire biblical Book of Leviticus. Rather, the midrash focuses only on the first word or words of each section of Leviticus and employs these as the bases for essays on specific themes. Leviticus Rabbah is commonly classified as a homiletical midrash. J. Heinemann, who did extensive work on the rabbinic homily and Leviticus Rabbah, described the two types of midrashim as follows:

> [T]he expositional midrash collects expositions, interpretations, and comments—as many as they can find—on each biblical verse or even each word or phrase and arranges them consecutively according to the order of the biblical text, the result being that more often than not there is no connection at all between the individual items that follow one another, because each of them refers to a different verse or phrase. But in Leviticus Rabbah no attempt is made to provide a running commentary on the whole of the biblical text; instead, each chapter or homily is devoted to one pericope and deals almost exclusively with its first verse or verses. Since each chapter limits itself to one brief passage, it can be developed to one clearly defined, specific subject, aspects of which are developed throughout the entire sermon.[1]

Heinemann also noted that the various sections of Leviticus Rabbah contain a "clear, formal structure. Each of them opens with a number of proems, followed by the 'body of the sermon' which enlarges upon the themes touched on in the former, concluding with a brief peroration, developed mostly to messianic hope."[2]

Leviticus Rabbah is not the only nonexpositional midrash; the Pesiqta deRav Kahana,[3] the Pesiqta Rabbatai,[4] and the Tanḥuma also fall into this category. In addition, the proem is a central feature of Genesis Rabbah as well as of Leviticus Rabbah. Unfortunately, the exact relationship of Leviticus Rabbah to these other midrashic collections is unclear, for the exact date of Leviticus Rabbah and the name of its final editor(s) are unknown to us.[5]

Because Leviticus Rabbah is organized around themes,[6] and not the content of Leviticus, it is possible to outline some of the topics found in the collection. Heinemann stated that the author of our midrash dealt "by implication with acute problems of his time."[7]

> Not only does he [the editor of Leviticus Rabbah] hold up the hope of redemption and demonstrate that Israel's subjugation to Roman rule is but temporary, he also summarily rejects the idea that the commandments are but a yoke and a burden—as was claimed by Christianity in its polemics against Judaism . . . [He] extolls those who observe the commandments loyally . . . Another question, arising again and again, is the great suffering of Israel in the past and in the present . . .
>
> Other sermons pose the problem of atonement after the destruction of the Temple and the suspension of the sacrificial cult. . . . Perhaps no less striking is the attitude taken by the author of the midrash towards any attempt to bring about Israel's liberation from the Roman yoke by means of an armed rebellion. Not only does he carefully refrain from mentioning any military action when describing the coming of the future redemption, he also disregards, minimizes, and plays down deeds of military prowess and heroism in the past.[8]

Our passage expounds Lev. 1:1: *And YHWH called to Moses from the Tent of Meeting.* Above, in our selection from Sifra, we saw one midrash to these words. Here, in our example from Leviticus Rabbah, we shall encounter a completely different treatment of this verse. While in Sifra several different issues were addressed, here virtually the whole midrash focuses on one theme, Moses. The proems and the "body" of the sermon all deal with Moses, his special nature and the fact that he was the best of the Jewish prophets, who were the best prophets in the world. No matter where the proem or the paragraph begins, it ends with Moses.

And [YHWH] called to Moses (Lev. 1:1).[9] Rabbi Tanḥuma the son of Ḥanilai opened [his discourse with Ps. 103:20]: *"Bless YHWH, O His messengers (ml'kyw), mighty ones who do His word, harkening to the voice of His word.* About whom does Scripture speak? If Scripture speaks about the upper beings [when it uses the word *ml'k*, this is superfluous], for is it not already said, *Bless YHWH, all*

His hosts (Ps. 103:21)? If Scripture speaks about the lower beings [this is awkward], for is it not already said, *Bless YHWH, O His messengers?* But [we have these two verses] because [all] the upper beings are able to fulfill the errands of the Holy One, blessed be He; therefore, it is said, *Bless YHWH, all His hosts.* But concerning the lower beings, because they are not [all] able to fulfill the errands of the Holy One, blessed be He, it is written, *Bless YHWH, O His messengers;* and [it is] not [written in Ps. 103:20] 'Bless YHWH *all* His messengers'; [therefore, Ps. 103:20 uses the term *messengers* to refer to the lower beings and the term *hosts* to refer to the upper beings].

"Another matter: [The] prophets are called messengers *(ml'kym)*. Thus it is written: *And He sent a messenger (ml'k) and He brought us forth from Egypt* (Num. 20:16). And was it an angel? Was it not Moses [whom He sent to lead us out of Egypt]? And why does Scripture call [Moses] a *ml'k?* [It employs this term so that] from here, [Num. 20:16, we may learn] that prophets are called messengers, *ml'kym.* Now, in the same way [it is written]: *And an angel (ml'k) of YHWH went up from Gilgal to Bochim* (Jdgs. 2:1). And was it really an angel? Was it not Phinehas? And why was he called an angel *(ml'k).* Said Rabbi Simeon: 'When the Holy Spirit rested on Phinehas, his face would burn like a torch, [and he would resemble an angel].' And the rabbis said: 'And what did Manoah's wife say to him? [She said,] *"Behold, a man of God came to me, and his appearance was like the appearance of an angel (ml'k)"* (Jdgs. 13:6). She thought he was a prophet, but he was really an angel; [therefore, we must assume a similarity between angels and prophets].' Said Rabbi Yoḥanan: 'There is a prototypical biblical verse [which proves] that prophets are called *ml'kym.* Thus it is written: *Then Haggai, the ml'k of YHWH, spoke to the people with YHWH's message (bml'kwt): " 'I am with you,' says YHWH"* (Hag. 1:13). Behold, you are forced to learn from this prototypical biblical verse that prophets were called *ml'kym,* [for here Haggai, the prophet, is specifically called a *ml'k,* and his message is designated as *ml'kwt*].'

"*Mighty ones who do His word* (Ps. 103:20). About what is Scripture speaking? Said Rabbi Isaac: 'Scripture speaks of those who observe the sabbatical year. It is customary that in this world, a man observes a commandment one day, one week, [or] one month, but does he keep it the rest of the days of the year? But this one [who keeps the sabbatical year] sees his field untilled and his vineyard untilled, and he gives [his] *arnona,* and he is silent. Can you point to a person greater than this? But if you say that [Scripture] does not speak of those who keep the sabbatical year, [here is proof that in fact it does speak of this one who keeps the sabbatical year]. It is said here, *Who do His word (dbr),* and it is said elsewhere [in Deut. 15:1]: *This is the matter (dbr) of the [year of] release.* Just as *dbr* which is said elsewhere [in Deut. 15:1 signifies] that Scripture is speaking about those who keep the sabbatical year, so also *dbr* which is said here [in Ps. 103:20 signifies] that Scripture is speaking about those who keep the sabbatical year.'

"*Who do His word, harkening [to the voice of His word]* (Ps. 103:20). Rabbi Huna in the name of Rabbi Aḥa [said]: 'Scripture speaks about Israel when they stood before Mount Sinai, for [there] the doing preceded the harkening, and they said: "*All which YHWH said we shall do and we shall harken to*" (Ex. 24:7).'

"*Harkening to the voice of His word.* Said Rabbi Tanḥum the son of Ḥanilai: 'It is customary that in this world a burden which is heavy for one is light for two, [and one that is heavy] for two is light for four. But is a burden which is heavy for sixty myriads light for one? [But in the case of Israel and Moses this was so!] All Israel stood before Mount Sinai and said: "*If we hear the voice of YHWH any more we shall die*" (Deut. 5:25). But Moses heard the voice of [YHWH's] speaking by himself, and he lived. Know that this is so, for of all those [assembled at Mount Sinai, YHWH] called to Moses alone; therefore, it is said: *And YHWH called to Moses* (Lev. 1:1).' "

Rabbi Abbahu opened [his discourse with Hosea 14:7]: "*They shall return and dwell beneath My shadow.* These are the proselytes, for they come and are protected under the shadow of the Holy One, blessed be He. *They shall grow grain* (Hos. 14:7) [means the proselytes] are made the essential part [of humanity] just like Israel, for thus you say: *Grain makes the young men flourish and new wine the maidens* (Zech. 9:17). *They shall blossom as the vine* (Hos. 14:7) [means] like Israel, for thus you say, *You brought a vine out of Egypt; You drove out the nations and planted it* (Ps. 80:9).

"Another matter: *They shall grow grain* [refers] to the Talmud. *They shall blossom as a vine* [refers] to the aggadah. *Their mention shall be like the wine of Lebanon* (Hos. 14:7). Said the Holy One, blessed be He, 'The names of the proselytes are as precious to Me as the libation wine which is placed before Me on the altar.' And why is [the altar]'s name called Lebanon? [It is called Lebanon] because it says, *That goodly mount, Lebanon* (Deut. 3:25). Taught Rabbi Simeon the son of Yoḥai: 'Why was [the altar]'s name called Lebanon? [It was called Lebanon] because it makes the sins of Israel white as snow. Thus it is written: *Though your sins are like scarlet, they shall be as white (mlbym) as snow* (Isa. 1:18).' Rabbi Ṭabyomi said: '[It was called Lebanon (lbnwn)] because every heart (lbbwt) rejoices over it; thus it is written: *His holy mountain, beautiful in elevation, is the joy of all the earth, Mount Zion, in the far north* (Ps. 48:3).' And the rabbis say: '[It is called Lebanon] because *[I have heard your prayer and your supplication, which you have made before Me; I have consecrated this house which you have built, and put My name there for ever;] My eyes and My heart (lby) will be there for all times* (I Kgs. 9:3).'

"Rabbi Simeon in the name of Rabbi Joshua the son of Levi and Rabbi Ḥama the father of Rabbi Hoshiya in the name of Rav [said]: 'The Book of Chronicles was given only for the purpose of interpretation. *And his Judite wife bore Jered the father of Gedor, Heber the father of Soco, and Jekuthiel the father of Zanoah. These are the sons of Bithiah, the daughter of Pharaoh, whom Mered married* (IChron. 4:18). *And his Judite wife;* this is Jochebed. And was she really from the tribe of Judah? Was she not from [the tribe] of Levi? So, why was her name called Judite? [She was called his Judite wife] because she produced Jews in the world. *Bore Jered (yrd);* this is Moses.' Rabbi Ḥananah the son of Pappa and Rabbi Simeon [discussed this interpretation]. Rabbi Ḥananah said: '[Moses was called Jered (yrd)], for he brought the Torah down (šhwryd) from the upper [world] to the lower [world].' Another matter: For he brought the *Shekhinah* down from the upper [world to the lower world]. Said Rabbi Simeon: 'Jered is an expression which means "leader" or "kingship." Thus you say: *May he have dominion (wyrd) from sea to sea, and from the River [Nile] to the ends of the earth* (Ps. 72:8). And it is written [elsewhere]: *For he had dominion (rwdh) over all the area across the river* (I Kgs. 5:4).' *The father of Gedor (gdwr).* Rabbi Hunah in the name of Rabbi Aḥa said: 'Many fence-makers (gwdrym) arose for Israel, and this one [Moses] was the father of them all.' *Heber (ḥbr).* [He was called Heber] for he joined (ḥybr) the Children [of Israel] with their Father who is in heaven. Another matter: [He is called] Heber, for he postponed (šh'byr) the coming of the severe punishments into the world. *The father of Soco (swkw).*

This [is Moses, the one who] was the father of all the prophets who used to foresee the future (*swkyn*) by means of the Holy Spirit. Rabbi Levi said: 'This is an Arabic expression. In Arabic they call a prophet a *skoya (skwyy)*.' *Jekuthiel*. Rabbi Levi and Rabbi Simeon [discussed this word]. Rabbi Levi said: '[Moses was called Jekuthiel (*yqwty'l*)] because he made the Children [of Israel] gain hope (*mqwyn*) in their Father who is in heaven.' Said Rabbi Simeon: 'When the Children [of Israel] gathered before God at the time of the [golden] calf, *the father of Zanoah (znwḥ)*, Moses, came and removed them (*hznyḥn*) from that transgression. Thus it is written: *[And he took the calf which they had made, and burnt it with fire, and ground it into powder,] and scattered it upon the water . . .* (Ex. 32:20).' *These are the children of Bithiah, the daughter of Pharaoh*. Rabbi Joshua of Siknin in the name of Rabbi Levi [said]: 'The Holy One, blessed be He, said to Bithiah, the daughter of Pharaoh, "Moses is not your son, but you call him your son. Likewise you, who are not my daughter, I shall call my daughter." ' *These are the children of Bithiah . . . whom Mered (mrd) married*. This is Caleb. Rabbi Abba the son of Kahanah and Rabbi Judah the son of Simeon [discussed this verse]. Rabbi Abba the son of Kahanah said: 'This one [Caleb] rebelled (*mrd*) against the advice of the spies, and this one [Pharaoh's daughter] rebelled against the command of her father [that all the male children of the Hebrews should be put to death]. Let he who rebelled come and marry her who rebelled.' Rabbi Judah the son of Simeon said: 'This one [Caleb] saved the sheep, and that one [Pharaoh's daughter] saved the shepherd. Let the one who saved the sheep come and marry the one who saved the shepherd.'

"Moses was called by ten names: Jered, Heber, Jekuthiel, the father of Gedor, the father of Soco, the father of Zanoah. Rabbi Judah the son of Rabbi Ilai said: 'His name is also [known as] Ṭobiah (*ṭwbyh*). Thus it is written: *And she saw he was a goodly child (ṭwb hw')* (Ex. 2:2) [which means] he [was called] Ṭobiah.' Rabbi Ishmael the son of Ami said: 'Also Shemaiah was his name.' Rabbi Joshua the son of Rabbi Nehemiah came and explained this verse: '*And the scribe Shemaiah the son of Nethanel, a Levite, recorded them in the presence of the king and the princes, and Zadok, the priest, and Ahimelek, the son of Abiathar* (I Chron. 24:6). [Moses was called] *Shemaiah (šm'yh)* because God (*yh*) listened (*šm'*) to his prayer. [Moses was called] *the son of Nethanel (bn ntn'l)* [because he was the] son *(bn)* to whom the Torah was given *(nytnh)* from [God's] hand to [his] hand. [Moses was called] *the scribe*, for he was the scribe of Israel [who first recorded the Torah. Moses was called] *a Levite*, for he was from the tribe of Levi. *In the presence of the king and the princes.* This is the King of kings, the Holy One, blessed be He, and his court [of angels]. *And Zadok, the priest.* This is Aaron [Moses' brother, who was the first] priest. *Ahimelek (᾽hy-mlk)* [refers to Aaron], for he was the brother (᾽h) of the king *(mlk)* [Moses]. *The son of Abiathar (bn 'bytr)* [refers to Moses, who was the] son *(bn)* [for whom] the Holy One, blessed be He, overlooked *(wytr)* the sin of the [golden] calf.' Rabbi Tanḥuma in the name of Rabbi Joshua the son of Qorḥa and Rabbi Nehemiah in the name of Joshua the son of Levi [said]: 'Even Levi was [Moses]' name [after] the original ancestor of his family; *And is not Aaron your brother, O Levi* (Ex. 4:14). And [finally] Moses [was the name of the Levite].' Behold, there are ten [names by which Moses is known]. The Holy One, blessed be He, said to Moses: 'By your life, of all the names by which you are called, I shall call you only by the name which Bithiah, the daughter of Pharaoh, called you': *And she called his name Moses* (Ex. 2:10). *And [YHWH] called [him] Moses* (Lev. 1:1)."

Rabbi Abin in the name of Rabbi Berekhyah the Elder opened [his discourse with Ps. 89:20]: *"Then You spoke in a vision to Your pious ones and said: 'I have set a crown (᾽zr) upon one who is mighty, I have exalted one chosen from the people.'* [He] speaks of Abraham, for He spoke with him through speech[es] and through vision[s]. Thus it is written: *After these things, the word of YHWH came to Abram in a vision saying* (Gen. 15:1). *To Your pious ones* [refers to Abraham, who is called pious in Mic. 7:20:] *You gave truth to Jacob and piety to Abraham. And said: 'I have set a crown upon one who is mighty* [refers to Abraham], for he killed four kings in one night. Thus it is written: *And he divided his forces against them at night* (Gen. 14:14). Said Rabbi Phineḥas: '[But did Abraham really kill them,] for can a man pursue those who have been killed? For it is written: *And he rose early and pursued them* (Gen. 14:14). Rather, learn [from this verse that] the Holy One, blessed be He, killed [them while] Abraham pursued [them].' *I have exalted one chosen from the people* [refers to Abraham, for it is said:] *You are He, YHWH, God who chose Abram and brought him forth from Ur of the Chaldees* (Neh. 9:7).

"[Ps. 89:20[speaks of David, who was spoken with by word[s] and by vision[s], for thus it is written: *In accordance with all these words and in accordance with all of this vision, Nathan spoke to David* (II Sam. 7:17). *To your pious ones* [refers] to David; [thus it is written:] *Preserve my life, for I am pious* (Ps. 86:2). *And You said: 'I have placed a crown upon the mighy ones.'* Rabbi Abba the son of Kahanah and the rabbis [discussed these words]. Rabbi Abba the son of Kahanah said: 'David fought thirteen wars.' But the rabbis said: '[He fought] eighteen [wars].' But there is no difference [between the opinion of Abba and that of the rabbis], for the one who said 'thirteen' [refers only to the wars which David fought] for the needs of Israel. The one[s] who said 'eighteen' [referred to] the five [wars David fought] for his own needs and to the thirteen [wars he fought] for the needs of Israel. *I have exalted one chosen from the people* [refers to David, for it is written:] *And He chose David, His servant, and took him* (Ps. 78:70).

"[Ps. 89:20] speaks of Moses, for He spoke with him through word[s] and vision[s], for it is written: *Mouth to mouth, I speak with him (Num. 12:8).* *To Your pious ones* [refers to Moses], for he was from the tribe of Levi, [and] it is written [about] him [Levi: *Give Levi] your Thummin and your Urim, to your pious one* (Deut. 33:8). *And You said: 'I have placed a crown on the mighty one'* [refers to Moses]. This is comparable to that which Rabbi Tanhuma the son of Hanilai said [above]: 'It is customary that in the world a burden which is heavy for one is light for two, [and one that is heavy] for two is light for four. But is a burden which is heavy for sixty myriads light for one? [But in the case of Israel and Moses this was so!] All Israel stood before Mount Sinai and said: *"If we hear the voice of YHWH any more we shall die"* (Deut. 5:25). But Moses heard the voice of [YHWH] speaking by himself, and he lived.' Know that it is so, for of all of them, the Word called to Moses alone, for it is written: *And [YHWH] called to Moses* (Lev. 1:1). *I have exalted one chosen from the people* [refers to Moses, for it is written: *Therefore, He said He would destroy them] had not Moses, His chosen one, stood in the breach before Him, to turn away His wrath from destroying them* (Ps. 106:23)."

Rabbi Joshua of Siknin in the name of Rabbi Levi opened [his discourse with Prov. 25:7]: *"For it is better to be told, 'come up here,' than to be put lower in the presence of the prince whom your eyes have seen.* Rabbi Aqiba taught this in the name of Rabbi Simeon the son of Azzai: 'Move back from your [normal] place [in the schoolhouse] two or three places and sit [there]. Move back so that they might say [to you] "come up." And do not go forward [to a place closer to the front], lest they say to you "move back." ' And thus did Hillel say: 'My degradation is my elevation; my elevation is my degradation.' What [scriptural verse provided the] reason [for Hillel's statement? Ps. 113:5–6 provided the basis: *Who is like YHWH, our God,] who is seated on high, who goes far down to look [upon the heavens and the earth?]* And you find that in the hour that the Holy One, blessed be He, was revealed to Moses in the midst of the [burning] bush, Moses hid his face from Him. Thus it is written: *And Moses hid his face* (Ex. 3:6). The Holy One, blessed be He, said to him: '*Now, come (lkh) and I will send you to Pharaoh'* (Ex. 3:10). Said Rabbi Eleazar: '[The term *lkh,* translated "come"] really [means] "you" (*lk*). [The addition of] the [letter] *he* at the end of the word ["come," *lkh,*] indicates that if you do not redeem them, no one else will redeem them.' At the [Reed] Sea [Moses] stood to the side. The Holy One, blessed be He, said to him: '*And you, raise your staff and spread forth your hand'* (Ex. 14:16), indicating that if you do not split it, no one else will split it. At Sinai [Moses] stood to the side. The Holy One, blessed be He, said to him: '*Go up, you and your brother Aaron'* (Ex. 24:1), indicating that if you do not go up, no one else will go up. At the Tent of Meeting [Moses] stood to the side. The Holy One, blessed be He, said to him: 'How long will you degrade yourself? You are the only one for whom the hour waits.' Know that this is so, for of all of them, the Word called to Moses, alone, for it is written: *And [YHWH] called to Moses* (Lev. 1:1)."

Rabbi Tanhuma opened [his discourse with Prov. 20:15]: "*There is gold, and abundance of costly stones; but the lips of knowledge are a precious jewel.* It is usual that in the world a man [who] possesses gold, silver, precious stones, pearls, and all desirable objects that are in the world does not possess knowledge. What benefit is there for him [in the things which he possesses]? They apply this maxim to him: '[If] you possess knowledge, what do you lack? [If] you lack knowledge, what do you possess?' *There is gold* [refers] to everyone's bringing gold as their Freewill-offering to the Tabernacle; thus it is written: *And this is the offering [which you shall receive from them: Gold . . .]* (Ex. 25:3). *And abundance of costly stones* [refers to] the Freewill-offering of the princes; thus it is written: *And the princes brought [onyx stones and stones to be set . . .]* (Ex. 35:27). *But the lips of knowledge are a precious jewel* [refers to Moses], for Moses grieved [and] said: 'Everyone else brought a Freewill-offering to the Tabernacle, but I did not bring [anything].' The Holy One, blessed be He, said to him: 'By your life, your words are more precious to Me than these [offerings].' Know that this is so, for of all of them, the Word called to Moses alone, for it is written: *And [YHWH] called to Moses* (Lev. 1:1)."

What is written above this subject in the section on the Tabernacle [Ex. 38:21 ff.]? *As YHWH commanded Moses* [is written]. To what [can this] be compared? [It can be compared] to a king who would command his servant and say to him: "Build me a palace." [While he was building, the servant] would write the king's name on each element [of the building]. He would build walls and would write the king's name on them; he would raise columns and would write the king's name on them; he would lay beams and would write the king's name on them. After a number of days, the king entered the palace, and on everything upon which he looked he found his name written. [The king] said: "All of this glory my servant created for me! Yet I am inside while he is outside!" [Then the king] called him, [requesting] that he should enter inside [to be with him]. Thus, when the Holy One, blessed be He, said to Moses: "Make Me a Tabernacle," upon every thing which he would make, [Moses] would write on it, *as YHWH commanded Moses.* [When] the Holy One, blessed be He, [entered the Tabernacle], He said: "All of this glory Moses has made for Me; but I am inside while he is outside." [Then] He called to him [requesting] that he should enter inside [to be with Him]; therefore, it is said: *And [YHWH] called to Moses* (Lev. 1:1).

Rabbi Samuel the son of Naḥman in the name of Rabbi Nathan said: 'Eighteen [times *As YHWH] commanded [Moses]* is written in the section about the Tabernacle, corresponding to the eighteen vertebrae of the spinal column." Corresponding [to these eighteen references in the section about the Tabernacle, the] sages, may their memory be for a blessing, established the eighteen benedictions which are in the *Tefilah.* [These eighteen references in the section about the Tabernacle] correspond [as well] to the eighteen references [to God's name] which are in the section of the *Shema'* [in the daily worship service. These eighteen references in the section about the Tabernacle] correspond [also] to the eighteen references [to God's name] which are in [Ps. 29, which begins] *Ascribe to YHWH, O heavenly beings.* Said Rabbi Ḥiyya the son of Ada: "[One begins to count the eighteen times that the phrase *as YHWH commanded*

Moses appears] only from *And with him was Oholiab the son of Ahisamach, of the tribe of Dan* (Ex. 38:23) until the end of the book [of Exodus]." To what may the thing be compared? [It may be compared] to a king who entered a country and with him were commanders, governors, and soldiers; but we do not know which of them is the most important. But he to whom the king turns his face and speaks, we know that he is the most important. Thus, everyone surrounded the Tent of Meeting: Moses, Aaron, Nadab, Abihu, and the seventy elders. But we do not know which of them is the most important. But from [the fact] that the Holy One, blessed be He, called to Moses and spoke with him, we know that he is the most important of all of them; therefore, it is said: *And [YHWH] called to Moses* (Lev. 1:1).

To what [can] the thing be compared? [It can be compared] to a king who enters a country. With whom will he speak first? Is it not to the market-supervisor of the country? Why [does the king speak to him first? It is because] he deals with [the essential requirements of] the life of the country, [for he deals with the sale of food]. Thus, Moses deals with the necessities of the life of Israel. He said to them: "This living thing you may eat, and this [living thing] you may not eat: *This you may eat of all that is in the sea* (Lev. 11:9); and this you may not eat. *These you shall have in abomination among the birds* (Lev. 11:13); these you shall have in abomination, and these you shall not have in abomination. *This is unclean for you* (Lev. 11:29); this is unclean, and this is not unclean." Therefore, it is said: *And [YHWH] called to Moses* (Lev. 1:1).

And [YHWH] called to Moses (Lev. 1:1). But to Adam did He not call? [Is it not said:] *And YHWH, God, called to Adam* (Gen. 3:9)? Rather, it is not improper for the King to speak to His tenant. *And [YHWH] spoke to him* (Lev. 1:1). But with Noah did He not speak? [Is it not said:] *And God spoke to Noah* (Gen. 8:15)? [But] it is not improper for the King to speak with His helmsman. *And [YHWH] called to Moses* (Lev. 1:1). But to Abraham did He not call? [Is it not said:] *And the angel of YHWH called to Abraham a second time* (Gen. 22:15)? [But] it is not improper for the King to speak with His inn-keeper. *And [YHWH] spoke to him* (Lev. 1:1). But with Abraham did He not speak? [Is it not said:] *And Abram fell on his face, and He spoke with him* (Gen. 17:3)? [But] it is not improper for the King to speak with His inn-keeper. "*And [YHWH] called to Moses,* but not in the way in which [He called to] Abraham. Concerning Abraham it is written, *And the angel of YHWH called to Abraham a second time from heaven* (Gen. 22:15) [which tells us that] the angel called and [only] the voice [of YHWH] spoke [to Abraham]. "But here," said Rabbi Abin, "said the Holy One, blessed be He, 'I am He Who calls, and I am He Who speaks: *I, even I, have spoken and called him, I have brought him, and he will prosper in his way* (Isa. 48:15).' "

From the Tent of Meeting (Lev. 1:1). Said Rabbi Eleazar: "Even though the Torah was given as a fence to Israel at Sinai, they were not punished [for violating its precepts] until it was repeated for them at the Tent of Meeting. It is a parable. [It can be compared] to an ordinance written and sealed and brought into a country. The people of the country were not punished [for violating the ordinance] until it was explained to them in the public baths of the country. Thus, even though the Torah was given to Israel at Sinai, they were not punished [for violating it] until it was repeated in the Tent of Meeting. Thus it is written: *Until I had brought it into my mother's house, and into the chamber of her that conceived me* (Cant. 3:4). *Into my mother's house*, this is Sinai. *And into the chamber of her that conceived me (hwrty)*, this is the Tent of Meeting, for from there Israel was commanded [to follow] the teaching [s *(hwr'h)* of the Torah]."

Said Rabbi Joshua the son of Levi: "If [the rest of] the nations of the world would have known how wonderful the Tent of Meeting was for them [Israel], they would have surrounded it with camps and fortifications. You find that before the Tabernacle was set up, [the rest of] the nations of the world would hear the voice of [God's] speech, and they would be frightened in their camps; thus it is written: *For who is there among all flesh who heard the voice of God and lived* (Deut. 5:23)."

Said Rabbi Simon: "The speech [of God] went forth [from the Tent of Meeting] with a double nature: life for Israel and the poison of death for [the rest of] the nations of the world. Thus it is said: *When you heard it and lived* (Deut. 4:33) [which means] you heard and lived, but [the rest of] the nations of the world heard [it] and died. For Rabbi Ḥiyya taught: '*From the Tent of Meeting* teaches [us] that the voice [of God] would stop and would not go outside of the Tent of Meeting.' "

Said Rabbi Isaac: "Before the Tent of Meeting was set up, prophecy was found throughout the nations of the world. After the Tent of Meeting was set up, [prophecy] was removed from among [the rest of the nations of the world]; thus it is written: *I held it and would not let it go* (Cant. 3:4)." They said to him [Isaac]: "Behold, Balaam prophesied, [and he was not an Israelite]." [Isaac] said to them: "He prophesied only for the good of Israel, [for it is said:] *Who can count the dust of Jacob* (Num. 23:10), *He has not beheld misfortune in Jacob* (Num. 23:23), *How fair are your tents, O Jacob* (Num. 24:5), *A star shall come forth from Jacob* (Num. 24:17), *By Jacob shall dominion be exercised* (Num. 24:19)."

What [difference] is there between the prophets of Israel and the prophets of [the rest of] the nations of the world? Rabbi Ḥama the son of Rabbi Ḥanina and Rabbi Issacar of the village of Mandi [discussed this question]. Rabbi Ḥama the son of Rabbi Ḥanina said: "The Holy One, blessed be He, revealed [Himself] to the prophets of [the rest of] the nations of the world only through partial speech; thus, what do you say? *And God called (wyqr) to Balaam* (Num. 23:4). But [He revealed Himself to] the prophets of Israel through a complete speech, for it is written: *And [YHWH] called (wyqr') to Moses* (Lev. 1:1)." Said Rabbi Issacar of the village of Mandi: "Should this [reception of prophecy] be their reward? This expression, *And He called (wyqr)*, is only an expression of uncleanness; thus you say, *But if there shall be a man among you who is not clean because of what happened (mqrh) at night* (Deut. 23:11). But [He revealed Himself to] the prophets of Israel through an expression of holiness, with an expression of cleanness, in a clear expression, in the [Hebrew] language with which the angels of service praise Him. Thus you say: *And they called (qr'), this one to that one and said* (Isa. 6:3)."

Said Rabbi Eleazar the son of Menaḥem: "It is written: *YHWH is far from the evil ones but He hears the prayers of the righteous* (Prov. 15:29). *Far from the evil ones*, these are the prophets of [the rest of] the nations of the world. *But he hears the prayers of the righteous*, these are the prophets of Israel. You find that the Holy One, blessed be He, revealed [Himself] to the prophets of [the rest of] the nations of the world only like a man who comes from a faraway land; thus you say: *They have come to Me from a faraway land, from Babylon* (Isa. 39:3). But [He revealed Himself to] the prophets of Israel immediately [without coming from a faraway place; thus it is written: *And YHWH] appeared [to him] and He called* (Gen. 18:1)."

Said Rabbi Yosi the son of Biba: "The Holy One, blessed be He, revealed Himself to the prophets of [the rest of] the nations of the world only at night, when normally human beings are separated from one another, [for it is said:] *Amid thoughts from visions of the night, when deep sleep falls upon men* (Job 4:13), and *Now a word was brought to me stealthily, my ear received a whisper of it* (Job. 4:12)." Rabbi Ḥanana the son of Pappa and the rabbis [discussed this matter]. Rabbi Ḥanana the son of Pappa said: "It is a parable. [It can be compared] to a king when he and his lover were placed in a hall and a curtain was between them. When he spoke with his lover, he doubled up the curtain and spoke to his lover." The rabbis said: "[It is comparable] to a king who had a wife and a concubine. When he walks with his wife, he walks freely and openly. When he walks with his concubine, he walks in secrecy. Thus, the Holy One, blessed be He, reveals Himself to the prophets of [the rest of] the nations of the world only at night, for it is written: *And YHWH came to Abimelech in a dream of the night* (Gen. 20:3). And it is written: *And God came to Laban the Arami in a dream of the night* (Gen. 31:24). *And God came to Balaam at night* (Num. 22:2). But [He revealed Himself to] the prophets of Israel during the day: *And he sat near the door of the tent in the heat of the day* (Gen. 18:1). *On the day when YHWH spoke to Moses in the Land of Egypt* (Ex. 6:28). *On the day that He commanded the Children of Israel* (Lev. 7:38). *These are the generations of Aaron and Moses on the day that YHWH spoke to Moses on Mount Sinai* (Num. 3:1)."

What is [the difference] between Moses and the rest of the prophets? Rabbi Judah the son of Ilai and the rabbis [discussed this matter]. Rabbi Judah said: "All [the other] prophets saw [their visions] through nine window panes. Thus it is written: *And like the vision which I saw was like the vision which I had seen when He came to destroy the city and like the vision which I had seen by the river of Cheber, and I fell on my face* (Ezek. 43:3). But Moses saw [his visions] through one window pane, *[With him I speak mouth to mouth] clearly and not in dark speech* (Num. 12:8)." But the rabbis said: "All [the other] prophets saw [their visions] through a dim glass, for it is written: *I spoke to the prophets, and I increased visions* (Hos. 12:11). But Moses saw [his visions] through a polished glass; thus it is written: *He beholds the form of YHWH* (Num. 12:8)." Rabbi Phinehas in the name of Rabbi Hoshiya [said: "It is comparable] to a king who revealed himself to his household only through his image, for in this world the Holy Presence reveals Herself to the special ones. But [with reference] to the world-to-come, what is written: *And the glory of YHWH will be revealed, and they shall see [it]* (Isa. 40:5)."

COMMENTS

Rabbi Tanḥuma the son of Ḥanilai opened. This is the first of five *petiḥot,* proems, which appear at the beginning of Leviticus Rabbah. The proem is a formal literary construction. It begins with a verse from the Bible, usually from Psalms or one of the other works of the third section of the Hebrew Bible, the Writings, or the Hagiographa. At first glance the opening verse appears to have little relationship with the opening of the biblical text upon which the midrash is supposed to comment. In fact, the proem moves from this opening verse to the beginning of the biblical section under consideration.[10] The theme of this particular proem is the identification of the person to whom Ps. 103:20 refers.

About what does Scripture speak. The midrash seeks a definition of the term *ml'k,* "messenger." The term is problematic because it can mean "angel" or simply "messenger;" that is, *ml'k* can refer either to a heavenly being or to an earthly creature. If Ps. 103:20 refers to heavenly beings, the midrash asks why does Ps. 103:21 state, *Bless YHWH, all His hosts?* Because the Bible does not merely repeat itself, we must assume that Ps. 103:20 and 103:21 do not state the same thing. The key word in the latter verse is *all* for that word indicates that Ps. 103:21 refers to the heavenly beings. If Ps. 103:21 refers to the heavenly beings, we can assume that Ps. 103:20 speaks of earthly messengers. The rest of the *petiḥah* will discuss the possible identities of the messenger mentioned in Ps. 103.20.

Another matter. At this point the midrash demonstrates that prophets are called by the term *ml'k.* Num. 20:16 states that God sent a *ml'k* to lead the Hebrews from Egypt. Because we know that Moses led the Hebrews from Egypt, we must conclude that Num. 20:16 teaches us that Moses, and by implication the other prophets, was called *ml'k.*

Said Rabbi Simeon. Jdgs. 2:1 employs the term *ml'k* but refers to Phinehas. Simeon notes that this term was applied to Phinehas because when the Holy Spirit rested on him, his face glowed like the face of an angel. Exactly why the *ml'k* in Jdgs. 2:1 is identified as Phinehas, the high priest, is unclear to me; however, this identification is made in Seder Olam Rabbah. The targum to this passage, the accepted Aramaic version of the prophetic books of the Bible, completed by the fourth century of the common era, translates *ml'k* with *nby',* "prophet." Rashi (11th cent.), the RaDaK (12th cent.), and the RaLBaG (13–14th cent.)[11] all identify the *ml'k* of Jdgs. 2:1 with Phinehas.

And the rabbis said. Although Manoah's wife thought a human being had been sent to her, Jdgs. 13:8 ff. makes it clear that in fact she had seen an angel, for when Manoah asks *YHWH, let the man of God whom You did send come again,* we are told that *God listened to the voice of Manoah, and the angel of God came again to the woman*—Because Manoah's wife could not tell the difference between a man of God, i.e., a prophet, and an angel, we must assume that they looked similar. The phrase *man of God* appears in connection with prophets such as Elijah and Elisha, cf. II Kgs. 1:13.

Said Rabbi Yoḥanan. Yoḥanan brings a verse in which not only is a specific prophet, Haggai, called a *ml'k* of YHWH, but also the message which he delivered is called a *ml'kwt* of YHWH. Thus, the Hebrew root *ml'k* is used to identify the prophet and his message.

Said Rabbi Isaac. Isaac argues that the *mighty ones* in Ps. 103:20 are those who keep the sabbatical years, for they must observe the commandment every day of the year even though it causes them financial hardship. As D. Sperber notes, "The Sabbatical (seventh) year carries with it a number of severe restrictions. Thus, it is forbidden to till the soil during this year; whatever grows (of itself) during this year is common property, even though it grew on privately owned land, etc. Such laws were extremely difficult to keep, and it took both advanced planning, firm resolve and a goodly measure of faith to abide by them."[12] According to M. Avi-Yonah, the *annona* "comprised above all the supply of wheat and cattle to the soldiers. . . . In the second half of the third century, the *arnona* became the financial mainstay of the Roman government. [The emperor] Diocletian [287–305 C.E.] succeeded in stabilizing the economic and political conditions of the [Roman] Empire. He made the *arnona* into a regular tax levied on the basis of a property valuation which was carried out every fifteen years. The *arnona* weighed most heavily on the peasants. The town-dwellers were affected only insofar as they owned land."[13] Thus, the one whose land lies fallow must still pay the tax according to the valuation of the land which was set in previous years, even though he does not have sufficient crops with which to pay the tax. Isaac employs a *gezarah shavah* to prove that Ps. 103:20 refers to the sabbatical year. According to this exegetical principle, two verses are juxtaposed if they contain the same word or phrase. When the two verses are brought into conjunction with each other, what applies to one verse also applies to the other. In this case, Ps. 103:20 is juxtaposed with Deut. 15:1 because both contain the Hebrew word *dbr*. Because the latter deals with the year of release, the sabbatical year, we must assume that the former also deals with the sabbatical year.

Rabbi Huna in the name of Rabbi Aḥa said. Huna suggests that the second phrase of Ps. 103:20 refers to Israel's standing at Mount Sinai because the order of the verbs in Ps. 103:20, *'śh* and *šm'*, parallels the order of the verbs in Ex. 24:7, *n'śh* and *nšm'*.

Said Rabbi Tanḥuma the son of Ḥanilai. Tanḥuma now brings us to the opening of Leviticus, for we have come to the end of the *petiḥah.* Tanḥuma suggests that the mighty one *harkening* to YHWH's voice was Moses. He offers a parable which demonstrates Moses' might. Normally, a burden which is heavy for sixty myriads, a reference to the number of those who left Egypt, Ex. 12:37, is also heavy for one. However, this is not true in the case of Moses and Israel, for the six hundred thousand Israelites who left Egypt were afraid to hear the voice of YHWH, while Moses alone listened to His voice. Therefore, YHWH called to Moses and not to the other Hebrews. We have a carefully constructed *petiḥah.* Tanḥuma opened the section with Ps. 103:20. First, the midrash establishes that the verse speaks of humans, even though it employs the term *ml'k.* Next, we discover that prophets are called by the term *ml'k.* Isaac offers an aside in which he argues that *mighty Ones* in Ps. 103:20 refers to those who keep the sabbatical year. Huna brings us back on track when he claims that Ps. 103:20 refers to Israel's standing before Mount Sinai. Tanḥuma then demonstrates that Ps. 103:20 explains that Moses was the mighty one who stood before YHWH at Mount Sinai and that his special character was the reason that he alone was called by YHWH at the opening of Lev. 1:1.

Rabbi Abbahu opened. Abbahu cites Hos. 14:7 and states that it refers to the proselytes, who dwell under YHWH's shadow after they have converted to Judaism.

They shall grow grain (yḥyw dgn). This could be read as follows: "They give life [as] wheat." Wheat was one of the essential foods of Palestine, Deut. 8:8. Mishnah *Berakhot* 6:5 states that the blessing over bread, which was made of grain, is the essential blessing one must make before eating a meal. This again underscores the importance of grain and grain-products for the Palestinians. Abbahu brings Zech. 9:17 as proof for the centrality of grain as a life-giving food. This verse which contains the phrase *dgn bḥwrym* has two possible interpretations, for *bḥwr* means both "young men" and "chosen." Thus, the verse could mean that grain gives life to the young men or that grain is the chosen produce. In any case, just as the grain is special, so also the converts to Judaism are special.

They shall blossom as the vine. This exegesis is unambiguous, for Ps. 80:9 describes Israel as *a vine*, and surely it was Israel whom God brought out of Egypt and planted in the Land of Canaan. Therefore, the proselytes shall prosper just as Israel has prospered.

Another matter. The opening of this section changes direction and speaks about the two major divisions of rabbinic lore: The Talmud (halakhah, law) and the aggadah (nonlegal material). The text probably means that just as grain is essential for life, so also the Talmud is essential for life. Just as grain brings joy and pleasure to the body, so also the aggadah brings spiritual enjoyment to the Jew.[14]

Said the Holy One, blessed be He. At this point the midrash moves back to the discussion of the proselytes. Hos. 14:7 states that *their mention shall be like the wine of Lebanon.* God said that this means that their names shall be as precious to Him as the wine which is placed on His altar. The rest of the section explains why the altar was called Lebanon; therefore, it explains God's statement. These comments are puns which connect *lbnn* with (1) "to make white," *mlbym*, and (2) "heart," *lb*.[15]

Rabbi Simeon in the name of Rabbi Joshua. At this point the midrash appears to go "off track," for here we learn that the names in Chronicles were written only to be interpreted. However, we must remember that immediately preceding the above discussion about the altar's being called Lebanon, God stated that the "names" of the proselytes were important to Him. That is the reason that this section on the names in I Chron. 4:18 appears here.

And his Judite wife. The midrash states that this is Jochebed, Moses' mother, Ex. 6:20. Even though she was from the tribe of Levi, Ex. 6:19, she was called a Judite, as if she were from the tribe of Judah, because she produced Jews through her son Moses.

Rabbi Ḥananah the son of Pappa and Rabbi Simeon. These two sages state that Jered, *yrd*, refers to Moses. Both employ puns; however, each bases his interpretation on a different Hebrew root. Ḥananah employs the root *yrd*, "to bring down," and states that Moses was called *yrd* because he brought the Torah down from the upper world to the lower world. An alternate interpretation suggests that Moses brought the *Shekhinah* down from the upper world to the lower world. Simeon used the root *rdh*, "to have dominion," and stated that *yrd* referred to Moses' having dominion over the Hebrews.

Rabbi Huna in the name of Rabbi Aḥa said. Huna states that Moses was called the father of Gedor, *gdwr*, because he was the father of the fence-makers *(gwdrym)*. The rabbis believed that in order to prevent people from violating the law, fences should be built around it to guard it. Often the rabbis enacted statutes which were designed to prevent people from accidentally violating a rule. For example, Mishnah *Berakhot* 1:1 states that one may recite the evening *Shemaʿ* until dawn; however, the sages ruled that one may recite the evening *Shemaʿ* only until midnight, in order to prevent one from actually reciting it after dawn. Here, the sages enacted a fence around the law. Their supposition was that if people were allowed to wait until dawn, they might inadvertently recite it after dawn; however, if people were forced to recite it before midnight, then even if they recited it after midnight they still would be able to recite it before dawn. According to Huna, the rabbinic injunctions, which were based on the Oral Torah which Moses received directly from God and transmitted to the rabbis, often served as fences around the Written Torah which God dictated to Moses and which Moses wrote down in the Torah scroll.[16]

Heber. This refers to Moses because he was the one who "joined," *ḥybr*, the Hebrews to God by transmitting God's word to them.

Another matter. This probably is also a pun, even though *ḥbr* and *'br* are spelled differently. This passage suggests that the *ayyin*, a guttural-sounding letter which is now silent, was pronounced similarly to the *ḥet*, another guttural letter, at the time that this comment was composed.

The father of Soco. Deut. 34:10 calls Moses a prophet. Again we have a pun, for Soco, *swkw*, is juxtaposed with the verb "to foresee," *skh*.

Rabbi Levi said. Levi also suggests that Soco refers to Moses' being called a prophet; however, he suggests that Soco refers to Moses' prophecy because it is similar to the Arabic word for "prophet."

Rabbi Levi and Rabbi Simeon. Levi suggests that Moses was called Jekuthiel, *yqwty'l*, because he made the Hebrews "hope," *qwt*, in God, *'l*. He properly has broken the theophoric name Jekuthiel into its two parts, *yqwty 'l*.

Said Rabbi Simeon. Something is wrong with the text. According to the style of this passage, the opening phrase, "Rabbi Levi and Rabbi Simeon," should introduce two comments, one by each of the sages, on the same word, Jekuthiel. However, Simeon discusses *the father of Zanoah*, not Jekuthiel. It appears that Simeon's original comment has been lost. Simeon argues that Moses was called *the father of Zanoah (zwnḥ)* because he removed the Jews from their transgression, *znḥ*, at the time of the golden calf. This exegesis is awkward, for it does not make clear why Moses was known as *the father* of Zanoah and not merely as Zanoah. The commentators suggest that Simeon meant to say that Moses was the father of the Children of Israel, whom he removed from the sin of the golden calf;[17] however, this explanation is less than satisfactory, given Simeon's comment as we now have it.

Rabbi Joshua of Siknin in the name of Rabbi Levi. We have another pun. Joshua reads Bithiah, *btyh*, as two words: *bt yh*, "the daughter of YH[WH]." Her name was "the daugher of YHWH" even though she was not Jewish, because she took Moses and called him her son. This comment returns us to the above theme that proselytes are important to God and that their names are precious to Him. The implication is that by taking Moses as her son, Pharaoh's daughter also accepted YHWH as her God.

Rabbi Abba the son of Kahanah said. Two sages now attempt to identify the husband of Pharaoh's daughter. I Chron. 4:18 gives his name as Mered, *mrd*. Both Abba and Judah state that this refers to Caleb. Abba employs a pun, for *mrd* means "to rebel." Just as Caleb rebelled against the other spies who reconnoitered the Land of Canaan, Num. 13:30, so also Pharaoh's daughter rebelled against her father's command, Ex. 1:16, for she did not allow Moses to die in the river. Therefore, it is logical to assume that the female rebel married the male rebel; that is, Pharaoh's daughter married Caleb.

Rabbi Judah the son of Simeon said. Although Judah agrees that Pharaoh's daughter married Caleb, he does not rely on a pun to prove his point; in fact, he totally ignores the name Mered. Judah argues that the two belonged together, for Caleb saved the sheep, the Children of Israel, by encouraging them to enter the Land of Canaan, while Pharaoh's daughter saved their shepherd, Moses. Therefore, it was appropriate that the two should marry each other.

Moses was called by ten names. The midrash continues the discussion of Moses' name. The previous paragraph explained that the six names in I Chron. 4:18 referred to Moses. The introduction to the present paragraph suggests that we must find four more names for Moses. Notice that this discussion about Moses' name is a development of the theme that God considers the names of the proselytes to be precious.

Rabbi Judah the son of Rabbi Ilai. Judah employs a pun, for Ex. 2:2 states that Moses was *a goodly child, twb hw'*; therefore, he was called Tobiah, *twb yh*, "the goodly one of YH[WH]."

Rabbi Ishmael the son of Ami said. Ishmael states that Moses was called Shemaiah; however, he does not offer a reason for his statement. This is supplied by Joshua's exegesis of I Chron. 24:6.

Rabbi Joshua the son of Rabbi Nehemiah came and explained. Joshua offers us several puns. Moses was called Shemaiah, *šm'yh*, because "YH[WH] listened," *šm' yh*, to his prayers. Moses was called the son of Nethanel, *bn ntn'l*, because he was the "son," *bn*, to whom "God," *'l*, "gave," *ntn*, the Torah. To this point we have ten names for Moses: Moses, Jered, Heber, Jekuthiel, the father of Gedor, the father of Soco, the father of Zanoah, Tobiah, Shemaiah, and the son of Nethanel. Even if Levite and Scribe are meant to be titles and not names, the rest of the paragraph applies the following names to Moses: Abiathar and Levi. Something is wrong with our text, for the opening reference to ten names does not fit with the midrash that we now have. It is probable that there was a tradition that Moses had ten names and that that tradition merely was added here because our passage discusses Moses' different names. Clearly, the reference to ten names is inappropriate to the text before us.[18]

Ahimelekh. Ahimelek refers to Aaron, for the name is divided into two parts: *'hy*, "brother of," *mlk*, "king." The rabbis took Deut. 33:5 as referring to Moses' kingship. *Thus YHWH was king in Jeshurun* means that YHWH appointed a king, Moses, in Jeshurun.[19]

The son of Abiathar. We again have a pun; *'bytr* is identified with the verb *wtr*.

Rabbi Tanhuma in the name of Rabbi Joshua. Ex. 4:14 is usually translated as follows: *Is there not Aaron, your brother, the Levite?* However, Tanhuma reads the verse as follows: "And is not Aaron your brother, O Levi"; therefore, Ex. 4:14 proves that Moses was called Levi.

The Holy One, blessed be He, said to Moses. At this point the *petihah* returns to the theme of God's considering the names of the proselytes as precious. Of all the names which were applied to Moses, God called him by the name given him by the assumed convert, Pharaoh's daughter. Therefore, Lev. 1:1 is read as follows: "And YHWH called him Moses." Again we have a carefully crafted proem. It opens with Hos. 14:7 and a discussion of the importance of converts to Judaism. God states that the non-Jewish names of the converts are precious, and, after an aside which discusses the fact that the altar is called Lebanon, the *petiḥah* discusses the several names which were applied to Moses. After discussing these names, the proem ends with Lev. 1:1, which proves that God considers the non-Jewish name given Moses by an assumed convert to be important, for of all the names which were applied to Moses, God chose to call him by the name given him by Pharaoh's daughter.

Rabbi Abin in the name of Rabbi Berekhya the Elder opened. Abin opens with Ps. 89:20, and this *petiḥah* attempts to identify to whom this psalm refers.

[He] speaks of Abraham. The first suggestion is that Ps. 89:20 refers to Abraham. Gen. 15:1 states that the word of YHWH came to Abraham in a vision, and this parallels *then You spoke in a vision.* Micah 7:20 states that God gave "piety," *ḥsd,* to Abraham, and this parallels *to your pious ones.* Gen. 14:1–16 discusses the war between Amraphel king of Shinar, Arioch king of Ellasar, Chedorlaomer, king of Elam, Tidal king of Goim and Bera king of Sodom, Birsha king of Gomorrah, Shinab king of Adman, Shemeber king of Zeboiim, and the king of Bela. The four defeated the five, sacked Sodom and Gomorrah, and took Lot, Abraham's nephew, as a captive. In response, Abraham fought and defeated the four kings. This parallels *I have set a crown upon one who is mighty.*

Said Rabbi Phineḥas. Phineḥas' comment is an aside which deals with Gen. 14:14, which was quoted in our section. Phineḥas claims that Abraham could not have killed the kings and pursued them. He concludes that in fact God pursued the kings while Abraham killed them. This is curious, for the biblical text clearly states that Abraham pursued the kings. There are some versions of the text which state that Abraham pursued the kings, while God killed them.[20]

Rabbi Abin continued. At this point we return to the identification of Abraham as the one to whom Ps. 89:20 refers. In Neh. 9:7, Abraham is identified as the one whom God chose, and this parallels *One chosen from the people.*

Ps. 89:20 speaks of David. The second suggestion is that Ps. 89:20 refers to David. II Sam. 7:17 states that the prophet Nathan spoke to David in accordance with the words and visions which he had received from God. This parallels *You spoke in a vision.* Ps. 86:1 opens with *A prayer of David;* therefore, the *I* in *I am pious* refers to David, and this parallels *To Your pious ones.*

Rabbi Abba the son of Kahanah said. Abba and the rabbis discuss David's wars, to which they believe the phrase *I have placed a crown upon the mighty one* referred. Abba states that David fought thirteen wars, while the rabbis said that he fought eighteen wars. In good rabbinic fashion, the text concludes that both numbers are correct. They are different only because Abba and the rabbis counted different wars. The former counted only the wars which David fought for Israel, while the latter counted the wars which David fought for Israel and those he fought for himself. Ze'av Wolf (19th cent.) identifies the eighteen wars as follows: I Sam. 17, I Sam. 18:27, I Sam. 18:30, I Sam. 19:8, I Sam. 23:5, I Sam. 27:8, I Sam. 27:8, II Sam. 5:6, II Sam. 5:20, II Sam. 5:25, II Sam. 8:1, II Sam. 8:2, II Sam. 8:3, II Sam. 8:5, II Sam. 8:14, II Sam. 11:18, II Sam. 12:29, II Sam. 21:16. Those which David fought for his own needs were I Sam. 18:27, I Sam. 27:8, I Sam. 27:8, II Sam. 5:6, II Sam. 5:25.[21] David Luria (18th–19th cent.) offers a slightly different list.[22] Margulies approves of the comment of one sage, who suggested that the five wars which David fought for himself were the first wars which he fought while Saul was king. The wars which he fought for Israel's needs were the wars he fought while he was king.[23]

I have exalted one chosen. Ps 78:70 states that *He chose David,* and this parallels *I have exalted one chosen from the people.*

Ps. 89:20 speaks of Moses. The midrash now suggests that Ps. 89:20 speaks of Moses, and this begins the end of the *petiḥah* Num. 12:8 states: *Mouth to mouth, I speak with him wmr'h.* The last word is usually translated "clearly"; however, it comes from the root *r'h,* "to see," and it could be interpreted as referring to a vision. The whole issue is curious, however, for Num. 12:6–8 states: *If there is a prophet among you, I, YHWH, make Myself known to him in a vision, I speak with him in a dream. Not so with My servant Moses, he is entrusted with all My house. Mouth to mouth . . .* In short, these verses suggest that God did *not* speak to Moses through dreams and visions, as He spoke to the other prophets. Again we have an example of the rabbis' taking a verse out of context and interpreting it in a way which fits what they want to say. Deut. 33:8 identifies Levi as God's pious one; the title is then placed on Moses, who was from the tribe of Levi. This parallels *To your pious ones;* however, the connection to Moses is rather weak.

This is comparable to that which Rabbi Tanḥuma the son of Ḥanilai said. This is an exact quotation of Tanḥuma's parable found above. The parable here illustrates Moses' might; above it illustrated Moses' harkening to YHWH. Here the parable is connected to the following phrase in Ps. 89:20: *I have set a crown on one who is mighty.* When the verse was applied to Abraham and David, two issues, kingship and military victory, were brought into the discussion. Here, with reference to Moses, the issue is Moses' ability to stand before YHWH while the rest of Israel stood in fear. At this point, the opening of Lev. 1:1 is cited. The *petiḥah* would have ended here had it not been for the fact that there was one more phrase in Ps. 89:20 with which the midrashist had to deal. The reference to Moses as the chosen one in Ps. 106:23 is juxtaposed with *I have exalted one chosen from among the people*. This *petiḥah* is fairly straightforward. We have three different interpretations of Ps. 89:20; the last connects Moses with the psalm. It is interesting to note, however, that of the three men proposed, Abraham, David, and Moses, the arguments which connected Moses with the person mentioned in the psalm are the weakest.

Rabbi Joshua of Siknin in the name of Rabbi Levi opened. Joshua opens with Prov. 25:7, a rather straightforward "wisdom-maxim" which advises against presumptuousness about one's status in the presence of princes.

Rabbi Aqiba taught about this. Aqiba advises against being presumptuous about taking one's seat in the rabbinic academy or in the court.[24] Clearly, the closer one sat to the front the more important was his status.

And thus did Hillel say. Hillel's statement, which fits nicely in this context, does not appear in any collections of the tannaitic period. It seems to be attributed to Hillel first in our present collection.[25] The point of Ps. 113:5–6 is that even one as exalted as YHWH goes below His station out of regard for others.

And you find that in the hour that the Holy One, blessed be He. The *petiḥah* now moves to Moses and exalts his humility. We find that at the burning bush, the Reed Sea, and Mount Sinai, Moses stood aside until he was called by YHWH. In no case did Moses presume to act until he was told to do so.

Said Rabbi Eleazar. In Ex. 3:10 the Hebrew word "come" is spelled *lkh* instead of the more normal way, *lk*. The word might also mean "for you," that is, "the task at hand is for you, Moses, alone." Thus, Eleazar claims that the extra letter at the end of the word emphasizes the special nature of Moses' duty: Moses, alone, was commanded to redeem Israel.

The Holy One, blessed be He, said to him. The point here seems to be the opening phrase, *and you*, and the constant repetition of the pronoun "you" in this verse.

The Holy One, blessed be He, said to him. I assume that the point here again is the word "you" and the word "your," for in both cases the emphasis is on Moses, even when speaking of Aaron.

At the Tent of Meeting. Even at the Tent of Meeting, after the burning bush, the Reed Sea, and Mount Sinai, Moses still stood to one side. God became impatient and asked Moses why he still was reluctant to come forward; therefore, *YHWH called to Moses* (Lev. 1:1). We have a short, but nicely constructed, *petiḥah*. It opens with a "wisdom-maxim" from Psalms which warns one not to be presumptuous in the presence of princes. After a short aside[26] which warns the rabbis not be presumptuous of their status in the schoolhouses or the court, the proem moves to Moses and stresses his humility. Moses never presumed to act; he always waited for God to call him or to tell him to do something. For that reason, at the Tent of Meeting, God had to call him, as we find in Lev. 1:1.

Rabbi Tanḥuma opened. Tanḥuma opens with Prov. 20:15, another "wisdom-maxim." This one stresses the value of knowledge over material wealth. Tanḥuma claims that a person may often have material wealth but lacks knowledge. He brings a popular proverb which states that material wealth without knowledge is worthless, while knowledge, even without material wealth, is a valuable possession.

There is gold. The items mentioned in Prov. 20:15 are now identified with the offerings the Hebrews brought to Moses for the building of the Tabernacle in the desert. The connections seem obvious, given the verses quoted.

But the lips of knowledge are a precious jewel. Upon seeing that everyone but himself brought a gift for the Tabernacle, Moses became sad. God responded that He considered Moses' words to be the most precious gift he had received. David Luria (18th–19th cent.) suggested that this refers to the words which Moses spoke to the craftsmen concerning the construction of the Tabernacle.[27] Ze'av Wolf (19th cent.) suggested that Moses' orders concerning the construction of the Tabernacle were among the precious things which God told Moses in the Torah. He connects *precious jewel, kly yqr,* with *the vessels of the Tabernacle, kly mškn.*[28]

Know that this is so. We know that God considered Moses' gift the most important, for God's word came to Moses alone, as we read in Lev. 1:1: *And YHWH called to Moses.* This short *petiḥah* opens with a "wisdom-maxim" which states that *the lips of knowledge are a precious jewel.* It ends by stating that God considered Moses' instructions about the building of the Tabernacle to be more precious than the material valuables which others brought for its construction. This is illustrated by the fact that God called to Moses alone.

What is written above this subject. The midrash asks about what is written prior to the opening of Lev. 1:1 in the section on the building of the Tabernacle with which the Book of Exodus ends. The text answers that the phrase *as YHWH commanded Moses* appears throughout that section. The midrash now explains why that phrase appears so often.

It can be compared to a king. The midrash uses a parable to explain why the phrase *as YHWH commanded Moses* appears so frequently. The parable concerns a king who has a palace built. While building the palace, the craftsman places the king's name on each part of the structure. The king is so pleased with the final product that he asks the craftsman to join him inside the palace, for the palace was clearly constructed for the glory of the king and not for the honor of the craftsman. Similarly, while Moses gave instructions concerning the building of the Tabernacle, he continually stressed that all was being done according to YHWH's directions. Thus, Moses also emphasized that the Tabernacle was for YHWH and not a monument to Moses or to the workers. YHWH was so pleased with the final results and with the fact that it was constructed solely for His honor that He asked Moses, and Moses alone, to join Him inside; therefore, He called to him to enter the Tent of Meeting in Lev. 1:1. This carefully crafted section, which continues the discussion of the Tabernacle with which the previous section ended, opens with the end of Exodus and ends with the opening of Leviticus.[29]

Rabbi Samuel the son of Naḥman said. Samuel states that the phrase *as YHWH commanded* appears eighteen times at the end of Exodus. He suggests that this corresponds to the eighteen vertebrae in the spinal column. Margulies notes that the construction of the Tabernacle is discussed twice in the Book of Exodus, Ex. 26 and Ex. 38. He states that in the latter section, the phrase *as YHWH commanded Moses* appears fourteen times: Ex. 39:1, 5, 7, 21, 26, 29, 31; Ex. 40:19, 21, 23, 25, 27, 29, 32. The phrase *according to all that YHWH commanded Moses* appears five times: Ex. 38:22, 39:32, 39:42, 39:43, and 40:16. Therefore, the phrase *YHWH commanded Moses* appears nineteen times at the end of the Book of Exodux.[30]

The eighteen benedictions. The central prayer of the Jewish worship service is the *Amidah* ("standing prayer"), also called the *Tefilah* ("prayer"). At present it consists of nineteen paragraphs; however, it seems to have had eighteen paragraphs originally. Samuel suggests that the eighteen sections of the prayer correspond to the eighteen times the phrase *YHWH commanded* appears at the end of the Book of Exodus.[31] Margulies suggests that the phrase and the *Tefilah* were juxtaposed because the *Tefilah* was meant to replace the sacrifices which were brought to the Temple/Tabernacle.[32]

Correspond to the eighteen references which are in the section of the Shemâ. In the worship service, the *Shemâ* consists of Deut. 6:4–9, Deut. 11:13–21, and Num. 15:37–41. The name YHWH appears twice in Deut.6:4, Deut. 11:17, and Num. 15:41. It appears once in Deut. 6:5, 11:13, 11:21, Num. 15:37, and Num. 15:39. The term *Elohim* appears three times in Num. 15:41, and once in Deut. 6:4, 6:5, 11:13, and Num. 15:40.

Which are in Ps. 29. The term YHWH does occur eighteen times in this psalm: twice in Ps. 29:1, 2, 3, 4, 5, 8, 10, and 11, and once in Ps. 29:7 and 29:9.[33]

Said Rabbi Ḥiyya the son of Ada. If, in fact, we count the verses as Ḥiyya suggests, we would eliminate Ex. 38:22 from Margulies's list and we would have eighteen appearances of the phrase.

To what may this thing be compared. This parable seems to be out of place, for it does not discuss the issue of the phrase *as YHWH commanded Moses.* It does, however, refer to the names of the people associated with Moses. Thus, it relates indirectly to the reference to Ex. 38:23, which contains the names of the principal craftsmen who built the Tabernacle. The connection would be better if Oholiab were included in the list of names at the end of the parable. I assume that the parable was not originally found in this setting. The parable makes the point that just as we learn about the king's most important advisor by watching to whom he speaks, also we learn about God's most important confidant by watching to whom He speaks. Because God spoke to Moses alone among all those who were assembled before the Tent of Meeting, we can learn that Moses was God's most important confidant.

To what may the thing be compared. Clearly this section wants to know to what God's speaking to Moses at the opening of Lev. 1:1 can be compared. The midrash answers that just as a king speaks first to the market-supervisor, because the latter is in charge of the country's food supply and therefore knows best the needs and the character of the country's inhabitants, so also God spoke to Moses, who was also in charge of Israel's food supply. It was Moses, after all, who delivered the dietary laws to Israel. With this we come to the end of the introductions to our section of Leviticus Rabbah.

And YHWH called to Moses. This section of the midrash notes that God called to others besides Moses—for example, to Adam, to Noah, and to Abraham. If this is so, how was Moses different from the other men to whom YHWH called?

But to Adam did He not call. Gen. 3:9 states that YHWH called to Adam. Should we conclude from this that Adam and Moses were equal? The midrash concludes that they were not equal, for Adam was God's tenant; that is, God had placed Adam in the Garden of Eden to care for it for Him, according to the rabbinic interpretation of Genesis 2. Therefore, God called to Adam the same way that a king calls to his tenant.

But with Noah did He not speak. Gen. 8:15 specifically states that God spoke to Noah, just as Lev. 1:1 states that He spoke with Moses; therefore, are we to conclude that these two men were equal? The midrash concludes that they were not equal, for Noah was God's helmsman when he built and sailed the ark. God spoke to Noah the same way that any king would speak with his helmsman.

But to Abraham did He not call. This section on Abraham begins like the others, for we learn that although the angel of YHWH called to Abraham, he was not equal to Moses. God called to Abraham the same way that any king would call to his inn-keeper, a reference to the events recorded in Gen. 18. However, this section continues in ways which the discussions of Noah and Adam did not. First, both elements of Lev. 1:1, calling and speaking, are related to Abraham. Second, the midrash ignores the first answer to the question, that Abraham was God's host, and states that God did not call to Abraham in the same way in which He called to Moses, because Gen. 22:15 states that the angel of YHWH, and not YHWH Himself, called to Abraham. In the case of Moses, however, as Rabbi Abin makes explicit, God Himself spoke directly to Moses. We learn from this passage that Moses is not comparable to Adam, Noah, and Abraham, even though God called to or spoke with each of the latter. They were not equal to Moses because God conversed with them the same way that any king would converse with any of his servants. The implication is that when God called to and spoke with Moses, He did not treat him in the way in which a king treats his servants.

From the Tent of Meeting. The midrash now moves from the opening phrases of Lev. 1:1 to the end of the verse. The midrash will now discuss the importance of the Tent of Meeting, not only for Israel, but also for the other nations of the world. Notice, however, that the rest of the midrash is carefully constructed. The discussion begins with the Tent of Meeting, moves to the subject of prophecy, and ends with a discussion of Moses as the superior prophet in Israel.

Said Rabbi Eleazar. Eleazar states that the Torah was given as a fence to protect Israel and to prevent her from violating God's will. Even though the Torah was given at Sinai, its punishments were not put into effect until it was repeated and taught to Israel at the Tent of Meeting. This is compared to a royal decree, which does not go into effect until it is made public and explained to the populace in a public place. This may be a reference to the fact that at Sinai the people did not go up to the mountain; in fact, they stayed away from it, Ex. 19–20. For this reason, the Torah was not expounded publicly at Sinai.

Into my mother's house. We are told that this phrase in Cant. 3:4 refers to Sinai. In Canticles Rabbah 8:2, Rabbi Berakhyah explains that Sinai was called *my mother's house* because "there Israel was like a newborn child." I have no way of knowing if Berakhyah's comment explains our text in Leviticus Rabbah.

And into the chamber of her that conceived me. Here we have a pun. The word *hwrty,* "conceived me," is taken as a form of *hwr'h,* "teaching." The text is read as follows: "And into the chamber of my instruction."

Said Rabbi Joshua the son of Levi. Joshua argues that if the rest of the nations of the world had known how important the Tent of Meeting would be to Israel, they would have prevented Israel from coming into it. Joshua states that before the Tent of Meeting was erected, even the non-Jewish nations of the world heard God's voice, although they were afraid of it. After the Tent was constructed, however, God spoke to Israel alone. Deut. 5:23 implies that there were people among all flesh, even among the non-Jews, who heard the voice of God; however, as the verse states, hearing God's voice could be a dangerous experience.

Said Rabbi Simeon. Simeon states that the word that came out from the Tent of Meeting had a double nature, bringing life to Israel and death to the rest of the nations of the world. I assume that Simeon means that God's word gave life to Israel, for they were the only ones who heard it. Therefore, they would have been the only ones who could have lived according to God's will. The word brought death to the non-Jews either because they no longer heard it once it came from the Tent of Meeting or because it pointed out to them how they were violating God's law. Alternately, this could refer to the reward of life in the world-to-come given to those who followed God's word and the withholding of this everlasting life from those who did not follow His commandments.

For Rabbi Ḥiyya taught. Ḥiyya takes the particle "from," *m*, as a limiting particle. It indicates a limit to the voice which was heard in the Tent of Meeting. This same interpretation appears anonymously in the passage from Sifra included in our anthology.[34]

Said Rabbi Isaac. Isaac also addresses the theme of the importance of the Tent of Meeting. He states that before the Tent was erected, prophecy was not limited to Israel but was found throughout the nations of the world. Cant. 3:4, which above was juxtaposed with the teaching of the Torah at Sinai and the Tent of Meeting, is also brought here with reference to the Torah. Isaac takes the verse to mean that God withheld his Torah from the non-Jews after the Tent of Meeting was constructed.

They said to him. "They" challenge Isaac's conclusion, for Balaam's prophecy is recorded in the Book of Numbers after the Tent had been constructed in Exodus and after God spoke to Moses from the Tent in Lev. 1:1. This means that non-Jewish prophets existed after the Tent had been erected.[35]

Isaac said to them. Isaac answers their objection by pointing out that Balaam was a special case. Balaam was allowed to prophesy after the Tent had been constructed because he spoke only for the benefit of Israel.

What difference is there between the prophets: The midrash now moves to a comparison between Israel's prophets and the prophets of the other nations. This topic is clearly related to Isaac's reference to the prophets of the other nations of the world.

Rabbi Ḥama the son of Rabbi Ḥanina said. Ḥama focuses on Num. 23:4. There we find the form *wyqr* for "he called." We would expect to find *wyqr'*. Apparently the former form has been affected by the lengthening of the vowel and the shift of the accent caused by the prefixed *w*.[36] In any case, Ḥama notes that the word is incomplete, for the final *aleph* is missing. He suggests that this means that God spoke to the prophets of the rest of the nations of the world in an incomplete manner; thus, their prophecy was less complete than the message of Israel's prophets.

Said Rabbi Issacar of the village of Mandi. Issacar is surprised that the non-Jews should have received the gift of prophecy at all. He suggests that the verb *wyqr* in Num. 23:4 is a form of the Hebrew root *qrh*, "event," not *qr'*, "call." He argues that it indicates uncleanness. Issacar employs a *gezarah shavah*. According to this exegetical principle, two verses are juxtaposed with each other if they contain the same word or phrase. After they are brought into conjunction with each other, what applies to one verse is applied to the other. In this case, the root *qrh* in Deut. 23:11 refers to a nocturnal emission which renders one unclean; therefore, *wyqr* in Num. 23:4 must also refer to something unclean. The root *qr'* which occurs in Lev. 1:1 refers to holiness, especially to the holy language with which the angels called to one another, for the root *qr'* also appears in Isa. 6:3.

Said Rabbi Eleazar the son of Menahem. Eleazar suggests that Prov. 15:29 tells us how God dealt with the prophets of Israel and those of the rest of the nations of the world. *YHWH is far from the evil ones* refers to His being far from the prophets of the rest of the world; however, His *hearing the prayers of the righteous* refers to His being close to Israel's prophets. Eleazar suggests that God revealed Himself to the non-Jewish prophets as a stranger. Isa. 39 discusses envoys from Babylonia who came to Isaiah and Hezekiah. To Eleazar, this suggests the way that the non-Jewish prophets approached God. However, God speaks to Israel's prophets Himself, like a friend, for we read that He appeared to Abraham and spoke directly to him. In Gen. 20:7 Abraham is called a prophet.

Said Rabbi Yosi the son of Biba. Yosi suggests that God appeared to the prophets of the rest of the nations of the world only at night, when people are normally separated from one another. Thus, Yosi agrees with Eleazar that God approached the prophets of the rest of the world, but not as directly or as closely as He approached Israel's prophets. Job 4:12–13 implies that people communicate indirectly, or at least not in the open, at night; therefore, we can see that God did not address the non-Jewish prophets with the same directness with which He communicated with Israel's prophets.

Rabbi Hanana the son of Pappa said. Hanana agrees with Yosi that God spoke to the prophets of the non-Jews indirectly. He compares it to one who is separated from his lover by a curtain. When he wishes to speak to his lover he does so directly, by doubling up the curtain. The implication is that when he wishes to speak to one other than his lover, he would not go to the trouble of opening the curtain. In the same way, God addresses Israel's prophets directly without any curtain between them; however, He "does not remove the curtain" when He speaks to the non-Jewish prophets.

The rabbis said. The rabbis agree that God addressed the non-Jewish prophets only at night, and they bring three verses which support this claim. Gen. 18:1 proves that He addressed Israel's prophets during the day, for this is the opening verse of God's visit to Abraham after the latter had been circumcised. Ex. 6:28 states that God spoke to Moses during the day, Num. 3:1 tells us that He spoke to Moses on Mount Sinai during the day, and Lev. 7:38 suggests that He spoke to Israel, in general, during the day.

What is the difference between Moses and the rest of the prophets. The above paragraphs have established the superiority of Israel's prophets over the prophets of the non-Jewish world. The midrash now demonstrates that Moses was the prophet among the Jews who received the most direct communications from God. In short, Moses is the best prophet among the best prophets. At this point the midrash returns to the major theme of this chapter, the superior character of Moses and God's direct communication with him. At this point the midrash has gone full circle, for it has returned to its opening theme.

Rabbi Judah said. Judah states that the other prophets saw God only through nine panes of glass; thus, His image would have been somewhat distorted. Ezek. 43:3 states: *wkmr'h hmr'h 'šr r'yty kmr'h 'šr r'yty bb'y lšht 't h'yr wmr'wt kmr'h 'šr r'yty 'l nhr kbr w'pl 'lpny.* The root *r'h,* "to see," appears nine times if we count the plural, *wmr'wt,* as two. This may be the basis for Judah's use of the number nine.

But Moses saw. Above we noted that the word *wmr'h,* "clearly," comes from the root *r'h,* "to see"; therefore, God communicated with Moses mouth to mouth and not in dark speech. In fact, the verse specifically states that Moses saw God's form. The root *r'h* appears once in this verse and implies that Moses saw God through only one pane of glass.

But the rabbis said. The rabbis seem to agree with Judah; however, they use a different image. All agree that the prophets besides Moses saw God less clearly than Moses saw Him. The rabbis suggest that the other prophets saw God as if through a clouded lense, while Moses viewed Him through a polished lense. Hos. 12:11 states: *I spoke to the prophets; it was I who multiplied visions, and through the prophets 'dmh.* The rabbis take *'dmh* from *dmh,* "likeness," and read the verse as follows: "I spoke to the prophets; it was I who spoke to them through multiple visions, and at their hand I made a likeness of Myself." Num. 12:8, on the other hand, specifically states that Moses saw the "form," *tmnt,* not the likeness, of YHWH.

Rabbi Phinehas in the name of Rabbi Hoshiya said. Phinehas suggests that God will actually reveal Himself to everyone in the same way. I assume that Phinehas implies that even Moses will have a more direct vision of God in the world-to-come. However, the difference between Moses' vision of God and that of the other prophets is comparable to a king who reveals himself completely only to the members of his immediate household.

CONCLUSIONS

This midrash is totally different from the others we have read. While the others were organized as commentaries to the various elements of the biblical text to which they were connected, the present collection focuses less on the biblical text than on a single theme: Moses. We have a number of small essays on Moses' special character. To see just how different Leviticus Rabbah is from the other midrashic collections we have examined, compare this selection with the one from Sifra which appears above, for both collections provide an exegesis of the same biblical verse. In Leviticus Rabbah, *parashah* one, the focus on Moses appears in both the *petiḥot* and the "body" of the text.

The opening proem begins with Ps. 103:20, *Bless YHWH, O His messengers (ml'kyw), mighty ones who do His word, harkening to the voice of his word.* The text first establishes that *ml'k* refers to humans. Next it demonstrates that the term is applied to the prophets. After Isaac's aside, which claims that the *mighty ones who do His word* are those who keep the sabbatical years, the text demonstrates that *who do His word, harkening* points to the events at Mount Sinai. The text ends by pointing to Moses' strength at Sinai.

The second proem focuses on the issue of "names," specifically Moses' names. It opens with Hos. 14:7, *They shall return and dwell beneath My shadow.* The text establishes that the verse refers to the proselytes, and we are told that God considers the proselyte's name to be precious. After an aside, which focuses on the altar's name, Lebanon, the text moves to a discussion of Moses' names. Most of the names in I Chron. 4:18 are applied to Moses. Those which are not applied to him are given to his mother, to Pharaoh's daughter, who saved him, and to the husband of Pharaoh's daughter; in short, all of the names in the verse are connected in some way to Moses. The name Tobiah is applied to Moses on the basis of Ex. 2:2, and all of the names in I Chron. 24:6 are related to Moses or to his brother, Aaron. The text ends by stating that God favored the name Moses because it was given him by a proselyte, Pharaoh's daughter.

The next proem opens with Ps. 89:20: *Then You spoke in a vision to Your pious ones and said: "I have set a crown upon one who is mighty, I have exalted one chosen from the people."* The text applies this verse to Abraham, David, and finally to Moses.

The next proem opens with Prov. 25:7: *For it is better to be told, "come up here," than to be put lower in the presence of the prince whom your eyes have seen.* After some advice given by Hillel and Aqiba, the text moves to a discussion of Moses. We are told that Moses never acted presumptuously; he always waited for God to tell him to act. This is why God had to call to him in Lev. 1:1.

The next proem opens with Prov. 20:15: *There is gold, and abundance of costly stones; but the lips of knowledge are a precious jewel.* The proem concludes by stating that Moses' words were more precious than all of the material wealth which the Israelites brought to Moses for the construction of the Tabernacle. Because this paragraph discussed the Tabernacle, the text next moves to a discussion of Moses' actions when he directed its construction. We are told that Moses made certain that the Tabernacle was built for the glory of God and not for his own glory or as a monument to those who did the actual work. God was so pleased with the final building, that He called to Moses to join Him inside. Because this section focused on the phrase *as YHWH commanded Moses*, the next section discusses the eighteen times which this phrase appears at the end of Exodus. Ḥiyya tells us that one begins the counting with Ex. 38:23, which mentions Oholiab and Ahisamach. This provides the occasion for the parable that one can tell a king's most important confidant by observing to whom he speaks first. This is compared to God's speaking to Moses at the Tent of Meeting even though there were others there, such as Aaron, his sons Nadab and Abihu, and the seventy elders.

The next paragraph again takes up the issue of God's calling to Moses. It concludes that God called to Moses because the latter was concerned with the basic necessities of Jewish life, the food supply.

We have seen that each of these sections was carefully constructed. Although they do not open with the technical term, *ptḥ*, they all function as *petiḥot*. We have also seen that the several paragraphs with which these "introductions" end are interrelated.

The "body" of the midrash also focuses on Moses. The first section suggests that God called to or spoke to Adam, Noah, and Abraham in the same way in which He called to and spoke to Moses at the opening of Lev. 1:1. However, God spoke to the former three the same way in which a king speaks to servants. God did *not* speak to Moses as a king speaks to His servants; therefore, Moses is different from the other "heroes" of the Bible.

The text now moves to the phrase *from the Tent of Meeting.* We are first told that the revelation at the Tent of Meeting was more public than the revelation at Sinai; therefore, the laws contained in the Torah took effect only at this time.

The text now states that if the rest of the nations of the world had known how Israel would benefit from the Tent of Meeting, they would not have allowed her to approach it. The point of the midrash is that before the erection of the Tent of Meeting prophecy was found in all the nations of the world; however, after its construction God spoke only through Israel's prophets. The text demonstrates that Israel's prophets had a more direct contact with God than did the prophets of the rest of the nations of the world, and it ends by claiming that Moses was the prophet in Israel who had the closest contact with God. In brief, Moses was the best prophet among the best prophets.

This section, like most of the sections in Leviticus Rabbah, according to Heinemann, ends with a discussion of the messianic future. The point seems to be that in the world-to-come we shall all be as close to God as was Moses.

The emphasis of the opening section of Leviticus Rabbah is Moses, the one to whom God spoke in Lev. 1:1. The issues of "calling" and "speaking" which were raised in Sifra, the issue of the force of God's voice, and the matter of the sacrifices, which were all discussed in Sifra, are not even raised here. We have before us a number of carefully constructed paragraphs whose subject is Moses, not the text of Lev. 1:1. We have seen that each paragraph is carefully constructed and that toward the end of the series of "introductions" the paragraphs are carefully woven together to give us a picture of Moses.

It has been common to describe the various sections of Leviticus Rabbah, especially the *petihot*, as sermons. However, a recent study by R. Sarason argues convincingly for the "literary" nature of these texts. Sarason states:

> A detailed study of the literary and stylistic traits of the document [Leviticus Rabbah] reveals that most of the *petihot* in LR are demonstrably editorial constructions; which is to say that the redactor(s) of this text has taken materials which to begin with were *not petihot* and made them into *petihot* for this document by the straightforward processes of rearranging the order of materials so that the Leviticus verse is at the end, and/or by adding at the end the appropriate *seder*-verse from Leviticus together with a stereotype transition-line to introduce this verse.[37]

Again, we have a carefully constructed text which reflects the rabbinic concerns with the Bible. In this case, the rabbis demonstrated that the revelation transmitted by Moses was the best revelation from God available to man. If we again take Moses as a code-word for "rabbi," we see here an attempt by the rabbis to validate their traditions. Given Sarason's article, there is no evidence before us that these were designed as public sermons. All we know is that this midrash was constructed by rabbis for their own purposes.

NOTES

1. J. Heinemann, "Profile of Midrash: The Art of Composition in Leviticus Rabbah," *Journal of the American Academy of Religion*, XXXIX, 2 (June 1971), 142–143.

2. Ibid., 153.

3. W. G. Braude and I. J. Kapstein (trans.), *Pesikta de-Rab Kahana: R. Kahana's Compilation of Discourses for Sabbaths and Festal Days* (Philadelphis, 1975).

4. See W. G. Braude (trans.), *Pesikta Rabbati: Discourses for Feasts, Fasts, and Special Sabbaths* (New Haven, 1968).

5. M. Margulies, *Midrash Wayyikra Rabbah* (Jerusalem, 1960), V, xii ff. H. Albeck, "The Midrash Leviticus Rabbah," in *Louis Ginzberg Jubilee Volume on the Occasion of His Seventieth Birthday* (New York, 1946), Hebrew section, 31 ff. Heinemann, 141.

6. Margulies, V, ix.

7. Heinemann, 148.

8. Ibid.

9. This translation is based on Margulies, 1–32.

10. See Chap. 6, note 9.

11. See their comments to Jdgs. 2:1.

12. D. Sperber, *Roman Palestine: 200–400: The Land* (Ramat-Gan, 1978), 14.

13. M. Avi-Yonah, *The Jews of Palestine: A Political History from the Bar Kokhba War to the Arab Conquest* (New York, 1976), 96.

14. For a romanticized discussion of the halakhah and aggadah, see H. N. Bialik, "Halakhah and Aggadah," *Contemporary Jewish Record* VIII (1944), 663–680. Reprinted in N. Glatzer (ed.), *Modern Jewish Thought: A Source Reader* (New York: 1977), 55–64.

15. See G. Vermes, *Scripture and Tradition in Judaism: Haggadic Studies* (Leiden, 1961), 26–39.

16. On the Oral Law and the Written Law, see J. Neusner, *The Rabbinic Traditions about the Pharisees before 70* (Leiden, 1971), III, 143–179.

17. See comment on *bn znwh*.

18. See the attempt of the traditional commentators, and Margulies, to explain the confused text and to find the "ten" names.

19. On Moses, see W. Meeks, *The Prophet-King: Moses Traditions and the Johannine Christology* (Leiden, 1967).

20. There is some question of exactly who pursued whom; see the traditional commentators on Phinehas' comment.

21. Ze'av Wolf on the wars.

22. See David Luria's discussion of David's wars.

23. Margulies, loc cit.

24. For an interesting discussion of who sits where in the schoolhouse and courts, see R. Goldenberg, "The Deposition of Rabban Gamliel II," *Journal of Jewish Studies*, XXIII (1972), 167–190.

25. Neusner, I, 275.

26. This aside may be appropriate because Moses is the paradigmatic rabbi; see J. Neusner, *A History of the Jews in Babylonia* (Leiden, 1965–70), III, Moses, passim.

27. David Luria on *kly yqr*.

28. Ze'av Wolf on *kly yqr*.

29. On the rabbinic parable, see Chap. 4, note 37.

30. Margulies on *k'šr ṣwh mšh*.

31. On the number of blessings in the *Amidah*, see K. Kohler, "The Origin and Composition of the Eighteen Benedictions," *Hebrew Union College Annual* I (1924), and L. Finkelstein, "The Development of the Amidah," *Jewish Quarterly Review*, N.S., XVI (1925/26). Both are reprinted in J. Petuchowski (ed.), *Contributions to the Scientific Study of Jewish Liturgy* (New York, 1970), 52–177.

32. See Margulies's comment on the connection between the *Tefilah* and the sacrifices, loc. cit.

33. See Palestinian *Berakhot* 4:3.

34. See Sifra's discussion of *from the Tent of Meeting*, supra, 25–26.

35. On Balaam, see H. Hoftizer, "The Prophet Balaam in a 6th-Century Aramaic Inscription," *Biblical Archaeologist*, XXXIX (1976), 11–17.

36. For a discussion of this problem in biblical Hebrew, see T. Lambdin, *Introduction to Biblical Hebrew* (New York, 1971), 107–127.

37. R. Sarason, "The Petihtot in Leviticus Rabbah: 'Oral Homilies' or Redactional Constructions?" *Journal of Jewish Studies: Essays in Honour of Yigael Yadin*, XXXIII, 1–2 (Spring–Autumn 1982), 559.

Index

RABBINIC LITERATURE

Mishnah

RABBINIC MASTERS

6